Leading Inclusion from the Inside Out

Leading Inclusion from the Inside Out

A Handbook for Parents and Early Childhood Teachers in Early Learning and Care, Primary and Special School Settings

Emer Ring, Lisha O'Sullivan,
Marie Ryan and Patricia Daly (eds)

Peter Lang
Oxford · Bern · Berlin · Bruxelles · New York · Wien

Bibliographic information published by Die Deutsche Nationalbibliothek
Die Deutsche Nationalbibliothek lists this publication in the Deutsche
Nationalbibliografie; detailed bibliographic data is available on the Internet at
http://dnb.d-nb.de.

A catalogue record for this book is available from the British Library.

Library of Congress Cataloging-in-Publication Data
Names: Ring, Emer, 1960- editor. | O'Sullivan, Lisha, 1976- editor. | Ryan,
   Marie, 1986- editor. | Daly, Patricia, 1953- editor.
Title: Leading inclusion from the inside out : a handbook for parents and
   early childhood teachers in early learning and care, primary and special
   school settings / Emer Ring, Lisha O'Sullivan, Marie Ryan, Patricia
   Daly.
Description: Oxford ; New York : Peter Lang, [2021] | Includes
   bibliographical references and index.
Identifiers: LCCN 2020045416 (print) | LCCN 2020045417 (ebook) | ISBN
   9781789971897 (paperback) | ISBN 9781789971903 (ebook) | ISBN
   9781789971910 (epub) | ISBN 9781789971927 (mobi)
Subjects: LCSH: Inclusive education. | Early childhood education. |
   Children with disabilities--Education (Early childhood)
Classification: LCC LC1200 .L3894 2021 (print) | LCC LC1200 (ebook) | DDC
   371.9/046--dc23
LC record available at https://lccn.loc.gov/2020045416
LC ebook record available at https://lccn.loc.gov/2020045417

Cover design by Brian Melville for Peter Lang.

ISBN 978-1-78997-189-7 (print) • eISBN 978-1-78997-190-3 (ePDF)
ISBN 978-1-78997-191-0 (ePub) • ISBN 978-1-78997-192-7 (mobi)

© Peter Lang Group AG 2021

Published by Peter Lang Ltd, International Academic Publishers,
52 St Giles, Oxford, OX1 3LU, United Kingdom
oxford@peterlang.com, www.peterlang.com

Emer Ring, Lisha O'Sullivan, Marie Ryan and Patricia Daly have asserted their right
under the Copyright, Designs and Patents Act, 1988, to be identified as Editors of this
Work.

All rights reserved.
All parts of this publication are protected by copyright.
Any utilisation outside the strict limits of the copyright law, without the permission of
the publisher, is forbidden and liable to prosecution.

This applies in particular to reproductions, translations, microfilming, and storage and
processing in electronic retrieval systems.

This publication has been peer reviewed.

Printed in Germany

Contents

List of Figures — ix

List of Tables — xi

Foreword — xiii

Glossary of Terms — xvii

Terminology — xix

Introduction

EMER RING

1 Introduction: Looking Towards a New Era of Leading Education for All from the Inside Out: The Potential of a Bioecological Lens in Creating Early Childhood Experiences Where Diversity Becomes the Norm — 3

The Child at the Centre

EMER RING, PAULA HARTE AND MAURICE HARMON

2 Making Children's Right to Participate Visible and Children's Voices Distinct in the Acoustic of Early Childhood Education — 31

MARIE DOHERTY

3 Children from Birth to 3 Years: Valuing and Supporting Our Earliest Learners, as They Begin Their Educational Journey 61

MARIE RYAN

4 Interactions Drive Development: What Does This Actually Mean for Practice? 95

Realising Inclusive Culture, Pedagogy and Practice

ANNA BARR AND PAULA HILLIARD

5 Realising and Building Partnership with Parents and Families 123

SHIRLEY HEANEY AND SARAH FEENEY

6 Wellbeing as Central to Including All Children in the Early Years 151

LISHA O'SULLIVAN

7 Play as a Pedagogy for All Children 181

SARAH KELLEHER AND EDEL FENLON

8 Making the Environment the Third Teacher 211

Leadership for Including All Children

SHARON SKEHILL

9 Leadership in the Early Learning and Care Setting 229

ANN DONNELLAN, MARGARET JOYCE AND RACHAEL RYAN

10 Leading and Implementing Whole-Setting and Individual
   Planning   255

PATRICIA M. DALY

11 Assessed Needs as Signposts for Learning and Development   279

Notes on Contributors   309

Index   317

Figures

Figure 1.1.	The Better Start Access and Inclusion Model (IDG 2015: 27)	7
Figure 1.2.	Indicators of High-Quality Early Childhood Education (Adapted from Melhuish 2015)	8
Figure 1.3.	Principles of an Inclusive Culture in an Early Childhood Education (Adapted from DCYA 2016)	13
Figure 2.1.	The Four General Principles Underpinning the United Nations Convention on the Rights of the Child (Ring et al. 2019a: 50)	35
Figure 2.2.	Theoretical Perspectives on Children's Learning and Development (Ring et al. 2018: 5)	39
Figure 2.3.	The Lundy Model of Participation (DCYA 2020b)	45
Figure 5.1.	The Application of Bronfenbrenner's Bioecological Model of Development to Realising and Building Partnerships with Parents and Families	127
Figure 5.2.	Quality Framework for Early Years Education (DES 2018: 16)	130
Figure 5.3.	A Summary of Key Principles to Support the Creation of Environments that Facilitate Building Relationships with Parents and Families (Grey et al. 2019)	131
Figure 5.4.	A Continuum to Support Partnerships with Parents (Goodall and Montgomery 2014)	133
Figure 6.1.	Continuum of Support within an Inclusive School Culture (NCSE 2018: 34)	160
Figure 9.1.	Lewin's Three-Step Process for Change (Adapted from Lewin 1947)	241

Tables

Table 1.1.	Competencies Associated with Providing Early Childhood Education for All Children	16
Table 5.1.	Inclusive Early Childhood Education Environment Self-Reflection Tool (EASNIE 2017c: 25)	144
Table 6.1.	The Seven Key Quality Characteristics of Early Childhood Education (Melhuish et al. 2015: 5)	158
Table 6.2.	Goals for an Anti-Bias Approach (Adapted from Derman-Sparks and the Anti-Bias Curriculum Task Force (1989) cited in DCYA 2016: 25)	167
Table 6.3.	Six Steps of the HighScope Problem-Solving Approach to Conflict Resolution (Adapted from Holt 2007: 49)	170
Table 8.1.	Key Terms Associated with the Pedagogy and Practice of a Reggio Emilia Approach to Early Childhood Education	214
Table 10.1.	Pointers for Developing a Collaborative Communication Culture	264
Table 11.1.	Elements of Behaviour Interactions in an Early Childhood Class	286
Table 11.2.	Functions of Behaviours that Challenge Adults	287
Table 11.3.	Physical Assessed Needs – Signposts and Supports	291
Table 11.4.	Assessed Needs with Intellectual Focus: Signposts and Supports	295
Table 11.5.	Common Supports Linked to Universal Design for Learning Elements	299

Foreword

An enduring puzzle of our times is why early childhood provision is the poor relation of public services and indeed how the significance of early childhood in primary schools is not always understood. Despite incontrovertible evidence from around the world that high-quality learning experiences for young children make economic and social sense – apart from the fact that it is the right thing to do – early childhood education is not resourced as it should be. It is ironic that Covid-19 has served to highlight the importance of child care, in enabling parents who are key works to continue working. Welcome though this greater appreciation is, little emphasis has been placed on the fundamental rationale that providing high-quality early childhood experiences for all of our children promotes child welfare and development, yields considerable long-term dividends and has particular importance for children from less advantaged backgrounds.

Inclusion represents another puzzle here. It beggars belief that in 2020 the case for inclusion still needs to be made. There has been progress from the days when those who were different were, at best, marginalised and frequently were villainised; but the uncomfortable reality of our times is that exclusion is still evident in our societies, including in the education sector which might be expected to lead the way. Despite a plethora of positive rhetoric, inclusion is not the taken-for-granted organising principle of educational provision that it ought to be, and we are still a far cry from ensuring that all early childhood settings and schools take effective account of the diverse situations of children and young people.

This book makes a signal contribution in respect of both of these puzzles. It may not resolve them entirely but, in making a powerful case for inclusive early childhood provision across early learning and care provision and the early years classes in primary and special schools, and demonstrating comprehensively how it can be achieved, it marks a significant step in moving the consensus forward.

The book has emerged from a remarkable development in Ireland. As part of a Government initiative to bolster early years provision, a programme was developed to equip all early years settings with a well-trained INclusion CO-ordinator. This entailed identifying existing members of staff and providing them with comprehensive, year-long professional development in all aspects of inclusive practice and especially leadership. Known as the LINC (Leadership for Inclusion in the Early Years) Programme, it was co-ordinated on a national basis by staff at Mary Immaculate College in Limerick and ran from 2016 to 2020. A second iteration of the programme is to commence in January 2021.

The heart of the Programme is a set of learning materials focussed on inclusive practices in early childhood settings and the role of leadership in achieving them. It utilises a blended learning approach, with the bulk of the materials delivered online. The Programme has been highly successful in terms of both student feedback and achievement. It has also won numerous awards for innovation in teaching and learning and for delivering online learning experiences.

This book draws on the exemplary materials of the LINC Programme to offer an authoritative account of thinking and practice in early childhood provision at early learning and care, primary and special school levels. Besides offering a robust account of what inclusion means, it provides a great deal of pertinent material on familiar topics such as partnership with parents, the pedagogical power of play and making effective use of the environment. More than that, however – and this is its particular contribution – it has a wealth of stimulating material on leadership for inclusion. Whether or not an early childhood setting – or any other setting for that matter – becomes truly inclusive depends critically on the quality of leadership available within the setting. Graduates of the LINC Programme have been true agents of change across the sector, and this book can play a signal role in developing the leadership skills the sector needs – and without which it will not thrive. Significantly the primary and special school sectors can now benefit from the exceptional success of the LINC programme.

This book will be a valuable resource not only for people who work in early education but also for national and local policy-makers and for parents. It makes a powerful case for expertise-driven provision, and sets out a wealth of practical guidelines and exemplars covering all aspects of provision but particularly leadership. Its clarity and focus mean that it has global resonance and will be a valuable resource far beyond the Irish shores.

Seamus Hegarty
Visiting Professor University of Warwick
Adjunct Professor University College Dublin

Glossary of Terms

ABA	Applied Behaviour Analysis
ABCs	Antecedents, Behaviours, Consequences
ABC	Anti-Bias Curriculum
AIM	Access and Inclusion Mode
APA	American Psychiatric Association
ASD	Autism Spectrum Differences. This terminology is specifically selected to underline the authors' position in employing positive and enabling language to acknowledge and celebrate differences.[1]
CECDE	Centre for Early Childhood Development and Education
CERAMIC	Centre for Early Childhood Research at Mary Immaculate College
CPD	Continuing Professional Development
DCYA	Department of Children and Youth Affairs
DES	Department of Education and Skills
DfE	Department for Education
DoH	Department of Health
EASNIE	European Agency for Special Needs and Inclusive Education
EC	European Commission
ECCE	Early Childhood Care and Education
ECEC	Early Childhood Education and Care
ECERS-E	Extension to the Early Childhood Environment Rating Scale
ECERS-R	Early Childhood Environment Rating Scale – Revised
ECI	Early Childhood Ireland
EIBI	Early Intensive Behavioural Intervention
ELC	Early Learning and Care
EPPE	Effective Provision of Pre-school Education Study
EPSEN Act	Education for Persons with Special Educational Needs Act
EYEI	Early Years Education-focused Inspection (EYEI)
GoI	Government of Ireland

---

1 Ring, E., Daly, P., and Wall, E. (eds) (2018). *Autism from the Inside Out: A Handbook for Parents, Early Childhood, Primary, Post-Primary and Special School Settings*. Oxford: Peter Lang.

HSE	Health Service Executive
IDG	Inter-Departmental Group
IECE	Inclusive Early Childhood Education
IEP	Individual Education Plan
INCO	INclusion CO-ordinator
ITE	Initial Teacher Education
LINC	Leadership for INClusion in the Early Years
MIC	Mary Immaculate College
MKO	More Knowledgeable Other
MU- Froebel Dept.	Maynooth University Froebel Department of Primary and Early Childhood Education
NCCA	National Council for Curriculum and Assessment
NCSE	National Council for Special Education
NEPS	National Educational Psychological Service
NFQ	National Framework of Qualifications
OECD	Organisation for Economic Co-operation and Development
OT	Occupational Therapist
PBS	Positive Behaviour Support
QQI	Quality and Qualifications Ireland
RtI	Response to Intervention
SESS	Special Education Support Service
SST	Sustained Shared Thinking
UDL	Universal Design for Learning
UN	United Nations
ZPD	Zone of Proximal Development

Terminology

Additional Needs	This terminology replaces the use of disability terminology in the publication to capture the manner in which specific needs trigger targeted resources.
	Where the term 'children with additional needs' is used in the publication, it includes children whose capacity to fully participate in education is limited, in some way, as a consequence of physical, sensory, cognitive, social and/or communicative differences.[1]
Better Start Access and Inclusion Model	The Better Start Access and Inclusion Model (Better Start AIM), is a cross-departmental initiative, led by the Department of Children and Youth Affairs (DCYA) and involving, *interalia*, the Department of Health (DoH) and the Department of Education (DES) in Ireland. The Better Start Aim provides for a model of Government-funded supports aimed at enabling children with specific additional needs to participate fully in pre-school mainstream settings alongside their peers. The model adopts a child-centred approach, through focusing on identifying and responding to each individual child's developmental level, abilities and needs rather than relying exclusively on formal diagnoses.
Early Learning	This refers to the period of 0–6 years for young children.
Early Learning and Care	Pre-school education in Ireland is provided in early learning and care settings.
Early Childhood Education	Early childhood education in Ireland comprises a split system, incorporating pre-school provision in early learning and care settings and primary and special school provision in junior and senior infant classes.

---

1   Ireland. (2004). *Education for Persons with Special Educational Needs Act, 2004*. Dublin: The Government Publications Office.

Early Childhood Teacher	Specifically early childhood teacher refers to the craft of teaching in pre-school, primary and special school settings. The concept of the early childhood teacher is influenced by Dewey's portrayal of the teacher as an interpreter and guide in providing the child with a myriad of opportunities to rediscover, re-enact and reconstruct his/her experience in high-quality early childhood settings (Dewey 1916).[2]
Early Childhood Education	This refers to the period of 0–6 years for young children.
Early Years	This refers to the period of 0–6 years for young children.
Family	Acknowledging that there is no definition of the family under international human rights law, the concept of family is interpreted in accordance with the principles infused through the United Nations Convention on the Rights of the Child (UNCRC) (UN 1989),[3] of recognising the plurality of family forms and their inextricable link with unique societal historical and contemporary influences.
Free Pre-school Programme	The free pre-school programme is a universal two-year pre-school programme available to all children who have turned 2 years and 8 months before September, provided they do not turn five years and six months at any point during the pre-school year. This is often referred to as the Early Childhood Care and Education (ECCE) programme.[4]

---

2 Dewey, J. (1916). *Democracy and Education*. New York, NY: The Free Press.
3 United Nations. (1989). *Convention on the Rights of the Child*. New York, NY: United Nations, <http://www.ohchr.org/EN/ProfessionalInterest/Pages/CRC.aspx>, accessed 12 January 2020.
4 Department of Children and Youth Affairs. (2019a). *Early Childhood Care and Education (ECCE) or Free Preschool*. Dublin: Department of Children and Youth Affairs, <https://www.gov.ie/en/publication/d7a5e6-early-childhood-care-and-education-ecce-or-free-preschool/?referrer=/cat/en/childcare/211.htm/>, accessed 21 January 2020.

Terminology

Inclusion	This publication adopts the definition of education for all articulated by the United Nations Educational, Scientific and Cultural Organisation (UNESCO) (2005).[5] Education for all means ensuring that all children have access to basic education of good quality. This implies creating an environment in schools and in basic education programmes in which children are both able and enabled to learn. Such an environment must be inclusive of children, effective with children, friendly and welcoming to children, healthy and protective for children and gender sensitive.
Parent	Parent in this publication encompasses the definition of parents as described in the Interpretation Section of the Education Act, 1998: 'parent' includes a foster parent, a guardian appointed under the Guardianship of Children Acts, 1964 to 1997, or other person acting in *loco parentis* who has a child in his or her care subject to any statutory power or order of a court and, in the case of a child who has been adopted under the Adoption Acts, 1952 to 1998, or, where the child has been adopted outside the State, means the adopter or adopters or the surviving adopter; (Ireland 1998: Section 2: Interpretation)[6]
Pre-school	This refers to provision in early learning and care settings prior to a child commencing primary school.

---

[5] United Nations Educational, Scientific and Cultural Organisation. (2005). *Guidelines for Inclusion: Ensuring Access to Education for All*. Paris: United Nations Educational, Scientific and Cultural Organisation, <http://www.ibe.unesco.org/sites/default/files/Guidelines_for_Inclusion_UNESCO_2006.pdf>, accessed 31 August 2020.
[6] Ireland. (1998). *Education Act, 1998*. Dublin: The Government Publications Office.

Introduction

EMER RING

Chapter 1 Introduction: Looking Towards a
New Era of Leading Education for All
from the Inside Out: The Potential of
a Bioecological Lens in Creating Early
Childhood Experiences Where Diversity
Becomes the Norm

Introduction

The current focus on inclusion is often traced to the Salamanca World Conference Declaration Statement, which asserted the familiar principle that regular education settings with an inclusive orientation are the most effective means of combating discriminatory attitudes, creating welcoming communities and achieving education for all (United Nations Educational, Scientific and Cultural Organisation (UNESCO) 1994). What is less well known is that the Salamanca Statement specifically referred to early childhood education, observing that:

> The success of the inclusive school depends considerably on early identification, assessment and stimulation of the very young child with special educational needs. Early childhood care and education programmes for children aged up to 6 years ought to be developed and/or oriented to promote physical, intellectual and social development and school readiness. (UNESCO 1994)

Research from national and international perspectives has continued to highlight the benefits of high-quality experiences in early childhood settings where all children are supported in achieving their potential (Ring,

Ryan and Burke 2018; Ring et al. 2019). However, ensuring the meaningful inclusion of all children is a complex, multifaceted process influenced by a wide range of historical political, economic and societal factors, reliant on, *interalia*, whole-setting attitudes, the foci of the teacher education continuum, an inclusive pedagogy and adequate resourcing. Fundamentally, inclusion challenges education systems globally to accommodate and respond positively to the complexity generated by human difference across a variety of contexts (O'Brien 2020). While in 1994, Ireland was one of ninety-two governments and twenty-five international organisations subscribing to the principles of the Salamanca Statement, the vision to create an inclusive education system in both the early learning and care (ELC) and school system remains a work in progress. This is not unique to the Irish context, as observed by the recent International Forum on Inclusion and Equity in Education: Every Learner Matters, celebrating the twenty-fifth anniversary of the Salamanca Statement. The Forum concluded that 'we are a long way from ensuring that all people, irrespective of their sex, age, race, or ethnicity, ability, location or other social characteristics, have equal opportunities for educational progress and lifelong learning' (UNESCO 2019). It continues to be highlighted that including all learners and ensuring each child has an equal and personalised opportunity to progress remains a challenge for all education systems globally (UNESCO 2017).

Believing that language is a significant contributor to progressing an education system where all children are valued equally, the authors have directed specific attention to the use of terminology in this publication. The terminology employed is inextricably linked to the power of language to shape our attitudes and the power of those attitudes to transform lives for better or worse. The authors are concerned that a language of deficit continues to be employed in describing children who are perceived to require extra or special inputs in order to progress through our education systems. The reality is that all children learn differently and at the twenty-fifth anniversary of the Salamanca Statement, we should be moving to a place where using terminology such as 'integration', 'inclusion', 'special', 'extra' or 'additional' is no longer relevant or necessary. The continued use of this terminology contributes to maintaining exclusionary practice in our education settings and in the broader society. The authors aspire to a future where the need for specific terminology is eradicated in favour of a system where education for all becomes a reality, and the differences that all of us have are equally acknowledged, understood, celebrated and accommodated. This publication therefore is underpinned by a philosophy of universality, within which difference and diversity are embedded, rather than disability and uniformity. However, the authors also acknowledge the need to provide explicit definitions of the manner in which this publication is applying the specific terminology that has characterised this field from its inception and these definitions are therefore clearly delineated in the Glossary of Terms, which follows the Foreword. Specifically early childhood teacher refers to the craft of teaching in pre-school, primary and special school settings. The concept of the early childhood teacher is influenced by Dewey's portrayal of the teacher as a guide and interpreter in providing the child with a myriad of opportunities to re-construct, rediscover, re-enact his/her experience in high-quality early childhood settings (Dewey 1916). Parent in this publication encompasses the definition of parents as described in the Interpretation Section of the Education Act, 1998:

> 'parent' includes a foster parent, a guardian appointed under the Guardianship of Children Acts, 1964 to 1997, or other person acting in *loco parentis* who has a child in his or her care subject to any statutory power or order of a court and, in the case of a child who has been adopted under the Adoption Acts, 1952 to 1998, or, where the child has been adopted outside the State, means the adopter or adopters or the surviving adopter; (Ireland 1998: Section 2: Interpretation)

Acknowledging that a definition of what specifically constitutes the family does not exist under international human rights law, the concept of family is interpreted in this publication with reference to the principles infused through the United Nations Convention on the Rights of the Child (UNCRC) (UN 1989), and recognises the plurality of family forms and their inextricable link with unique societal historical and contemporary influences.

Inclusion in Early Childhood Education in Ireland: A Work in Progress

Stemming from a historical legacy, children in Ireland experience a split system of early childhood education (Ring et al. 2016). Traditionally access to education was associated with a child's entry to primary school, in a context where the mother in the home was viewed as being responsible for the education and care of pre-school children (Ring, O'Sullivan and Wall 2020). A predominantly private and costly pre-school system developed, leading to the need for government investment in recent years to support the professionalisation of the system in Ireland, and the provision of two free pre-school years through the universal early childhood scheme for children aged 0–6 (Department of Children and Youth Affairs (DCYA) 2019a; Ring et al. 2020). While the official school-starting age in Ireland is six, almost 40 per cent of 4-year-olds and almost all 5-year-olds are enrolled in the infant classes in primary schools (Department of Education and Skills (DES) 2020). Early childhood education is therefore provided at pre-school level in ELC settings and at primary and special school level in junior and senior infant classes.

In the absence of a robust legislative basis for, or a constitutional right to pre-school education, the provision of targeted resources to support all children in ELC settings has not, until recently, been prioritised by successive governments. The Inter-Departmental (IDG) Report on Supporting Access to the Early Childhood Care and Education (ECCE) Programme for Children with a Disability was launched in November 2015 (IDG 2015). This report provided for a new model of Government-funded supports aimed at enabling children deemed to have additional needs stemming from a disability to participate fully in pre-school mainstream settings alongside their peers. The model, referred to as the Better Start Access and Inclusion Model (Better Start AIM), is a cross-departmental initiative, led by the DCYA and involving, *interalia*, the Department of Health (DoH) and the DES. The Better Start AIM is based on national and international research evidence, and was developed following extensive consultation with a wide range of stakeholders, including the parents of children with additional needs. In accordance with best practice, the seven-level model detailed in Figure 1.1 adopts a child-centred approach through focusing on identifying and responding to each individual child's developmental level, abilities and needs rather than relying exclusively on formal diagnoses.

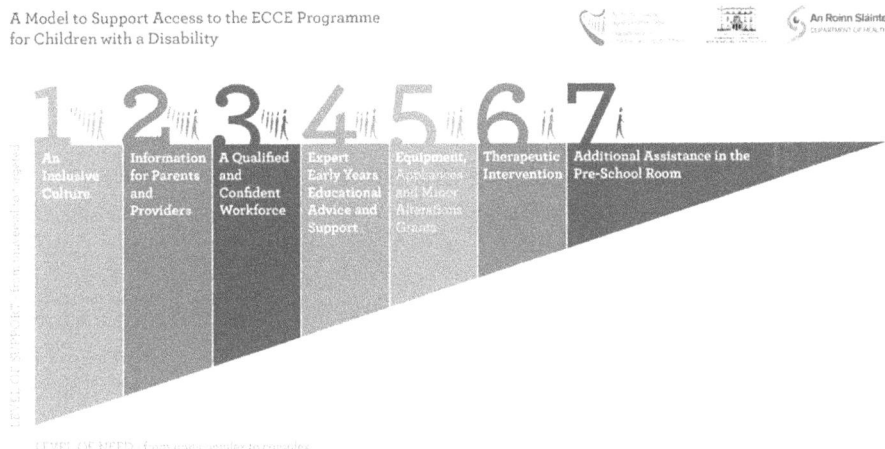

Figure 1.1. The Better Start Access and Inclusion Model (IDG 2015: 27)

The seven levels of support range from universal (Levels 1–3) to targeted supports (Levels 4–7) based on the needs of the individual child, and are consonant with the key components of quality early childhood education. While each of the levels is presented in the model separately, they are intrinsically linked with each other, and in auditing progress, these links emerge as a key strength of the model (DCYA 2019b). Initial evaluations of the model suggest that the model is having a significant impact on providing support for the inclusion of all children in ELC settings (DCYA 2019b; Ring et al. 2019).

Many of the authors involved in this publication have been involved in designing, delivering and evaluating a teacher education programme located at Level 3 on the Better Start AIM. The LINC Programme was developed by a Consortium led by Mary Immaculate College (MIC) and including Early Childhood Ireland (ECI) and Maynooth University – Froebel Department of Primary and Early Childhood Education (MU-Froebel Dept.) to contribute to the qualified and competent workforce envisaged at Level 3 of the Better

Start AIM (Ring et al. 2019). The LINC programme focuses specifically in facilitating the creation of a new role of INclusion CO-ordinator (INCO) in each ELC setting registered for the free pre-school scheme[1] (DCYA 2019a; Ring et al. 2019). Successful graduates of the programme acquire a Level 6 (Higher Education) Special Purpose Award, which enables them to successfully perform the role of INCO in an ELC setting. Designed to provide for 900 students annually from September 2016, the LINC programme is delivered in nine regional centres through a blended format, comprising face-to-face classroom-based sessions and online delivery. The programme is aligned with Aistear – the Early Childhood Curriculum Framework (National Council for Curriculum and Assessment (NCCA) 2009), the Aister/Síolta Practice Guide (NCCA 2015) Síolta, the National Quality Framework (Centre for Early Childhood Development and Education (CECDE) and the Diversity, Equality and Inclusion Charter and Guidelines for Early Childhood Care and Education (DCYA 2016). Specifically the LINC programme is embedded in best practice with regard to the indicators of high-quality early childhood experiences identified by Melhuish (2015) and summarised in Figure 1.2. The programme also maintains a particular focus on listening to and responding to the voice of the child.

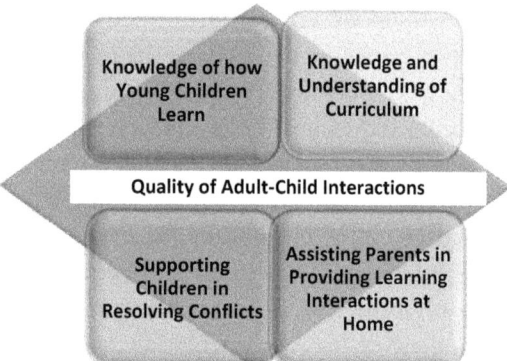

Figure 1.2. Indicators of High-Quality Early Childhood Education (Adapted from Melhuish 2015)

1 The free pre-school programme is a universal two-year preschool programme available to all children who have turned 2 years and 8 months before September, provided they do not turn 5 years and 6 months at any point during the preschool year (DCYA 2019a).

Up to 1998, access to primary education only was guaranteed by the State through the provisions of Article 42 of the Constitution of Ireland (Bunreacht na hÉireann), which explicitly stated that the 'State shall provide for free primary education' (Ireland 1937). In the absence of education legislation, parents of children with special educational needs sought recourse to the courts in order to secure the constitutional right of their children to primary education, with the courts effectively becoming the guardian of each child's right to free primary education until the late nineties. In 1998, with the enactment of the Education Act, 1998, a statutory obligation was placed on the State to provide all persons, including those with disabilities, with access to education appropriate to their needs (Ireland 1998).

Subsequently in the Irish context, a raft of education legislation has continued to consolidate the right of all children from their entry to primary school to an education appropriate to their needs and abilities. In 2000, The Education (Welfare) Act, 2000, provided an entitlement for all children to a certain minimum education, and the Equal Status Acts, 2000–2004, prohibited discrimination on nine specific grounds, including disability (Ireland 2000; Ireland 2000–2004). In 2004, the Education for Persons with Special Educational Needs (EPSEN) Act, 2004, specified the statutory right of children with special educational needs to avail of, and benefit from, an inclusive education, while also noting the centrality of parental involvement (Ireland 2004). Subsequently the Disability Act, 2005, aimed at children aged 0–5 years, provided for an independent assessment of a child's individual needs, an associated service statement, and an independent redress and enforcement process (Ireland 2005). Interestingly inclusive education is not defined in the legislation. Parallel to these seismic developments in education legislation, the establishment of the National Council for Special Education (NCSE) under the EPSEN Act, 2004, provided for an independent statutory body, with a range of functions including, conducting and commissioning relevant research; dissemination of best practice information related to special education; co-ordinating and planning special education support services; providing special education-focused policy advice to the Minister for Education and Skills; compiling information for parents with regard to their entitlements and those of their children; assessing and reviewing the resources required and ensuring the availability of a continuum of special education provision. In 2017, a special education teacher allocation was introduced to provide for a unified single allocation of additional teaching support to each school based on the school's educational profile (DES 2017a; 2017b). This model emerged following limitations identified by the NCSE that required attention in order to ensure all schools had access to an equitable, balanced and sustainable model of additional teaching support and thereby ensure that appropriate provision for all children was firmly located within an inclusive whole-school context and structure (Lynch et al. 2020). Aligned with the continuum of support framework, the revised model of teaching support allocates resources based on the acknowledgement that transient or long-term additional support along a continuum from mild to severe may be required based on an individual child's needs (DES 2007). An inclusive-whole-school framework is identified as promoting good practice in identifying children's needs, effective teaching and learning for all children; the promotion of positive collaborative relations between schools, parents and children; maintaining a focus on prevention and early intervention and ensuring children's outcomes and achievements are monitored, recorded and regularly reviewed (DES 2017b). In the school context, therefore, a focus is maintained on the provision of universal support at classroom level, school support level and school support plus level, with a key focus maintained on the critical importance of children with the most significant level of need having access to the requisite and highest level of support (Lynch et al. 2020). While it is acknowledged that not all provisions of both the EPSEN Act, 2004, and the Disability Act, 2005, have been fully commenced, the existing legislative and policy contexts in Ireland indicate a commitment to providing access to education appropriate to their needs for all children across the school system. At primary level, Looking at Our School 2016; A Quality Framework for Primary Schools, published by the DES Inspectorate, indicates a clear expectation that schools cultivate a commitment to inclusion, equality of opportunity and the holistic development of each child, throughout all dimensions of school life (DES 2016).

It is evident that while there is commitment to the development of an inclusive early childhood education system at pre-school, primary and special school levels in Ireland, challenges remain in terms of bridging the gap between policy aspirations and practice (Harris 2020). In *Leading Inclusion from the Inside Out: A Handbook for Parents and Early Childhood Teachers in Early Learning and Care, Primary and Special School Settings*, the authors share their experience in supporting the creation of early childhood spaces for all children in ELC, primary and special school settings and focus on continuing to bridge the gap that remains between policy and practice.

Inclusion: An Elusive Concept?

Education systems globally continue to struggle with identifying a universally agreed definition of inclusion. The integration movement, acknowledged as the precursor to inclusion, emerged in the 1960s as expressed in legislation across many countries, including, Italy, Denmark and the United States (US) in the 1970s (Hegarty 1993). According to Warnock (1982), the introduction of the term 'special educational needs' coincided with the integration movement and an effort to dispel the belief that special education was possible only in separate special provision. With concerns developing that integration necessitated making additional arrangements to existing provision in order to accommodate children with special educational needs, inclusion emerged as the embodiment of the belief in education for all. The emergence of inclusion as an ideology is reflected in the Salamanca Statement and promotes a societal zeitgeist focused on acknowledging and accommodating human differences and eliminating exclusionary practices, labelling and stigmatisation (UNESCO 1994). While the ideology is laudable in terms of its focus on advancing social justice, enhancing human rights and cultivating equity in educational provision, the emergence of a position that associates inclusion with having to do something additional for particular groups of children risks disconnecting and isolating groups of children and reinforcing stigma (O'Brien 2020). O'Brien highlights the dangers inherent in the normalisation of a labelling culture, cautioning that while labels are useful in highlighting group typicality and signposting potential needs, they do not capture individual differences and dispositions. Finally the focus in the Salamanca Statement of inclusion being equated solely with mainstream education settings remains problematic in terms of associating inclusion with a place rather than on key principles that should inform educational provision such as equity and respect for others (Hegarty 2001; Ring 2019).

The authors of *Leading Inclusion from the Inside Out: A Handbook for Parents and Early Childhood Teachers in Early Learning and Care, Primary and Special School Settings* acknowledge the complexity and competing values inherent in the concept of inclusion and subscribe to the definition of education for all articulated by UNESCO (2005: 10)

> Education for all means ensuring that all children have access to basic education of good quality. This implies creating an environment in schools and in basic education programmes in which children are both able and enabled to learn. Such an environment must be inclusive of children, effective with children, friendly and welcoming to children, healthy and protective for children and gender sensitive.

In operationalising this definition, the authors endorse the principles of an inclusive culture identified in the Diversity, Equality and Inclusion Charter and Guidelines for Early Childhood Care and Education (DCYA 2016). These principles are summarised in Figure 1.3.

In research conducted by Daly and colleagues, a special needs assistant (SNA) supporting children in a special school noted that the focus of her

Looking Towards a New Era of Leading Education   13

Figure 1.3. Principles of an Inclusive Culture in an Early Childhood Education
(Adapted from DCYA 2016)

work was around making a child's world 'bigger not smaller' (Daly et al. 2016: 144). In essence therefore, *Leading Inclusion from the Inside Out: A Handbook for Parents and Early Childhood Teachers in Early Learning and Care, Primary and Special School Settings* is designed to support early childhood teachers across ELC, primary and special school settings in making each child's world bigger and dismantling exclusionary practices that combine and contribute to the unacceptable oppression of vulnerable individuals and specific groups in our society (Slee 2019). An inclusive system is committed to education for all children through cultivating responsive environments and a pedagogy located within the principles of universal design for learning (UDL) (Centre for Applied Special Technology (CAST) 2018; Ring et al. 2019). The principles on which this publication is based go beyond a focus on removing the barriers to learning experienced by particular groups of children and focus instead on providing a curriculum that can be accessed, understood and engaged in by learners.

The Potential of a Bioecological Lens in Making Children's World Bigger

While society and education systems have made progress towards providing equal opportunities for all children, the journey to creating truly inclusive systems continues. Slee (2019: 909), emphasising the importance of belonging, observes that the ongoing 'struggle to achieve a condition of belonging in education by and for children with disabilities exposes the deep structure of social exclusion that is represented in and reproduced by schooling'. Slee (2019) reminds us of the often forgotten fact that the beneficiaries of inclusion are not those who continue to be the objects of separation but rather all members of society. Adopting a bioecological lens provides us with the opportunity to interrogate the concept of belonging and situate the biopsychosocial model within an interactionist/ecological perspective, while simultaneously reminding us of the importance of focusing on both the child and the broad range of environmental factors impacting on each child (Desforges and Lindsay 2010). It is suggested that viewing inclusion through a bioecological lens can support educators in understanding and addressing the complexity of inclusion and the multiple dimensions contributing to including all children in our education systems.

The idea of a bioecological lens can be traced to the work of Bronfenbrenner (1979), which moved away from theoretical models of children's learning and development, focusing exclusively on the child, and instead suggested that all relationships in each child's ecosystem impact on the child's learning and development. The value of this approach in creating an education system where all children are enabled to achieve their potential was recently affirmed by the European Agency for Special Needs and Inclusive Education (EASNIE) and by research commissioned by the NCCA exploring research-informed theoretical approaches for children's learning and development (EASNIE 2017a; 2017b; 2017c; Ring et al. 2019).

Following an extensive review of the literature on effectively providing for inclusion in the early years, the EASNIE concluded that understanding the complex evolving influences on children stemming from children's interactions with the systems that surround them and the influence of the interrelations between these systems on how children learn and develop is vital to providing for an effective inclusive early childhood system (EASNIE 2017a; 2017b; 2017c; 2017d). Ensuring that the perspective of the child is located at the centre of this model and combined with a research-based inclusive pedagogy remains the responsibility of educators.

Adopting a bioecological lens, the LINC Consortium identified the key competencies in Table 1.1 associated with cultivating effective inclusive culture, practices and pedagogy for all children in the early years (LINC Consortium 2016–2020). These competencies reflect the convincing research evidence that the characteristics of children's relationships with their primary caregivers and the context within which this relationship occurs exert the strongest influence on children's developmental pathways and their present and future wellbeing (DeCandia et al. 2020).

The competencies identified in Table 1.1 emerge as inter-connected rather than mutually exclusive and are addressed extensively throughout this publication. Central to the effectiveness and influence of these competencies in creating inclusive early childhood settings in practice is an understanding of the complexity of and influence of leadership for inclusion in children's early years.

Table 1.1. Competencies Associated with Providing Early Childhood Education for All Children

A.	An Inclusive Culture
1	All children are welcome.
2	All children are valued.
3	A focus is placed on promoting respectful interactions.
4	There are high expectations for all children.
5	Partnership with parents/carers is actively promoted.
6	Difference is acknowledged and celebrated.
7	The environment accommodates the needs of all children.
8	All policies are inclusive policies.
B.	**Inclusive Practice**
1	Transitioning to and from the setting is a positive experience for children, families and staff.
2	Support for children with additional needs is co-ordinated.
3	Staff members are encouraged to avail of continuing professional development opportunities.
4	All staff are aware of their roles and responsibilities in relation to the promotion of inclusive practice.
5	The expertise of staff is acknowledged and utilised.
C.	**An Inclusive Pedagogy**
1	Children's experiences are planned with the needs of all children in mind.
2	Strategies are in place to promote the participation of all children in learning.
3	A range of appropriate pedagogical approaches is used to support the holistic development of all children.
4	Play and playful learning are key features of practice for all children.
5	All children's communication and interaction are promoted.
6	All children's views are valued and responded to.

7	Early identification of children who require additional support is central to practice.
8	A variety of approaches to observation, recording and assessment is in place.
9	Early years educators plan, implement and evaluate children's learning in partnership with children, parents/carers and relevant others.
10	Positive relationships are understood and nurtured.
11	Children's specific assessed needs are understood as 'signposts' that support children's learning and development.
12	External assistance is elicited where required to support the setting in meeting children's additional needs.

Leading Inclusion for Children in the Early Years: Whose Responsibility?

The increasing administrative, management and pedagogical complexity of leading educational contexts has necessitated a re-conceptualisation of leadership across ELC and school settings (Harris and Spillane 2008; Ring et al. 2019). Distributed leadership refocuses the traditional understanding of leadership as being the sole responsibility of the manager to distributing the responsibility for leadership across an organisation (Leithwood et al. 2007; O'Donovan 2016). Distributed leadership envisages a relational, interactive, reciprocal and dialogical process with trust as a decisive component in cultivating leadership practice (Harris and Spillane 2008). A commitment to administrative, management and pedagogical leadership has consistently been identified as the crucial determinant of the success or failure of creating inclusive education environments (Ring 2010; Fitzgerald 2018). Increasingly research is isolating and interrogating the central importance of pedagogical leaders in early childhood education and their fundamental role in ensuring that all children are supported in achieving their full potential (Coughlin and Baird 2013; Carroll-Meehan, Bolshaw and Hadfield 2019). Pedagogy itself is the practice we engage in every day as educators, informed by our understanding of how children learn and the philosophy of education we aspire to. Pedagogy therefore is firmly located in the learning and teaching process and pedagogical leadership is concerned with leading this process. According to Coughlin and Baird (2013: 1), pedagogical leaders 'see themselves as partners, facilitators, observers and co-learners alongside educators, children and families'.

Distributed leadership provides an opportunity for ELC settings and schools to reduce the challenges presented by the increasing administrative, management and pedagogical complexity of leading educational contexts. Specifically, pedagogical leadership acknowledges the contribution of the early childhood teacher in leading inclusive pedagogy and contributing to the whole-setting's inclusive culture and practice. Leading inclusion for children in the early years therefore remains a shared and distributed responsibility.

The Structure of the Book

Reflecting the bioecological lens described above, each section of the book is inherently linked, and presented in three inter-connected sections focused on placing the child at the centre of the ecosystem, realising inclusive pedagogy and leadership for including all children.

The Child at the Centre

In the three chapters of this section, the critical importance of placing the child at the centre of decision-making in early childhood education is highlighted. In Chapter 2, Ring, Harte and Harmon identify the threefold rationale for capturing the voices of all children as being a matter of human rights and social justice; optimising children's learning and development and being central to the concept of democracy in education. The authors provide a range of strategies to support parents and early childhood teachers in meaningfully harnessing all children's voices at home, in ELC, primary and special school settings. An insight into the unique nature and learning capacity of children from birth to three (babies and toddlers) is explored from a theoretical perspective in Chapter 3 and a picture painted by Doherty of what this might look like in practice. Practical implications and strategies are provided for supporting babies and toddlers at home and in ELC settings in order to optimise and enhance children's learning, wellbeing and development from the beginning. The potential of pedagogical interactions for enhancing learning and development, with a particular focus on children's cognitive development, learning and thinking is considered by Ryan in Chapter 4. Ryan positions the concept that interactions drive development as an inclusive principle located at the fulcrum of providing education for all children and provides signposts, which can be applied by parents, early childhood and primary teachers to support children as they commence their education voyage.

Realising Inclusive Culture, Pedagogy and Practice

The first chapter in this section deliberately focuses on realising and building partnership with parents and families. Barr and Hillard highlight the importance of developing a seamless connection between home and the education setting for all children in Chapter 5. The authors suggest a number of strategies to support early childhood teachers in enhancing communication with parents and families; parental involvement in decision-making and parental engagement in children's learning. Wellbeing is explored in the context of the inclusion of all children by Heaney and Feeney in Chapter 6. Practical strategies are suggested, which can promote children's wellbeing, while simultaneously enhancing the inclusive culture in children's early learning experiences. The role and responsibility of the adult in nurturing children's wellbeing are interrogated and signposts for practice identified. Play is suggested as a pedagogy that can support all children in a child-centred way and that builds on individual interests and celebrates diverse ways of exploring, meaning making and knowing by O'Sullivan in Chapter 7. The significance of clearly articulating what playful learning looks like, in practice, is addressed, in addition to the contribution of play to children's wellbeing, self-regulation and social competence. Strategies for promoting inclusive play and for using Aistear: The Early Childhood Curriculum Framework (NCCA 2009) as a tool to support the development of inclusive play provision, are provided. In the final chapter of this section, Kelleher and Fenlon examine research related to the impact the environment potentially has on children's learning, development and wellbeing; and strategies are identified to support the meaningful participation of all children in the context of harnessing the potential of the 'environment as the third teacher'.

Leadership for Including All Children

The final section explores the role of leadership in leading and coordinating inclusive practice and whole-setting and individual planning. In Chapter 9, Skehill explores the key features of effective leadership for inclusion which underpin the LINC Programme. The barriers for INCOs in the Irish context are examined and the manner in which the LINC programme supports INCOs in navigating these challenges is detailed. The chapter explores what it means to be an INCO in practice; the skills required, the process of facilitating change and the core responsibilities of the role. Practical guidance is offered for early childhood teachers and INCOs and key signposts for practice are identified in terms of communicating with colleagues; facilitating diversity, equality and inclusion; sharing information with parents and professional colleagues and harnessing the voice of the child. The critical importance of whole-setting and individual planning in ensuring the inclusion of all children is detailed by Donnellan, Joyce and Ryan in Chapter 10. The chapter identifies a range of planning frameworks to support whole-setting and individual planning in ELC, primary and special school settings. The final section of Chapter 10 deliberates on the importance of including the child's voice in the planning process. Strategies are identified for the reader to support the practice of consultation with children. In the final chapter of the book, Daly focuses on children's assessed needs as signposts for learning and development rather than defining features of a child's ability. Daly helpfully connects patterns in recommended supports to the concept of UDL that facilitates early childhood teachers in cultivating early childhood settings where all children are enabled to flourish.

Conclusion

Education remains UNESCO's top priority because of its status as a basic human right and its potential to build peace and propel sustainable development (UNESCO 2017). It is clear that despite the many efforts to create education settings where all children experience an authentically inclusive environment, challenges remain (Ring 2019; Slee 2019; O'Brien 2020). Dewey's linking of democracy to pedagogy continues to be a key influence on cultivating an education in, and for, democracy as an aspiration of powerful and transformative education systems (Dewey 1916). Inclusive education is closely linked to this aspiration as 'a franchise of an education in, and for democracy' (Slee 2019: 910). However, creating spaces where all children belong, can only be authenticated by a commitment to inclusion evidenced in the habits of an inclusive pedagogy firmly located in inclusive culture and practice. In *Leading Inclusion from the Inside Out: A Handbook for Parents and Early Childhood Teachers in Early Learning and Care, Primary and Special School Settings*, the authors hope to contribute to the creation of an inclusive early childhood system through supporting early childhood teachers in ELC, primary and special school settings in their quest for an inclusive pedagogy that removes barriers and enables all children and families to flourish. In essence this publication looks towards a new era where leading inclusion from the inside out progresses to leading all children's early childhood experiences from the inside out.

Bibliography

Bronfenbrenner, U. (1979). *The Ecology of Human Development: Experiments by Nature and Design*. Cambridge, MA: Harvard University Press.

Carroll-Meehan, C., Bolshaw, P., and Hadfield, E. (2019). 'New Leaders in Early Years: Making a Difference for Children in England', *Early Child Development and Care*, 3, 416–429.

Centre for Applied Special Technology. (2018). *Universal Design for Learning Guidelines Version 2.2*. Cambridge, MA: Harvard Graduate School of Education, <http://udlguidelines.cast.org>, accessed 31 August 2020.

Centre for Early Childhood Development and Education. (2006). *Síolta: The National Quality Framework for Early Childhood Education*. Dublin: Centre for Early Childhood Development and Education, <http://siolta.ie/media/pdfs/final_handbook.pdf>, accessed 20 October 2019, accessed 29 October 2010.

Coughlin, A. M., and Baird, L. (2013). *Pedagogical Leadership*. London: London Bridge Child Care Services & Kawartha Child Care Services, <http://www.edu.gov.on.ca/childcare/Baird_Coughlin.pdf>, accessed 25 January 2020.

Daly, P., Ring, E., Egan, M., Fitzgerald, J., Griffin, C., Long, S., McCarthy, E., Moloney, M., O'Brien, T., O'Byrne, A., O'Sullivan, S., Ryan, M., Wall, E., and Madden, R. (2016). *An Evaluation of Education Provision for Children with Autistic Spectrum Disorder in the Republic of Ireland*. Trim: National Council for Special Education, <https://dspace.mic.ul.ie/handle/10395/2273>, accessed 16 January 2020.

DeCandia, C. J., Volk, K. T., Unick, G. J., and Donegan, L. R. W. (2020). 'Developing a Screening Tool for Young Children Using an Ecological Framework', *Infants & Young Children*, 33(4), 237–258.

Department of Children and Youth Affairs. (2016). *Diversity, Equality and Inclusion Charter and Guidelines for Early Childhood Care and Education*.

Dublin: Department of Children and Youth Affairs, <https://assets.gov.ie/38186/c9e90d89d94b41d3bf00201c98b2ef6a.pdf>, accessed 20 October 2019.

Department of Children and Youth Affairs. (2019a). *Early Childhood Care and Education (ECCE) or Free Preschool*. Dublin: Department of Children and Youth Affairs, <https://www.gov.ie/en/publication/d7a5e6-early-childhood-care-and-education-ecce-or-free-preschool/?referrer=/cat/en/childcare/211.htm/>, accessed 21 January 2020.

Department of Children and Youth Affairs. (2019b). *An End of Year One Review of the Access and Inclusion Model (AIM)*. Dublin: Department of Children and Youth Affairs, Dublin: Department of Children and Youth Affairs, <https://aim.gov.ie/wp-content/uploads/2019/10/aim-end-of-year-one-review.pdf>, accessed 21 January 2020.

Department of Education and Skills. (2007). *Special Educational Needs: A Continuum of Support*. Dublin, Department of Education and Skills, <https://www.education.ie/en/Schools-Colleges/Services/National-Educational-Psychological-Service-NEPS-/neps_special_needs_guidelines.pdf>, accessed 06 September 2020.

Department of Education and Skills. (2016). *Looking at our School 2016: A Quality Framework for Primary Schools*. Dublin: Department of Education and Skills, <https://www.education.ie/en/Publications/Inspection-Reports-Publications/Evaluation-Reports-Guidelines/Looking-at-Our-School-2016-A-Quality-Framework-for-Primary-Schools.pdf>, accessed 30 August 2020.

Department of Education and Skills. (2017a). *Circular No 0012/2017. Circular to the Management Authorities of all Mainstream Primary Schools Special Education Teaching Allocation*. Athlone: Department of Education and Skills, <https://www.education.ie/en/Circulars-and-Forms/Active-Circulars/cl0013_2017.pdf>, accessed 21 January 2020.

Department of Education and Skills. (2017b). *A New Model for Allocating Special Education Teachers to Mainstream Schools*. Dublin: Department of Education and Skills, <https://www.education.ie/en/The-Education-System/Special-Education/a-new-model-for-allocating-special-education-teachers-to-mainstream-schools.pdf>, accessed 21 January 2020.

Department of Education and Skills. (2020). *Primary Education*. Dublin: Department of Education and Skills, <https://www.education.ie/en/The-Education-System/Primary/>, accessed 30 August 2020.

Desforges, M., and Lindsay, G. (2010). *Procedures Used to Diagnose a Disability and to Assess Special Educational Needs: An International Review*. Trim: National Council for Special Education, <https://ncse.ie/wpcontent/uploads/2014/10/5_NCSE_Diag_Ass.pdf>, accessed 26 January 2020.

Dewey, J. (1916). *Democracy and Education*. New York, NY: The Free Press.
European Agency for Special Needs and Inclusive Education. (2017a). *Inclusive Early Childhood Education: New Insights and Tools – Contributions from a European Study* (M. Kyriazopoulou, P. Bartolo, E. Björck-Åkesson, C. Giné, and F. Bellour, eds). Odense, Denmark: European Agency for Special Needs and Inclusive Education, <https://www.european-agency.org/resources/publications/inclusive-early-childhood-education-new-insights-and-tools-contributions>, accessed 21 January 2020.
European Agency for Special Needs and Inclusive Education. (2017b). *Inclusive Early Childhood Education: New Insights and Tools – Final Summary Report* (M. Kyriazopoulou, P. Bartolo, E. Björck-Åkesson, C. Giné, and F. Bellour, eds). Odense, Denmark: European Agency for Special Needs and Inclusive Education, <https://www.european-agency.org/sites/default/files/IECE-Summary-ENelectronic.pdf>, accessed 21 January 2020.
European Agency for Special Needs and Inclusive Education. (2017c). *Inclusive Early Childhood Education: Literature Review* (F. Bellour, P. Bartolo, and M. Kyriazopoulou, eds). Odense, Denmark: European Agency for Special Needs and Inclusive Education, <https://www.european-agency.org/sites/default/files/IECE%20Literature%20Review.pdf>, accessed 21 January 2020.
European Agency for Special Needs and Inclusive Education. (2017d). *Inclusive Early Childhood Education Environment Self-Reflection Tool* (E. Björck-Åkesson, M. Kyriazopoulou, C. Giné, and P. Bartolo, eds). Odense, Denmark: European Agency for Special Needs and Inclusive Education, <https://www.european-agency.org/sites/default/files/IECE%20Environment%20Self-Reflection%20Tool.pdf>, accessed 21 January 2020.
Fitzgerald, J. (2018). 'Leading Learning for Children with Autism Spectrum Difference'. In Ring, E., Daly, P., and Wall, E., (eds), *Autism from the Inside Out: A Handbook for Parents, Early Childhood, Primary, Post-Primary and Special School Settings*, pp. 243–264. Oxford: Peter Lang.
Harris, A. (2020). 'We Are Failing too Many Children with Disabilities in Mainstream Schools', *Irish Times*, Tuesday January 14, <https://www.irishtimes.com/news/education/we-are-failing-too-many-children-with-disabilities-in-mainstream-schools-1.4128732>, accessed 21 January 2020.
Harris, A., and Spillane, J. (2008). 'Distributed Leadership through the Looking Glass', *Management in Education*, 22(1), 31–34.
Hegarty, S. (1993). 'Reviewing the Literature on Integration', *European Journal of Special Needs Education*, 8(3), 94–200.
Hegarty, S. (2001). 'Inclusive Education – A Case to Answer', *Journal of Moral Education*, 30(3), 243–249.

Inter-Departmental Group. (2015). *Supporting Access to the Early Childhood Care and Education Programme for Children with a Disability*. Dublin: Inter-Departmental Group, <http://nda.ie/nda-files/Supporting-Access-to-the-Early-Childhood-Care-and-Education-for-Children-with-a-Disability.pdf>, accessed 21 January 2020.

Ireland. (1937). *Bunreacht na hÉireann. Constitution of Ireland*. Dublin: Government Publications Office, <https://www.gov.ie/en/publication/d5bd8c-constitution-of-ireland/>, accessed 11 January 2020.

Ireland. (1998). *Education Act, 1998*. Dublin: The Government Publications Office.

Ireland. (2000). *Education (Welfare) Act, 2000*. Dublin: The Government Publications Office.

Ireland. (2000–2004). *The Equal Status Acts 2000 to 2004*. Dublin: The Government Publications Office.

Ireland. (2004). *Education for Persons with Special Educational Needs Act 2004*. Dublin: The Government Publications Office.

Ireland. (2005). *The Disability Act 2005*. Dublin: The Government Publications Office.

Leadership for INClusion in the Early Years Consortium. (2016–2020). *Competencies Associated with Providing for Inclusion in the Early Years*. Mary Immaculate College, Limerick: Leadership for INClusion in the Early Years Consortium.

Leithwood, K., Mascall, B., Strauss, T., Sacks, R., Memon, N., and Yashkina, A. (2007). *Distributing Leadership to Make Schools Smarter*. Toronto: University of Toronto, Ontario Institute for Studies in Education.

Lynch, H., Ring, E., Boyle, B., Moore, A., O'Toole, C., O'Sullivan, L., Brophy, T., Frizelle, P., Horgan, D. and O'Sullivan, D. (2020). *Evaluation of In-School and Early Years Therapy Support Demonstration Project*. Trim: National Council for Special Education, https://ncse.ie/wp-content/uploads/2020/11/Demo-project-evaluation-fInal-for-web-upload.pdf , accessed 04 January 2021.

Melhuish, E. (2015). What *Matters in the Quality of ECCE? Answer: Interactions Drive Development'. Organisation for Economic Development and Co-Operation Meeting (OECD)*, Early Childhood Education and Care International Policy Event, 28 October 2015, Chartered Accountants House, Pearse Street, Dublin 2: Pobal, <https://www.youtube.com/watch?v=2U1z0C6EUbw>, accessed 21 January 2020.

National Council for Curriculum and Assessment. (2009). *Aistear: The Early Childhood Curriculum Framework*. Dublin: National Council for Curriculum and Assessment, <https://www.ncca.ie/en/early-childhood/aistear>, accessed 29 October 2019.

National Council for Curriculum and Assessment. (2015). *Aistear/Síolta Practice Guide*. Dublin, National Council for Curriculum and Assessment, <www.ncca.ie/en/Practice-Guide>, accessed 29 October 2019.

O'Brien, T. (2020). 'Has Inclusion become a Barrier to Inclusion?', *Support for Learning*, 35(3), 299–311.

O'Donovan, M. (2016). *Distributed Leadership. Professional Development Service for Teachers*, <https://pdst.ie/sites/default/files/Distributed%20Leadership%20Web%20Version.pptx>, accessed 25 January 2020.

Ring, E. (2010). *An Evaluation of the Effects of an Autistic Spectrum Disorder-Specific Post-Graduate Certificate Continuing Professional Development Programme on Practice in Six Schools*. St. Patrick's College (Dublin City University): Dublin (Unpublished Ph.D. Thesis).

Ring, E. (2019). *Reflections on the Journey from Exclusion to Inclusion and Beyond*, National Association of Boards of Management in Special Education Conference 2019: 50 Years On: Creating a Brighter Future Together, 10 October 2019, Sheraton Hotel, Athlone, Ireland.

Ring, E., Grey, T., O'Sullivan, L., Corbett, M., Sheerin, J., and Heeney, T. (2019). *Universal Design Guidelines for Early Learning and Care Settings: Literature Review*. Dublin: Department of Children and Youth Affairs, <https://aim.gov.ie/wp-content/uploads/2019/06/universal-design-guidelines-for-elc-settings-literature-review-2.pdf>, accessed 31 August 2020.

Ring, E., Kelleher, S., Breen, F., Heeney, T., McLoughlin, M., Kearns, A., Stafford, P., Skehill, S., Campion, K., Comerford, D., and O'Sullivan, L. (2019). *Interim Evaluation of the Leadership for Inclusion in the Early Years (LINC) Programme*. Limerick: Mary Immaculate College, <https://documentcloud.adobe.com/link/track?uri=urn:aaid:scds:US:d8c95d7d-2d75-40a8-9f65-b6582908c08d>, accessed 6 January 2019.

Ring, E., Mhic Mhathúna, M., Moloney, M., Hayes, N., Breathnach, D., Stafford, P., Carswell, D., Keegan, S., Kelleher, C., McCafferty, D., O'Keeffe, A., Leavy, A., Madden, R., and Ozonyia, M. (2016). *An Examination of Concepts of School Readiness among Parents and Educators in Ireland*. Dublin: Department of Children and Youth Affairs, <https://dspace.mic.ul.ie/handle/10395/2344>, accessed 16 January 2020.

Ring, E., O'Sullivan, L., Ryan, M., and Burke, P. (2018). *A Melange or a Mosaic of Theories? How Theoretical Perspectives on Children's Learning and Development can Inform a Responsive Pedagogy in a Redeveloped Primary School Curriculum*. Dublin: National Council for Curriculum and Assessment, <https://www.ncca.ie/media/3863/seminar_four_er_los_mr_pb_paper.pdf>, accessed 16 January 2020.

Ring, E., O'Sullivan, L., and Wall, E. (2020). 'Resisting the "Schoolification Epidemic" in Early Childhood Education: Why the "3Rs" of Rights. Research and Reflection Must Continue to Be the Propellers for Re-Conceptualising Initial Early Childhood Teacher Education'. In Lin, M. and Jones, I., (eds), *Critical Issues in Early Childhood Education: Volume 2 – International Perspective*, pp. 1–22. Charlotte, NC: Information Age Publishing.

Slee, R. (2019). 'Belonging in an Age of Inclusion', *International Journal of Inclusive Education*, 23(9), 909–922.

United Nations. (1989). *Convention on the Rights of the Child*. New York, NY: United Nations, <http://www.ohchr.org/EN/ProfessionalInterest/Pages/CRC.aspx>, accessed 12 January 2020.

United Nations Educational, Scientific and Cultural Organisation. (1994). *The Salamanca Statement and Framework for Action on Special Needs Education*, Adopted by the World Conference on Special Needs Education: Access and Quality, Salamanca, Spain, 7–10 June 1994, Paris: United Nations Educational, Scientific and Cultural Organisation, <https://unesdoc.unesco.org/ark:/48223/pf0000098427>, accessed 21 January 2020.

United Nations Educational, Scientific and Cultural Organisation. (2005). *Guidelines for Inclusion: Ensuring Access to Education for All*. Paris: United Nations Educational, Scientific and Cultural Organisation, <http://www.ibe.unesco.org/sites/default/files/Guidelines_for_Inclusion_UNESCO_2006.pdf>, accessed 31 August 2020.

United Nations Educational, Scientific and Cultural Organisation. (2017). *A Guide for Ensuring Inclusion and Equity in Education*. Paris: United Nations Educational, Scientific and Cultural Organisation, <https://unesdoc.unesco.org/ark:/48223/pf0000248254>, accessed 25 January 2020.

United Nations Educational, Scientific and Cultural Organisation. (2019). *International Forum on Inclusion and Equity in Education: Every Learner Matters*. Paris: United Nations Educational, Scientific and Cultural Organisation, <https://unesdoc.unesco.org/ark:/48223/pf0000371096>, accessed 21 January 2020.

Warnock, M. (1982). 'Children with Special Needs in Ordinary Schools: Integration Revisited', *Education Today*, 32(3), 56–62.

The Child at the Centre

EMER RING, PAULA HARTE AND MAURICE HARMON

Chapter 2 Making Children's Right to Participate Visible and Children's Voices Distinct in the Acoustic of Early Childhood Education

ABSTRACT

The competencies associated with early childhood teacher education for inclusion identified in the Leadership for INClusion in the Early Years (LINC) competency framework focus on embracing best practice around valuing and welcoming all children to child-centred stimulating environments, where positive interactions are prioritised and supported (LINC 2016–2020). Central to creating inclusive environments is the value that is placed on cultivating an atmosphere where children know that their voices are valued, listened and responded to, and can make a difference. Article 12 of the United Nations (UN) Convention on the Rights of the Child (UNCRC) explicitly states that children have the right to have their opinions taken into account and their views respected in relation to decision-making that affects them, while in Ireland, children's right to have their voices heard and allocated due weight is further acknowledged in the Constitution (Ireland 1937; 2012; UN 1989). In this chapter, research concerning the value of creating early childhood environments where children's right to participate is visible and where children's voices are embedded in the acoustic and fabric of the setting is explored, and strategies provided to support early childhood teachers in meaningfully harnessing all children's voices in early learning and care (ELC), primary and special school settings.

Introduction

We are now almost all aware of Article 12 of The United Nations (UN) Convention on the Rights of the Child (UNCRC), which states that children have the right to have their opinions taken into account, their views respected in decision-making that affects them and these views given due weight in accordance with their age and maturity (UN 1989).

We know that prioritising children's participation impacts positively on their self-esteem and confidence, promotes their overall development, resilience, autonomy, independence and social competence (National Council for Curriculum and Assessment (NCCA) 2009; Lansdown 2005; Ring et al. 2018). Aistear: The Early Childhood Curriculum Framework reminds us that 'The child's ability to communicate is at the very heart of early learning and development' (NCCA 2009: 2). Critically the creation of early childhood environments where affordances are created to support all children in participating and communicating in a myriad of ways is central to providing for inclusive environments where diversity becomes the norm. Ensuring all children are viewed as equal participants in early childhood education contributes to the creation of settings where children's rights are acknowledged and children's views valued. In Ireland, our vision and commitment to realising children's rights is expressly articulated in Better Outcomes, Brighter Futures: The National Policy Framework for Children and Young People 2014–2020 (Department of Children and Youth Affairs (DCYA) 2014), which states that:

> Our vision is for Ireland to be one of the best small countries in the world in which to grow up and raise a family, and where the rights of all children and young people are respected, protected and fulfilled; where their voices are heard and where they are supported to realise their maximum potential now and in the future (DCYA 2014: vi)

While including the right of the child to participate and have his/her voice listened and responded to is articulated as a key principle across global education policy and practice contexts, ensuring that this participation remains meaningful continues to present challenges for education systems (Ring and O'Sullivan 2016). We may not always be convinced that the child's contribution matters; we may be challenged in finding ways to listen to young children or children who are perceived as learning differently and we may consider that encouraging children to express their views has the potential to undermine adult authority (Clark and Moss 2011). However, we must remind ourselves that children now have a non-negotiable right to participate and have their views valued and responded to. As early childhood teachers, we are obliged to find ways to ensure that children's participation and voices have an equal prominence with adult voices in early childhood education. In this chapter the implications of Article 12 of the UNCRC (UN 1989) in policy, legislative and practice contexts will be discussed. Research related to the impact of prioritising children's participation in early childhood education on their overall development will be interrogated, and the Lundy Model of Child Participation applied specifically to early learning and care (ELC), primary and special school settings (DCYA 2015a). Practical strategies will be identified to support early childhood teachers in making children's right to participate visible and children's voices distinct in the acoustic and fabric of early childhood education.

Key Signposts: Introduction

- Article 12 of The United Nations (UN) Convention on the Rights of the Child (1989) states that children have the right to have their opinions taken into account and their views respected in decision-making that affects them (UN 1989).
- Prioritising children's participation impacts positively on their self-esteem and confidence, promotes their overall development, resilience, autonomy, independence and social competence (National Council for Curriculum and Assessment (NCCA) 2009; Lansdown 2005).
- Ensuring children are viewed as equal participants in early childhood education contributes to the creation of settings where children's right to participate is acknowledged and children's views valued.
- While including the right of the child to participate and have his/her voice listened and responded to is articulated as a key principle in national and international education policy and practice contexts, ensuring that this participation remains meaningful continues to present challenges for education systems (Ring and O'Sullivan 2016).
- As early childhood teachers, we are obliged to find ways to ensure that children's voices have an equal prominence with adult voices in the acoustic and fabric of early childhood education.

The Policy, Legislative and Practice Context: Children's Rights Emerging from the Shadows

Hayes and Bradley (2009) put forward that it is only in the latter half of the last century that the discourse of children's rights has begun to become embedded in national and international policy, legislative and practice contexts. In 2007, Kilkelly observed that multiple barriers to securing children's rights in Ireland existed, highlighting children's invisibility; a failure to listen to children's voices; absence of a child focus, a rights basis and child proofing, in addition to inadequate administrative and political structures, as among these barriers. Linked to the barriers in realising children's rights identified by Kilkelly (2007) are the societal images of childhood, whereby children were historically viewed as being dependant on, and subservient to, adults (Sorin 2005). The move to the current concept of the child as agentic and viewed as competent, confident and capable of sharing power with adults can be traced to evolving societal ideologies and the simultaneous development of a robust corpus of research related to children's early learning and development (Ring, O'Sullivan and Harmon 2021).

Following World War II, and a global concern that the atrocities and suffering characteristic of both world wars would not re-occur, an international focus on human rights emerged and the Universal Declaration of Human Rights (UDHR) was announced by the UN General Assembly in Paris on 10 December 1948 (UN 1948). Human rights are described by Kilkelly (2007: 18) as being 'based on the fundamental principle that all people are equal, and equally deserve to have their rights and freedoms respected'. Concerned that children's rights needed to be expressly articulated, the UNCRC was proclaimed in 1989 and ratified by Ireland on 28 September 1992. Testimony to the reach of the UNCRC, is that it is now the most extensively ratified convention in international law, which comes with a duty to implement its provisions (Ring et al. 2019a). McGoldrick (1991) heralded the UNCRC as an important milestone in the development of civilisation through its articulation of the rights of the child as

Making Children's Right to Participate Visible

a fundamental and universal concept. The UNCRC is consonant with the concept of the child's holistic and harmonious development through a non-hierarchical integration of the economic, social, cultural, civil and political rights of the child underpinned by the four general principles summarised in Figure 2.1 (Ring et al. 2019a).

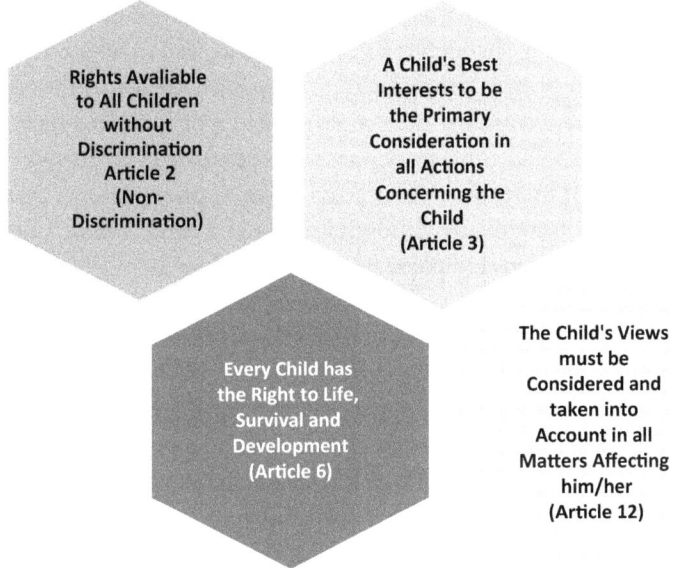

Figure 2.1. The Four General Principles Underpinning the United Nations Convention on the Rights of the Child (Ring et al. 2019a: 50)

Specifically related to this chapter is the application of Article 12 to children's early education experiences across ELC, primary and special school contexts. Article 12.1 expressly states that:

> State Parties shall assure to the child who is capable of forming his or her own views the right to express those views freely in all matters affecting the child, the views of the child being given due weight in accordance with the age and maturity of the child. (UN 1989: Article 12.1)

Of particular relevance to children's early childhood experiences, in accordance with the principle of non-hierarchical integration, is that the participation rights articulated in Article 12 are reflected across the convention, notably in Article 13 (Freedom of Expression); Article 14 (Freedom of Thought, Conscience and Religion); Article 15 (Freedom of Association and Peaceful Assembly) and Article 17 (Access to Information) (Ring et al. 2019a). However as international conventions are not legally binding through ratification, the degree to which they are incorporated into policy, law and practice by individual member states remains the sole determinant as to whether the rights and freedoms prescribed in international conventions are realised (Ring et al. 2019a).

In Ireland, an increasingly concerted effort at policy level is discernible in relation to recognising children's rights as a fundamental concept in policy development and implementation (Government of Ireland (GoI) 2000; DCYA 2014; 2015a; 2015b; GoI 2018a; 2018b; Comhairle na nÓg (translated as Young Voices. Local Issues) 2019). Evidence of a commitment at policy level to including children's voices in decision-making is clearly discernible in the establishment of Hub na nÓg (translated as Young Voices in Decision Making) to support the implementation of the National Strategy on Children and Young People's Participation in Decision Making (2015–2020) (DCYA 2015a; DCYA 2020a). Hub na nÓg, as a national centre of excellence and co-ordination, supports government departments, state agencies, and non-government organisations to include children's voices in decision-making issues that affect their lives, and maintains a particular focus on eliciting the voices of those children who are seldom heard (DCYA 2020a). Through ratifying the UNCRC, monitoring its implementation and establishing the Ombudsman for Children's Office (OCO) in 2004 under the Ombudsman for Children Act 2002, Ireland displays a commitment to promoting children's rights (Ireland 2002; DCYA 2013). On 10 November 2012, a referendum was held to amend the Irish Constitution (Bunreacht na hÉireann), with a majority of voters supporting the inclusion of Article 42A, which recognises and affirms the natural and imprescriptible rights of all children and the State's duty, in so far as is practicable to protect and vindicate those rights through its laws (Ireland 1937; 2012). In relation to early childhood education, key practice-focused and framework documents supporting early childhood teachers across ELC, primary and special contexts are focused on providing children with a wide range of opportunities to share their experiences, thoughts, ideas and feelings in a variety of ways and for a variety of purposes. Acknowledging the importance of providing children with a range of modes of communication in the early years, where freedom of expression is promoted and where children are listened and responded to is evident in, *interalia*, Aistear: The Early Childhood Curriculum Framework (NCCA 2009); Síolta: The National Quality Framework for Early Childhood Education (Centre for Early Childhood Development and Education (CECDE) 2006); Aistear/Síolta Practice Guide (NCCA 2015); Diversity, Equality and Inclusion Charter and Guidelines for Early Childhood Care and Education (DCYA 2016a); Looking at Our Schools: A Quality Framework for Primary Schools (Department of Education and Skills (DES) 2016a); Action Plan for Education 2016–2019 (DES 2016b). A Guide to Early Years Education Inspection (DES 2018) and the Primary Language Curriculum (NCCA 2019).

At this juncture, the message from the policy, legislative and practice context is that children's rights are indeed emerging into the light. In terms of Article 12 of the UNCRC therefore, we as early childhood teachers have a responsibility to consider and take into account each child's view in all matters affecting him/her in ELC, primary and special school contexts.

> Key Signposts: The Policy, Legislative and Practice Context: Children's Rights Emerging from the Shadows
>
> - Multiple barriers to securing children's rights in Ireland existed, including children's invisibility; a failure to listen to children's voices; absence of a child focus, a rights basis and child proofing and inadequate administrative and political structures as being among these barriers (Kilkelly 2007).
> - The move to the current concept of the child as agentic and viewed as competent, confident and capable of sharing power with adults can be traced to evolving societal ideologies and the simultaneous development of a robust corpus of research related to children's early learning and development (Ring, O'Sullivan and Harmon, 2021).

- Following World War II, an international focus on human rights emerged described by Kilkelly (2007: 18) as being 'based on the fundamental principle that all people are equal, and equally deserve to have their rights and freedoms respected'.
- The United Nations Convention on the Rights of the Child (UNCRC) was proclaimed in 1989 and ratified by Ireland on 28 September 1992 and is now the most extensively ratified convention in international law (Ring et al. 2019a).
- Of particular relevance to children's early childhood experiences, in accordance with the principle of non-hierarchical integration, is that the participation rights articulated in Article 12 of the UNCRC are reflected across the convention.
- At this juncture, the message from the policy, legislative and practice context is that children's rights are indeed emerging into the light. We as early childhood teachers have a responsibility to consider and take into account each child's view in all matters affecting him/her in ELC, primary and special contexts, primary and special school contexts (DCYA 2014; Graham 2017).

Research on Children's Learning and Development in the Early Years: The Power and Potential of Participation

Ensuring the meaningful participation of all children in high-quality early childhood settings is critical, with research on children's early learning and development confirming that providing spaces where children can meaningfully participate remains a key determinant of this high-quality (Melhuish et al. 2015). Ring et al. (2018), exploring the current theoretical perspectives on children's learning and development, summarised in Figure 2.2, concluded that enabling each child to flourish requires a broader focus than curriculum alone.

Making Children's Right to Participate Visible

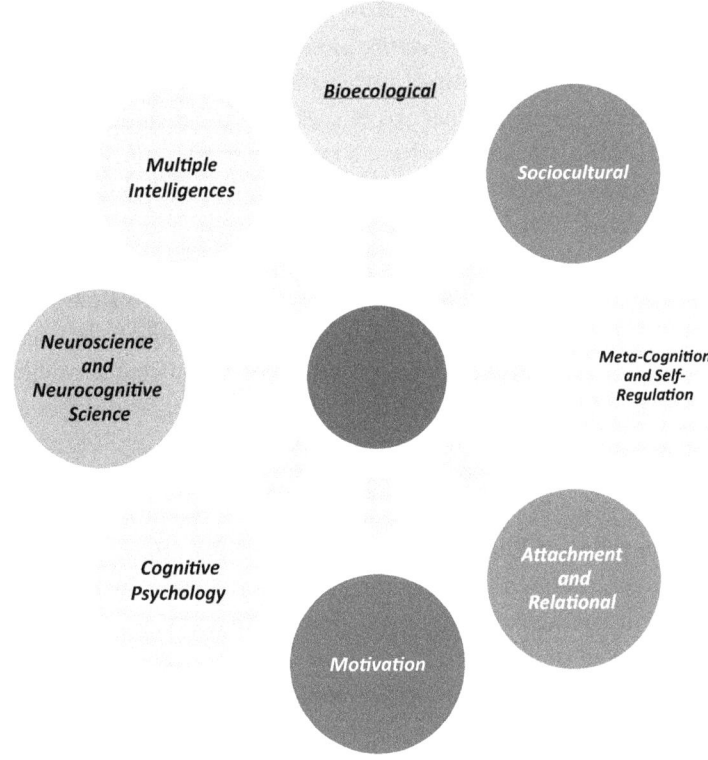

Figure 2.2. Theoretical Perspectives on Children's Learning and Development (Ring et al. 2018: 5)

Stemming from an exploration of a wide range of literature focused on Bioecological (Bronfenbrenner and Morris 1998; European Agency for Special Needs and Inclusive Education (EASNIE) 2017; Edwards, Gandini and Forman 2012); Sociocultural (Vygotsky 1962; 1978; Veraska and Van Oers 2011) MetaCognition and Self-Regulation (Vygotsky 1978; Whitebread 2010; 2012; Blair and Raver 2015; Whitebread et al. 2017); Attachment (Bowlby 1988; Sabol and Pinta 2012; Verissimo et al. 2017); Motivation (Maslow 1943; Deci and Ryan 2008; Hidi 2015) Cognitive

Psychology (Willingham 2009; Rosenshine 2012) Neuroscience and Neurocognitive Perspectives (Goswami 2004; Melhuish et al. 2015) and Multiple Intelligences (including Learning Styles) perspectives (Silver et al. 1997; Gardner 2006; Kirschner 2017), the authors concluded that 'classroom climate and relationships have a tangible impact on readiness and ability to engage with new learning', noting that 'the relational aspect of pedagogy remains critical' (Ring et al. 2018: 48).

In interrogating the theoretical perspectives in the literature, the authors suggest individual themes can be combined to form a mosaic that teachers can draw on to inform children's learning and development in educational settings (Ring et al. 2018). A recurrent theme through the mosaic of theories identified was the contention that learning is not a passive exercise but rather that it requires learners to be actively engaged in the processing required to optimise learning, with the focus remaining on the child's thinking while he/she is engaged in the process. Teaching that is grounded in children's experiences is more likely to engage children and impact positively on their learning and development. While the role of the adult in facilitating children's learning and development is pivotal, it remains critical that children are supported by the adult in regulating and planning elements of their own learning experiences. The research further suggests that participation is key to providing for children's effective learning and development and that language-rich environments where talk and discussion are valued and prioritised are essential. Capturing, including and responding to children's voices therefore promotes children's meaningful participation in ELC and school environments, thus enabling all children to achieve their potential. Ring and colleagues (2018) conclude that democratic spaces should be provided in classrooms to incorporate both a pedagogy of voice and a pedagogy of listening and that both adults and children develop a shared understanding that children have a voice within the curriculum.

> **Key Signposts: Research on Children's Learning and Development in the Early Years: The Power and Potential of Participation**
>
> - Enabling each child to flourish requires a broader focus than curriculum alone with classroom climate and relationships having a tangible impact on readiness and a child's ability to engage with new learning and the relational aspect of pedagogy remaining critical (Ring et al. 2018).
> - Learning is not a passive exercise but rather it requires learners to be actively engaged in the processing required to optimise learning, necessitating a focus remaining on the child's thinking while he/she is engaged in the process (Hayes and Kernan 2012).
> - The adult has a pivotal role in facilitating children's learning and development through supporting children in regulating and planning elements of their own learning experiences (CECDE 2006).
> - The key in providing for children's effective learning and development lies in language-rich environments, where talk and discussion are valued and prioritised as an essential part of participation (Locke and Locke 2013).
> - Capturing, including and responding to children's voices promotes children's meaningful participation in ELC and school environments, thus enabling all children to achieve their potential (Kendall 2019).

Participation for All Children or Limited by Age and Maturity?

The provisions of Article 12.1 of the UNCRC ostensibly set boundaries to all children being capable of forming their own views through including limitations on children's participation in expressly referring to 'the child who is capable of forming his or her own views' in addition to 'the views of the child being given due weight in accordance with the age and maturity of the child' (UN 1989: Article 12.1). According to Deegan (2015), the voice of the child remains a contested and unresolved phenomenon associated with unanswered questions around who speaks, how they speak, why they speak and in what contexts they should speak. However, since 1989, a wide range of research in the area of early childhood and inclusive education has confirmed that all children irrespective of age or ability have a voice, and that as educators we have a responsibility to elicit children's voices (Daly et al. 2016; Ring 2016; Ring and O'Sullivan 2016; Ring et al. 2016; Turner 2017; GoI 2018b; Grey et al. 2019; Ring et al. 2019a; Ring et al. 2019b; Lynch et al. 2020).

Research on effective learning and teaching continues to highlight the critical importance of all children contributing to the process and the accommodation, incorporation and value placed on this contribution (Ring 2016; Ring et al. 2018). Dewey (1916: 55), in highlighting the concept of the child as a co-constructor of knowledge, emphasised the importance of all members of a group having 'an equable opportunity to receive and take from others'. At a time when globally education systems are committing to prioritising democracy as a central concept in education, ensuring all children participate in this process becomes an imperative.

Lansdown observes that the benefits of providing for all children's participation are significant, advising that 'adults need to acquire a greater humility in recognising that they have a great deal to learn from children' (2005: 40). From the beginning all children, irrespective of age or ability, display a desire to communicate and have their voices listened and responded to (NCCA 2009; Lansdown; 2011). The realisation of participation for all children is dependent on our commitment as educators to embed an innovative pedagogy of voice and a corresponding pedagogy of listening in our ELC, primary and special school settings (CECDE 2006; NCCA, 2009) The rationale for capturing the voices of all children is therefore threefold in terms of being a matter of human rights and social justice; optimising children's learning and development and central to the concept of democracy in education.

> **Key Signposts: Participation for All Children or Limited by Age and Maturity?**
>
> - The provisions of Article 12.1 of the United Nations Convention on the Rights of the Child (UNCRC) ostensibly set boundaries to all children being capable of forming their own views through including limitations on children's participation in expressly referring to 'the child who is capable of forming his or her own views' in addition to 'the views of the child being given due weight in accordance with the age and maturity of the child' (UN 1989: Article 12.1).
> - Since 1989, a wide range of research in the area of early childhood and inclusive education has confirmed that all children irrespective of age or ability have a voice and that as educators we have a responsibility to elicit children's voices (Daly et al. 2016; Ring 2016; Ring and O'Sullivan 2016; Ring et al. 2016; Turner 2017; Government of Ireland (GoI) 2018b; Grey et al. 2019; Ring et al. 2019a; Ring et al. 2019b; Lynch et al. 2020).
> - Research on effective learning and teaching continues to highlight the critical importance of all children contributing to the process and the accommodation, incorporation and value placed on this contribution (Ring 2016; Ring et al. 2018).
> - At a time when globally education systems are committing to prioritising democracy as a central concept in education, ensuring all children participate in this process becomes an imperative.
> - From the beginning all children, irrespective of age or ability, display a desire to communicate and have their voices listened and responded to (Murray 2019).

A Way Forward: Adopting the Lundy Model to Reflect Each Setting's Unique Ethos and Mission

A democratic education system acknowledges the importance of the child's voice and recognises that prioritising participation enhances children's self-esteem and confidence, promotes their overall development and develops their sense of autonomy, independence, social competence and resilience (Rinaldi 2012; Whitebread and O'Sullivan, 2012; Martin et al. 2015). If those involved in ELC, primary and special school settings are truly committed to providing for children's participation, a model to begin to access voice and facilitate participation is offered by Laura Lundy at the School of Education, Queen's University, Belfast. Lundy has developed a rights-based model of child participation that has potential benefit for education settings. Lundy's model focuses on ensuring all children's views are valued and respected (Lundy 2007). This model aligns well with Aistear – the Early Childhood Curriculum Framework (NCCA 2009), Síolta, the National Quality Framework (CECDE 2006) and the Primary School Curriculum (NCCA 1999; 2019).

The Lundy Model of Participation (Figure 2.2) highlights four components that are necessary to ensure that Article 12 of the UNCRC is achieved. These components include: space, voice, audience and influence. Lundy (2007) suggests that children should be given the opportunity to share their views through the provision of a safe and familiar location, in which they are:

- encouraged to express their views and are given opportunities to both form and express their views on what matters to them;
- allocated a voice through being facilitated in expressing their views freely;
- assured of their voices being heard by an audience and given due weight, as they have a right to be heard by those who have power to make decisions;
- assured of having their views responded to in order that they understand their views have influence in their environment. (Lundy 2007)

The Lundy Model of Participation was adopted by the DCYA (2015a; 2020b) in the National Strategy on Children and Young People's Participation in Decision-Making (2015–2020).

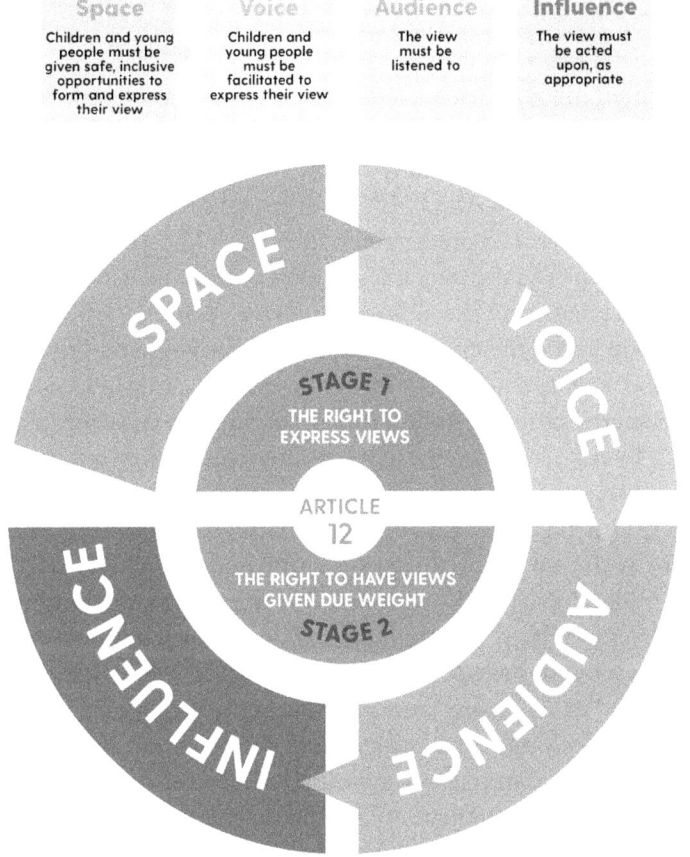

Figure 2.3. The Lundy Model of Participation (DCYA 2020b)

Providing Space for Children to Form and Express Their Views

Operationalising the Lundy Model of Participation begins with the creation of a safe and inclusive space for children to express their views. This space is a pre-requisite for children to articulate their authentic views, in a secure environment (Lundy 2007). Each child attending an ELC, primary or special school setting is a learner in his/her own right; therefore, each child has a right to equality of learning within that environment (Children's Rights Alliance (CRA) 2019). Pairman and Terreni (2001) suggest that the physical, temporal and interactional dimensions of the environment are particularly relevant for young children. The physical environment is concerned with the organisation of physical space, embedding of routines and predictability for the child constitutes the temporal environment and the interactional environment focuses on the quality of relational pedagogy the child experiences. Providing enhanced physical, temporal and interactional spaces, with engaging and organised materials and activities supported by competent and caring educators, creates a vibrant environment in which children can form and express their views.

Physical spaces should allow children the freedom to play and explore with unrestricted access to inclusive indoor and outdoor play facilities that are purposefully designed to accommodate the needs of all learners (Ring et al. 2019a). Enriching early childhood environments include a variety of developmentally appropriate, challenging and engaging play and curriculum-related materials that afford young children opportunities to interact with their peers and adult (CECDE 2006). Children are thus supported in expressing their preferences through their choice of and engagement with materials and spaces in their environment (NCCA 2015a; 2015b). In this context also, the creation of spaces such as a cosy corner or an area with reduced stimulation can support children in expressing their need for calming experiences and the reduction of stressors in the environment that may be impacting on their wellbeing. Creating accessible spaces in the early childhood environment that are physically and emotionally safe for children to explore also beneficially supports children in managing their own self-regulation (Rosanbalm and Murray 2017). Cultivating positive interactions through a commitment to a relational pedagogy provides a frame of reference and the security necessary for children to confidently contribute to the discourse in the setting.

> **Key Signposts: Providing Space for Children to Form and Express Their Views**
>
> - Operationalising the Lundy Model of Participation begins with the creation of a safe and inclusive space for children to express their views. This space is a pre-requisite for children to articulate their authentic views, in a secure environment (Lundy 2007).
> - The physical, temporal and interactional dimensions of the environment are particularly relevant for young children (Pairman and Terreni 2001).
> - Physical spaces should allow children the freedom to play and explore with unrestricted access to inclusive indoor and outdoor play facilities that are purposefully designed to accommodate the needs of all learners (Ring et al. 2019a).
> - Children are supported in expressing their preferences through their choice of and engagement with materials and spaces in their environment (Mac Naughton and Williams (2009).
> - Providing enhanced physical, temporal and interactional spaces with engaging and organised materials and activities supported by competent and caring educators creates a vibrant environment in which children can form and express their views (Sluss 2015).

Facilitating Children in Articulating Their Views

Harris and Menatakis (2013) note that not everyone expresses themselves in the same way and once a safe space has been created, as educators we have a responsibility to give due consideration to how each child's voice can be heard. Voice can be articulated in a variety of ways and is not restricted to the spoken word. Hence, from the minute we are born, as human beings, we display an innate desire to communicate, be listened to, responded to and as a result, young babies continuously communicate with us through eye-contact, movements and babbling (Chomsky 1986; Bruner 2009). It is clear that all children, irrespective of age or capacity have views and it is our responsibility as educators to find ways to capture and include these views. It is imperative therefore that multiple means of expression are facilitated and that the apparently silent voices in the setting are listened to (Harmon 2018).

In facilitating children to articulate their views, our role as educators is to become expert listeners, remembering that listening cannot be equated with hearing and as expert listeners, we remain in a constant state of alert, consistently observing how a child is communicating with us. Cooper (2010) indicates young children communicate their thoughts, ideas and feelings in a myriad of ways through physical movement, gestures, sounds, humming, singing, laughing, smiling, crying and expressing preferences for particular activities, materials, places and people. Through staying 'attuned' to how children are communicating with us, we become expert, responsive and more effective educators (French 2019).

> **Key Signposts: Facilitating Children in Articulating Their Views**
>
> - Not everyone expresses themselves in the same manner, but once a safe space has been created by educators they have a responsibility to give due to contemplation as to how each child's voice can be heard and facilitated (NCCA 2015a; 2015b).
> - Young babies continuously communicate with us through eye-contact, movements and babbling. It is clear that all children, irrespective of age or capacity have views and it is our responsibility as educators to find ways to capture and include these views (Carr and Lee 2019).

- In facilitating children to articulate their views, our role as educators is to become expert listeners, remembering that listening cannot be equated with hearing (Mainstone-Cotton 2019).
- Children communicate their thoughts, ideas and feelings in a myriad of ways through physical movement, gestures, sounds, humming, singing, laughing, smiling, crying and expressing preferences for particular activities, materials, places and people (Webster Stratton and Reid 2004).
- By being mindful of children's the myriad of ways children communicate with us, we become expert, responsive and more effective educators (Nutbrown 2018).

Ensuring Children's Voices Have an Audience and that They Understand Their Views Have Influence

A principal reason for the development of the Lundy Model was to emphasise that children have a right to an audience that listens and that they are reassured their voices have the potential to effect change (Lundy 2007). This can happen in a variety of ways, sometimes those who listen can effect changes, on other occasions, they may be required to open channels of communication to ensure that the voice is communicated in the appropriate forum. For Lundy, it is moving beyond just listening, to listening with purpose. Purposeful listening allows educators to be open to and challenged by what is articulated, and where appropriate to act for the benefit of the children. The concept of influence is captured by the phrase 'due weight' in Article 12 of the UNCRC (UN 1989). For Lundy (2007) influence is key; children must understand they have influence, and therefore when inviting children to share their views, they must be informed who the audience is, and receive information on how that audience received their view. If the children feel that their voice has influence and is respected, it will develop a culture where children's voices are valued and meaningfully considered (National Early Years Access Initiative 2012).

Children that feel safe, cared for and actively listened to are more likely to be successful learners and achieve their full potential (Macartney 2016). Therefore, it is vital for all those working with young children to be warm, genuine, empathetic, considerate, understanding and supportive. Children's participation supports not only a sense of belonging and inclusion but, most importantly, develops their understanding of how they themselves can be agents of change (Beneke et al. 2019).

> **Key Signposts: Ensuring Children's Voices Have an Audience and that They Understand Their Views Have Influence**
>
> - A principal reason for the development of the Lundy Model was to emphasise that children have a right to an audience that listens and that they are reassured their voices have the potential to effect change (Lundy 2007).
> - Purposeful listening allows educators to be open to and challenged by what is articulated, and where appropriate to act for the benefit of the children (Rodd 2012).
> - Children must be enabled to understand they have influence and therefore when inviting children to share their views, they must be informed who the audience is, and receive information as to how that audience received their views (Purdon 2016).
> - Children's participation supports a sense of belonging and inclusion but, most importantly, develops children's understanding of how they themselves can be agents of change (DCYA 2014).

Conclusion

While progress is being made in promoting and providing equal opportunities in an education system where all children are included, a foundational element must be the centrality of the child and the place the child's voice is given in that learning environment. This chapter has explored the right of children to participate and have their voice listened and responded to as key principles in national and international education policy, legislation and practice. The barriers to child participation are acknowledged and the Lundy Model of Participation, located in Article 12 of the UNCRC, combined with research in early childhood education, are interrogated to suggest a way forward in realising children's right to participate (UN 1989; Lundy 2007). Providing for the four dimensions of space; voice; audience; influence suggested by Lundy (2007) has the potential to foster early childhood education environments where the voices of all children are embedded. The chapter confirms the threefold rationale for capturing the voices of all children as being a matter of human rights and social justice; optimising children's learning and development and being central to the concept of democracy in education.

Bibliography

Beneke, M. R., Newton, J. R., Vinh, M., Blanchard, S. B., and Kemp, P. (2019). 'Practicing Inclusion, Doing Justice: Disability, Identity, and Belonging in Early Childhood', *ZERO TO THREE Journal*, 39(3), 26–34.

Blair, C., and Raver, C. C. (2015). 'School Readiness and Self-Regulation: A Developmental Psychobiological Approach', *Annual Review of Psychology*, 3, 711–731.

Bowlby, J. (1988). *A Secure Base: Clinical Applications of Attachment Theory*. London: Routledge.

Bronfenbrenner, U., and Morris, P. A. (1998). 'The Ecology of Developmental Process'. In W. Damon and R. M. Lerner (eds), *Handbook of Child Psychology: Vol. 1. Theoretical Models for Human Development* (5th ed.), pp. 993–1028. New York, NY: John Wiley.

Bruner, J. (2009). *Actual Minds, Possible Words*. Cambridge. MA: Harvard University Press.

Carr, M., and Lee, W. (2019). *Learning Stories in Practice*. London: SAGE Publications Ltd.

Centre for Early Childhood Development and Education. (2006). *Síolta: The National Quality Framework for Early Childhood Education*. Dublin: Centre for Early Childhood Development and Education, <http://siolta.ie/media/pdfs/final_handbook.pdf>, accessed 08 September 2020.

Children's Rights Alliance. (2019). *5 Rights in Early Childhood, Children's Rights Alliance Report Card 2019*. Dublin: Children's Rights Alliance, <https://www.childrensrights.ie/sites/default/files/submissions_reports/files/Chapter-5-Rights-in-Early-Childhood.pdf>, accessed 30 January 2020.

Chomsky, N. (1986). *Knowledge of Language: It's Nature, Origin and Use*. New York, NY: Praeger.

Clark, A., and Moss, P. (2011). *Listening to Young Children: The Mosaic Approach* (2nd ed.). London: National Children's Bureau Enterprises Ltd.

Comhairle na nÓg. (Young Voices. Local Issues). (2019). *Our Voices Our Schools*. Dublin: Comhairle na nÓg, <https://www.ourvoicesourschools.ie/>, accessed 12 January 2020.

Cooper, J. (2010). *The Early Years Communication Handbook: A Practical Guide to Creating a Communication Friendly Environment*. London: Practical Pre-School Books.

Daly, P., Ring, E., Egan, M., Fitzgerald, J., Griffin, C., Long, S., McCarthy, E., Moloney, M., O'Brien, T., O'Byrne, A., O'Sullivan, S., Ryan, M., Wall, E., and Madden, R. (2016). *An Evaluation of Education Provision for Children with Autistic Spectrum Disorder in the Republic of Ireland*. Trim: National Council for Special Education, <https://dspace.mic.ul.ie/handle/10395/2273>, accessed 16 January 2020.

Deci, E. L., and Ryan, R. M. (2008). 'Self-Determination Theory: A Macrotheory of Human Motivation, Development and Health', *Canadian Psychology*, 49(3), 182–185.

Deegan, J. (2015) 'Keynote Address: Ways of Accomplishing Pedagogies of Voice', *Irish Association of Teachers in Special Education, 27th Annual Conference: Our School Community: Promoting Resilience and Wellbeing*, 12–13 June 2015. Dublin: All Hallows College, Drumcondra, Dublin.

Department of Children and Youth Affairs. (2013). *Ireland's Consolidated Third and Fourth Reports to the UN Committee on the Rights of the Child*. Dublin: Department of Children and Youth Affairs, <https://www.childrensrights.ie/resources/ireland%e2%80%99s-consolidated-third-and-fourth>, accessed 12 January 2020.

Department of Children and Youth Affairs. (2014). *Better Outcomes, Brighter Futures: The National Policy Framework for Children and Young People 2014–2020*. Dublin: Department of Children and Youth Affairs, <https://assets.gov.ie/23796/961bbf5d975f4c88adc01a6fc5b4a7c4.pdf>, accessed 04 July 2020.

Department of Children and Youth Affairs (2015a). *National Strategy on Children and Young People's Participation in Decision-making, 2015–2020*. Dublin: Department of Children and Youth Affairs, <https://assets.gov.ie/24462/48a6f98a921446ad85829585389e57de.pdf>, accessed 29 January 2020.

Department of Children and Youth Affairs. (2015b). *A Practical Guide to Including Seldom-Heard Children and Young People in Decision-Making*. Dublin: Department of Children and Youth Affairs, <https://www.comhairlenanog.ie/wp-content/uploads/2014/10/Seldom-Heard-toolkit.pdf>, accessed 8 January 2020.

Department of Children and Youth Affairs. (2016). *Diversity, Equality and Inclusion Charter and Guidelines for Early Childhood Care and Education*. Dublin: Department of Children and Youth Affairs, <https://assets.gov.ie/38186/c9e90d89d94b41d3bf00201c98b2ef6a.pdf>, accessed 20 October 2019, accessed 04 July 2020.

Department of Children and Youth Affairs. (2020a). *What Is Hub na nÓg?*. Dublin: Department of Children and Youth Affairs, <https://www.hubnanog.ie/what-is-hub-na-nog/>, accessed 12 January 2020.

Department of Children and Youth Affairs. (2020b). *The Lundy Model*. Dublin: Department of Children and Youth Affairs [Personal Correspondence 05 October 2020].

Department of Education and Skills. (2016a). *Action Plan for Education (2016–2019): Department of Education and Skills Strategic Statement*. Dublin: Department of Education and Skills, <https://www.education.ie/en/Publications/Corporate-Reports/Strategy-Statement/Department-of-Education-and-Skills-Strategy-Statement-2016-2019.pdf>, accessed 02 October 2020.

Department of Education and Skills. (2016b). *Looking at Our School 2016: A Quality Framework for Primary Schools*. Dublin: Department of Education and Skills, <http://schoolself-evaluation.ie/primary/wp-content/uploads/sites/2/2016/08/Looking-at-Our-School-2016-A-Quality-Framework-for-Primary-Schools_English_WEB.pdf>, accessed 04 July 2020.

Department of Education and Skills. (2018). *A Guide to Early Years Education Inspection*. Dublin: Department of Education and Skills, <https://www.education.ie/en/Publications/Inspection-Reports-Publications/Evaluation-Reports-Guidelines/guide-to-early-years-education-inspections.pdf>, accessed 04 July 2020.

Dewey, J. (1916). *Democracy and Education*. New York, NY: The Free Press.

Edwards, C., Gandini, L., and Forman, G. (eds) (2012). *The Hundred Languages of Children* (3rd ed.). Santa Barbara, CA: Praeger.

European Agency for Special Needs and Inclusive Education. (2017). *Inclusive Early Childhood Education: Literature Review* (F. Bellour, P. Bartolo, and

M. Kyriazopoulou, eds). Odense, Denmark: European Agency for Special Needs and Inclusive Education, <https://www.european-agency.org/sites/default/files/IECE%20Literature%20Review.pdf>, accessed 03 July 2020.

French, G. (2019). *Key Elements of Good Practice to Support the Learning and Development of Children from Birth to Three*. Dublin: National Council for Curriculum and Assessment, <https://ncca.ie/media/4123/key-elements-of-good-practice-to-support-the-learning-and-development-of-children-birth-three-drgfrench.pdf>, accessed 02 October 2020.

Gardner, H. (2006). *Multiple Intelligences*. New York, NY: Basic Books.

Goswami, U. (2004). 'Neuroscience and Education', *British Journal of Educational Psychology*, 74, 1–14.

Government of Ireland. (2000). *The National Children's Strategy 2000–2010: Our Children, Their Lives*. Dublin: The Government Publications Office, <https://www.lenus.ie/bitstream/handle/10147/574860/nationalchildrensstrategysummary.pdf?sequence=1&isAllowed=y>, accessed 04 July 2020.

Government of Ireland. (2018a). *First Five: A Whole-of-Government Strategy for Babies, Young Children and Their Families 2019–2028*. Dublin: The Government Publications Office, <https://assets.gov.ie/31184/62acc54f4bdf4405b74e53a4afb8e71b.pdf>, accessed 04 July 2020.

Government of Ireland. (2018b). *First Five: Report on the National Consultation with Young Children*. Dublin: The Government Publications Office, <https://assets.gov.ie/34574/2b9355febe2542ac871aa69d2fc4a96a.pdf>, accessed 04 July 2020.

Graham, I. (2017). *Realising Potential Equality, Diversity and Inclusive Practice in Early Years*. Dublin: Barnardos.

Grey, T., Corbett, M., Sheerin, J., Heeney, T., Ring, E., and O'Sullivan, L. (2019). *Universal Design Guidelines for Early Learning and Care Settings*. Dublin: Department of Children and Youth Affairs in collaboration with the Centre for Universal Design, National Disability Authority, <https://aim.gov.ie/wp-content/uploads/2019/06/universal-design-guidelines-for-elc-settings-introduction-1.pdf>, accessed 6 January 2019.

Harmon, M. (2018). *'I am a Catholic Buddhist': The Voice of Children on Religion and Religious Education in an Irish Catholic Primary School Classroom*, Unpublished Doctoral Thesis. Dublin: Dublin City University, <http://doras.dcu.ie/22639/>, accessed 06 February 2020.

Harris, P., and Mentakis, H. (2013). *Children as Citizens: Engaging with the Childs Voice in Educational Settings*. London: Routledge.

Hayes, N., and Bradley, D. (2009). *Right by Children: Children's Rights and Rights Based Approaches to Policy Making in Early Childhood Education and Care: The Case of Ireland*. Technological University Dublin: Irish Research

Council Humanities and the Social Sciences, <https://arrow.tudublin.ie/cgi/viewcontent.cgi?article=1037&context=cserrep>, accessed 02 October 2020.

Hayes, N. and Kernan, M. (2012). *Engaging Young Children: A Nurturing Pedagogy*. Dublin: Gill and Macmillan.

Hidi, S. (2015). 'Revisiting the Role of Rewards in Motivation and Learning: Implications of Neuroscientific Research', *Educational Psychology Review*, 28(1), 61–93.

Ireland. (1937). *Bunreacht na hÉireann. Constitution of Ireland*. Dublin: Government Publications Office, <https://www.gov.ie/en/publication/d5bd8c-constitution-of-ireland/>, accessed 11 January 2020.

Ireland. (2002). *Ombudsman for Children Act 2002*. Dublin: The Government Publications Office.

Ireland. (2012). *Thirty-First Amendment of the Constitution (Children) Act 2012*. Dublin: The Government Publications Office.

Kendall, L. (2019). 'Supporting All Children to Reach Their Potential: Practitioner Perspectives on Creating an Inclusive School Environment', Education, 47(6), 678–691.

Kilkelly, U. (2007). *Barriers to the Realisation of Children's Rights in Ireland*. Cork: University College Cork, <https://www.oco.ie/app/uploads/2007/05/Barrierstorealisationofchildren_x0027_srights1.pdf>, accessed 12 January 2020.

Kirschner, P. A. (2017). 'Stop Propagating the Learning Styles Myth', *Computers and Education*, 106(1), 166–171.

Lansdown, G. (2005). *Can You Hear Me: The Right of Young Children to Participate in Decisions Affecting Them, Working Papers in Early Childhood Development (Working Paper 36)*. The Hague: Bernard Van Leer Foundation, <http://www.bibalex.org/Search4Dev/Files/282624/114976.Pdf>, accessed 12 January 2020.

Lansdown, G. (2011). *Every Childs Right to Be Heard: A Resource Guide on the UN Committee on the Rights of the Child; General Comment No. 12*. New York, NY: UNICEF <https://www.unicef.org/files/Every_Childs_Right_to_be_Heard.pdf>, accessed 02 October 2020.

Leadership for INClusion in the Early Years Consortium. (2016–2020). *A Competency Framework for Inclusion in Early Childhood Education and Care*. Mary Immaculate College, Limerick: Leadership for INClusion in the Early Years Consortium.

Locke, A., and Locke, D. (2013). *Teaching Speaking and Listening: One Step at a Time*. London: Bloomsbury Publishing.

Lynch, H., Ring, E., Boyle, B., Moore, A., O'Toole, C., O'Sullivan, L., Brophy, T., Frizelle, P., Horgan, D. and O'Sullivan, D. (2020). *Evaluation of In-School and*

Early Years Therapy Support Demonstration Project. Trim: National Council for Special Education, https://ncse.ie/wp-content/uploads/2020/11/Demo-project-evaluation-fInal-for-web-upload.pdf , accessed 04 January 2021.

Lundy, L. (2007). 'Voice Is Not Enough: Conceptualizing Article, 12 of the UNCRC', *British Educational Research Journal*, 33(6), 927–942.

Macartney, B. (2016). *Early Childhood Education and Barriers to Inclusivity: Working Toward a Fairer System, a Background Paper Prepared for Child Poverty Action Group (CPAG)*, <https://ieag.org.nz/assets/Uploads/Early-Childhood-eductaion-barriers-to-inclusivity-.pdf>, accessed 30 January 2020.

Mac Naughton, G. and Williams, G. (2009). *Teaching Young Children: Choices in Theory and Practice* (2nd ed.). Maidenhead: Open University Press.

Mainstone-Cotton, S. (2019). *Listening to Young Children in Early Years Settings*. London: Jessica Kingsley Publishers.

Martin, S., Forde, C., Dunn Galvin, A., and O'Connell, A. (2015). *An Examination of Children and Young People's Views on the Impact of Their Participation on Decision-Making*. Dublin: Department of Children and Youth Affairs.

Maslow, A. H. (1943). 'A Theory of Human Motivation', *Psychological Review*, 50(4), 370–396.

McGoldrick, D. (1991). 'The United Nations Convention on the Rights of the Child', *International Journal of Law, Policy and the Family*, 5(2), 132–169.

McNaughton, G., and Williams, G. (2009). *Teaching Young Children: Choices in Theory and Practice*. Maidenhead: Open University Press.

Melhuish, E., Ereky-Stevens, K., Petrogiannis, K., Ariescu, A., Penderi, E., Rentzou, Tawell, A., Leseman, P., and Broekhuisen, M. (2015). *A Review of Research on the Effects of Early Childhood Education and Care (ECEC) upon Child Development*, CARE Project; Curriculum Quality Analysis and Impact Review of European Early Childhood Education and Care (ECEC), <http://ecec-care.org/fileadmin/careproject/Publications/reports/new_version_CARE_WP4_D4_1_Review_on_the_effects_of_ECEC.pdf>, accessed 04 July 2020.

Murray, J. (2019). 'Hearing Young Children's Voices', *International Journal of Early Years Education*, 27(1), 1–5.

National Council for Curriculum and Assessment. (1999). *Primary School Curriculum*. Dublin: The Stationery Office, <https://curriculumonline.ie/getmedia/93de2707-f25e-4bee-9035-92b00613492e/Introduction-to-primary-curriculum.pdf>, accessed 04 July 2020.

National Council for Curriculum and Assessment. (2009). *Aistear: The Early Childhood Curriculum Framework*. Dublin: National Council for Curriculum and Assessment, <https://www.ncca.ie/en/early-childhood/aistear>, accessed 04 July 2020.

National Council for Curriculum and Assessment. (2015a). *Aistear/Síolta Practice Guide*. Dublin: National Council for Curriculum and Assessment, <www.ncca.ie/en/Practice-Guide>, accessed 04 July 2020.

National Council for Curriculum and Assessment. (2015b). *Creating and Using the Learning Environment*. Dublin: National Council for Curriculum and Assessment, <https://www.aistearsiolta.ie/en/creating-and-using-the-learning-environment/>, accessed 02 October 2020.

National Council for Curriculum and Assessment. (2019). *Primary Language Curriculum*. Dublin: National Council for Curriculum and Assessment, <https://www.curriculumonline.ie/getmedia/2a6e5f79-6f29-4d68-b850-379510805656/PLC-Document_English.pdf>, accessed 12 January 2020.

National Early Years Access Initiative. (2012). *Professional Pedagogy Project: Supporting Every Childs Right to Education – An Educator's Handbook*. Donegal: Donegal County Childcare Committee.

Nutbrown, C. (2018). *Early Childhood Educational Research: International Perspectives*. London: SAGE Publications Ltd.

Pairman, A., and Terreni, L. (2001). *If the Environment Is the Third Teacher What Language Does She Speak*. Wellington: Ministry of Education, <http://spotidoc.com/doc/741536/if-the-environment-is-the-third-teacher-what-language-doe>, accessed 04 July 2020.

Purdon, A. (2016). 'Sustained Shared Thinking in an Early Childhood Setting: An Exploration of Practitioners' Perspectives', Education, 3(13), 269–282.

Rinaldi, C. (2012). 'The Pedagogy of Listening: The Listening Perspective from Reggio Emilia'. In C. Edwards, L. Gandini, and G. Foreman (eds), *The Hundred Languages of Children* (3rd ed.), pp. 233–246. Santa Barbara, CA: Praeger.

Ring, E. (2016). 'Why the Voice of the Child Matters for Education in the 21st Century'. In *Conference Proceedings* (6th ed.), pp. 667–672. Padova: Libreria Universitaria.

Ring, E., and O'Sullivan, L. (2016). 'The Importance of Including the Child's Voice in the Transition Process: Signposts from a National Evaluation of Concepts of School Readiness in Ireland', *Children's Research Digest*, 2(3), 37–44.

Ring, E., Grey, T., O'Sullivan, L., Corbett, M., Sheerin, J., and Heeney, T. (2019a). *Universal Design Guidelines for Early Learning and Care Settings: Literature Review*. Dublin: The Government Publications Office, <https://aim.gov.ie/wp-content/uploads/2019/06/universal-design-guidelines-for-elc-settings-literature-review-2.pdf>, accessed 12 January 2020.

Ring, E., Mhic Mhathúna, M., Moloney, M., Hayes, N., Breathnach, D., Stafford, P., Carswell, D., Keegan, S., Kelleher, C., McCafferty, D., O'Keeffe, A., Leavy, A., Madden, R., and Ozonyia, M. (2016). *An Examination of Concepts of School*

Readiness among Parents and Educators in Ireland. Dublin: Department of Children and Youth Affairs, <https://dspace.mic.ul.ie/handle/10395/2344>, accessed 16 January 2020.

Ring, E., O'Sullivan, L., and Harmon, M. (2021). 'The Concept of the Child, Pedagogy, Curriculum and Accountability in Early Childhood Education for a Post-Covid 19 World: Insights from Dewey's Philosophy'. In J. Avilia, A. G. Rud, L. Waks, and E. Ring (eds), *Routledge International Studies in the Philosophy of Education: The Contemporary Relevance of John Dewey's Theories on Teaching and Learning: Deweyan Perspectives on Standardization, Accountability and Assessment in Education*. New York, NY: Routledge, [In preparation].

Ring, E., O'Sullivan, L., O'Keeffe, S., Ferris, F., and Wall, E. (2019b). *An Evaluation of Teach Me As I Am Early Years Programme*. Dublin: AsIAm, <https://asiam.ie/wp-content/uploads/2019/04/TeachMeAsIAm-booklet.pdf>, accessed 16 January 2020.

Ring, E., O'Sullivan, L., Ryan, M., and Burke, P. (2018). *A Melange or a Mosaic of Theories? How Theoretical Perspectives on Children's Learning and Development can Inform a Responsive Pedagogy in a Redeveloped Primary School Curriculum*. Dublin: National Council for Curriculum and Assessment, <https://www.ncca.ie/media/3863/seminar_four_er_los_mr_pb_paper.pdf>, accessed 16 January 2020.

Rodd, J. (2012). *Leadership in Early Childhood: The Pathway to Professionalism* (4th ed.). Maidenhead: Open University Press.

Rosanbalm, K. D., and Murray, D. W. (2017). *Promoting Self-Regulation in Early Childhood: A Practice Brief, Office for Planning, Research and Evaluation, Administration for Children and Families Brief #2017-79*. Washington, DC: Office of Planning, Research, and Evaluation, Administration for Children and Families, US Department of Health and Human Services, <https://fpg.unc.edu/sites/fpg.unc.edu/files/resources/reports-and-policy-briefs/PromotingSelf-RegulationIntheFirstFiveYears.pdf>, accessed 04 July 2020.

Rosenshine, B. (2012) 'Principles of Instruction: Research-based Strategies that All Teachers Should Know', *American Educator*, Spring 2012, 12–39, <https://www.aft.org/sites/default/files/periodicals/Rosenshine.pdf>, accessed 03 July 2020.

Sabol, T. J., and Pianta, R. C. (2012). 'Recent Trends in Research on Teacher–Child Relationships', *Attachment & Human Development*, 14(3), 213–231.

Silver, H., Strong, R., and Perini, M. (1997). 'Integrating Learning Styles and Multiple Intelligences', *Educational Leadership*, 55(1), pp. 22–27, <http://www.ascd.org/publications/educational-leadership/sept97/vol55/num01/

Integrating-Learning-Styles-and-Multiple-Intelligences.aspx>, accessed 04 July 2020.
Sluss, J. (2015). *Supporting Play in Early Childhood: Environment, Curriculum and Assessment* (2nd ed.). Stamford, CT: Cengage Learning.
Sorin, R. (2005). 'Changing Images of Childhood: Reconceptualising Early Childhood Practice', *International Journal of Transitions in Childhood*, 1(1), 1–21.
Turner, S. (2017). *How Do Primary School Teachers Strategically Ensure that the Voice of the Child Is Heard*, Unpublished Master's Thesis. Limerick: Mary Immaculate College, University of Limerick.
United Nations. (1948). *A Universal Declaration of Human Rights*. Paris: United Nations, <https://www.un.org/en/ga/search/view_doc.asp?symbol=A/RES/217(III)>, accessed 12 January 2020.
United Nations. (1989). *Convention on the Rights of the Child*. New York, NY: United Nations, <http://www.ohchr.org/EN/ProfessionalInterest/Pages/CRC.aspx>, accessed 29 October 2019, accessed 12 January 2020.
Veraksa, N., and Van Oers, B. (2011). 'Early Childhood Education from a Russian Perspective', *Early Years Education*, 19(1), 5–17.
Verissimo, M., Torres, N., Silva, F., Fernandes, C., Vaughn, B. E., and Santos, A. J. (2017). 'Children's Representations of Attachment and Positive Teacher–Child Relationships', *Frontiers in Psychology*, 8, <https://www.frontiersin.org/articles/10.3389/fpsyg.2017.02270/full>, accessed 03 July 2020.
Vygotsky, L. (1962). *Thought and Language*. Cambridge, MA: Harvard University Press.
Vygotsky, L. S. (1978). *Mind in Society. The Development of Higher Psychological Processes* (M. Cole, V. John-Steiner, S. Scribner, and E. Souberman, eds). Cambridge, MA: Harvard University Press.
Webster-Stratton, C., and Reid, M. J. (2004). 'Strengthening Social and Emotional Competence in Young Children-The Foundation for Early School Readiness and Success: Incredible Years Classroom Social Skills and Problem-Solving Curriculum', *Infants & Young Children*, 17(2), 96–113.
Whitebread, D. (2010). 'Play, Metacognition and Self-Regulation'. In P. Broadhead, J. Howard, and E. Wood, E. (eds), *Play and Learning in the Early Years*, pp. 161–176. London: Sage.
Whitebread, D. (2012). *Developmental Psychology and Early Childhood Education*. London: Sage.
Whitebread, D., and O'Sullivan, L. (2012). 'Preschool Children's Social Pretend Play: Supporting the Development of Metacommunication, Metacognition and Self-Regulation', *International Journal of Play*, 1(2), 197–213.

Whitebread, D., Neale, D., Jensen, H., Liu, C., Lynneth Solis, S., Hopkins, E., Hirsh-Pasek, K., and Zosh, J. (2017). The Role of Play in Children's Development: A Review of the Evidence (Research Summary), The LEGO Foundation, <https://www.legofoundation.com/media/1065/play-types-_-development-review_web.pdf>, accessed 30 January 2020.

Willingham, D. T. (2009). *Why Don't Students Like School?*. San Francisco, CA: Jossey-Bass.

MARIE DOHERTY

Chapter 3 Children from Birth to 3 Years: Valuing and Supporting Our Earliest Learners, as They Begin Their Educational Journey

> One of the greatest gifts we are given at birth is potential and the greatest harm we can do to babies and young children is to take away from them their chance to achieve their full potential whatever that may be. (Robinson 2003: 183)

ABSTRACT
There is a general consensus across the literature that the first three years of a child's life hold momentous potential for learning and development. Everything young children learn in the early years of life impacts on their future. It is very important that we adequately value this important learning period in a child's life and realise this significant potential for learning and development.

In this chapter, an insight into the unique nature and learning capacity of children from birth to 3 years (babies and toddlers) will be explored from a theoretical perspective and a picture painted of what this might look like in practice. Practical implications and strategies will be provided for supporting babies and toddlers at home and in early learning and care (ELC) settings in order to optimise and enhance children's learning, wellbeing and development.

Introduction

First Five: A Whole-of-Government Strategy for Babies, Young Children and their Families 2019–2018 (Government of Ireland (GoI) 2018), places babies as 'learners' from birth. It proposes that all ELC centre-based settings or home-based, private or community locations in which children participate irrespective of the stage of life a child is at will be equally considered, resourced and quality assured. It respects this period from birth to starting school as an important and unique phase of a child's learning journey. This mirrors key messages in Better Outcomes, Brighter Futures: The National Policy Framework for children and young people 2014–2020, which firmly acknowledges and recognises that children are learners from birth (Department of Children and Youth Affairs (DCYA) 2014).

> Children are learning from birth. Their life chances are shaped and enhanced through support for their early learning and development. Their early experiences of parental love and attention lay the foundation for their future development. Children's capacity for learning depends on having caring adults who understand how to support their learning and development. (DCYA 2014:81)

This document also proposes that

> There is a need for a special focus on the period that spans from the ante-natal period to 2 years of age, during which time the social and emotional architecture of the brain is being formed. (DCYA 2014: 81)

Aistear: The Early Childhood Curriculum Framework (National Council for Curriculum and Assessment (NCCA) 2009) and Síolta: The National Quality Framework for Early Childhood Education (Centre for Early Childhood Development and Education (CECDE) 2006) likewise clearly acknowledge that children are learning from birth. These frameworks are based on the belief that children are competent and confident learners from birth. Aistear: The Early Childhood Curriculum Framework is designed to support early childhood experiences for all children in Ireland from birth to 6 years (NCCA 2009). The birth to 3 age group, while implicitly included throughout the document, are only referenced specifically in the sample learning opportunities within each of the four themes that characterise Aistear. Síolta: The National Quality Framework for Early Childhood Education (CECDE 2006) was designed to evaluate and support the improvement of quality across all aspects of practice in early learning and care (ELC) settings where children aged birth to 6 years are present. This framework aspires everyone working with children from birth to 6 years to consistently reflect on the quality of the experiences they provide for the children in their ELC setting. The 'Signposts for Reflection' in this framework prompt early childhood teachers to consider their practice for children aged birth to 18 months and children aged 12 to 36 months within all the components of the quality standards. Aistear presents learning using 3 overlapping age groups comprising babies (birth to 18 months); toddlers (12 months to 3 years) and young children (2 1/2 to 6 years). Síolta uses the same overlapping age groups (CECDE 2006), without mentioning terminology. The United Nations Convention on the Rights of Children clearly interprets the right to education as something that commences at birth (UN 1989; 2006) and recent research continues to highlight the quality of children's experiences during all children's early years and importantly children's unique learning capacity at this phase of development (Melhuish et al. 2015; Asmussen et al. 2018; Ring et al. 2018).

> Key Signposts: Introduction
>
> - The first three years of a child's life hold momentous potential for learning and development.
> - There is a need for a special focus on the period that spans from the ante-natal period to 2 years of age, during which time the social and emotional architecture of the brain is being formed (DCYA 2014: 81).
> - This period from birth to starting school is a very important and unique phase of a child's learning journey (DCYA 2014).
> - Young children's capacity for learning depends on having caring adults who understand how to support their learning and development (DCYA 2014).
> - Research continues to highlight the importance of quality learning experiences during all children's early years and importantly children's unique learning capacity at this phase of development (Melhuish et al. 2015; Asmussen et al. 2018; Ring et al. 2018).

The Unique Learning Capacity of Children from Birth to Three Years

The literature illuminates the importance, uniqueness and amazing learning capacity of children from birth to 3 years. In fact, Asmussen et al. (2014) would stress that there is no other phase in human development where such radical changes happen. Scientific findings from a varied range of disciplines ratify that the most important foundations of health, wellbeing and capacity take shape in the earliest years of life (Shonkoff et al. 2012). Rinaldi (2005) believes that from the moment of birth everyone begins that journey of making sense of the world which continues all through life, while Mathers et al. (2014) highlight this period of life as significant in the development of internalised emotions.

> The first three years of life are when emotional foundations for our being are laid down. It is a key period in developing internalised emotions and feelings about how lovable we are. (Mathers et al. 2014: 37)

It is during these earliest years of a child's life that they learn how to interact with others and the environment. They learn to be imaginative and adventurous and begin to make sense of their world, and themselves. The environments that children experience in these early years need to be extremely nurturing and inspiring to ensure that they have the best possible learning outcomes as they grow older (Dalli et al. 2011; Maguire-Fong 2015). Recent neurobiological research illustrates clearly how it is in these earliest years that the steepest rate of growth in synapses and neurological pathways takes place (Gopnik 2011; 2016; Mathers et al. 2014). Bernard Van Leer (2018) calls attention to the importance of this period from conception to around a child's third birthday (the first 1,000 days of life) and points out that the brain develops much more rapidly during this unique phase in a child's life, with substantial numbers of neural connections created in response to stimulus, affection and security from caregivers. Essentially, to build neural connections and strengthen children's brains, it is critical that carers and early childhood teachers smile, touch, talk, tell stories, provide opportunities to listen to music, share and read books, and engage in play with babies and toddlers (Lagercrantz 2016). Underpinning the child's unique learning capacity during this period is a raft of theoretical and research-based literature that provides us with signposts on supporting and optimising all children's learning and development at this time.

> **Key Signposts: The Unique Learning Capacity of Children from Birth to 3 Years**
>
> - There is no other period in human development where such major changes occur (Mathers et al. 2014; Asmussen et al. 2018).
> - Scientific findings from a range of disciplines have confirmed that the most important foundations of health, wellbeing and capacity take shape in the earliest years of life (Shonkoff et al. 2012).
> - The first 1,000 days of life is a unique period of time, when the brain develops most rapidly and emotional foundations are laid down.
> - The environments that children experience in these early years need to be extremely nurturing and inspiring to ensure that they have the best possible learning outcomes as they grow older (Dalli et al. 2011; Maguire-Fong 2015).
> - Smiling, touching, talking, storytelling, listening to music, sharing and reading books, and engaging in play with babies is crucial for building neural connections and supporting a child's brain (Lagercrantz 2016).

Applying a Theoretical Lens to Young Children's (Birth–3 Years) Learning and What This Looks Like in Practice

Lindon and Brodie (2016) highlight that developmental and psychological learning theories and neuroscience have had a substantial influence on more progressive concepts of how young children learn and on early educational practice. The idea that babies and toddlers investigate, experiment and explore in order to build concepts, knowledge and skills originates in the work of pioneers such as Vygotsky (1896–1934), Piaget (1886–1980) and Bruner (1915–2016). Contemporary research continues to build and expand on the work of these pioneers (Ring et al. 2018).

Cognitive and Constructivist Learning Theories

There is no doubt that Vygotsky's (1896–1934) sociocultural theory has had a crucial influence on educational theory and practice internationally. He strongly believed that learning and development are connected and that this is evident from the child's very first day of life. Babies, toddlers and young children's learning and development depends largely on interaction with people and the objects available within individual children's cultural context. Vygotsky suggested that babies, toddlers and young children construct their own knowledge, and that all human mental activity is the result of social learning (culture). This core principle that development and learning cannot be separated from social context is important (Vygotsky 1980). Vygotsky introduced the zone of proximal development (ZPD) theory and the role of the more knowledgeable other (MKO) (Featherstone 2017). This theory locates the adult or more experienced other as central to supporting and building on what children already know. This can be done by adults providing, timely careful prompts, which can bridge that gap between what the children can achieve on their own and with assistance. Vygotsky also believed that every child is born with essential learning tools such as memory and attention, which enable high-level learning, and that children's environmental contexts have a big influence on what children learn and how they learn it.

Piaget (1886–1980) is another great influencer, who has dramatically shaped educational practice. He believed and proposed that children's cognitive ability was a series of assimilations and accommodations which were needed to build up their knowledge of the world. Piaget was the first person to offer a theory on the development of young children's thinking. He believed that their thinking begins before they have acquired the language to express their thoughts. In Piaget's view language is simply a tool used to develop and enhance thinking. Gray and MacBlain (2017) claim that Piaget's stages of development, which emerged from his close observation of babies and toddlers continue to be the basis for work in child development, health and education today. His theories were revolutionary at the time and are invaluable to our understanding of young children's behaviour. His studies of very young children's cognitive structures (birth-3 years) and development became known as schemas. Schemas are where young children learn through repeatedly acting on objects and materials in their environment. Piaget describes this behaviour such as young children putting objects next to each other (proximity) or putting them in a series (order). These observable behaviours can be seen where children are enclosing objects, tightening or loosening objects, cutting, rotating, folding or unfolding objects.

Piaget believed that it is

> Through these repetitive actions children build up working theories … they do this by assimilating new content into their current models or structures (schemas) and then sometimes they have to accommodate their actions and knowledge when something unexpected happens. (Piaget 1956: 453)

Much of Chris Athey's (2007) research and work expanded on Piaget's concept of schemas. She describes them in her book as patterns of repeatable actions that lead to early categories and then to logical classifications. Athey believes that very young children are able and competent, and they are always seeking out new content to assimilate into their current structures (or schemas). Nutbrown (2013), Goldschmied and Jackson (2004), Bruce (2004), Gerber (2002) and, more recently, Arnold (2010), Grenier (2014) and Hughes (2016) have all shown a huge interest in Piaget's concept of schemas and the development of very young children's play behaviours, and explorations with objects. Arnold (2010) points out that these schemas provide us with a clear formula of when these behaviours can be seen and believes that they can be visible in children between the ages of 2 to 5 years and in time become recognised foundations of learning. Gerber (2002) concurs with Arnold (2010) and also believes that babies can achieve mastery by continuing the same activity over and over again. It is important that early childhood teachers understand when they see babies and toddlers repeat an action many, many times, that it may not mean they are bored but involved in a deeper learning process.

Elinor Goldschmied (1910–2009) pioneered object play ('treasure basket' and 'heuristic' play) for children under 3 years. Hughes (2016) admits that this approach to object play for babies and toddlers has a big impact on their learning, in encouraging them to concentrate and providing them with opportunity to explore. Treasure baskets are specifically for babies (aged 5 to 10 months) who have reached that milestone and can sit unattended. Heuristic play is for young mobile children (aged 10 to 20 months). Being mobile offers children a lot more opportunities to explore and find objects themselves that interest them. The word 'heuristic' derives from the Greek 'eurisko' which just means 'serves to discover' or 'gain an understanding of' (Hughes 2016). This describes exactly what babies and toddlers are engaged in as they handle, explore and experiment with objects. They can be observed emptying, filling up, placing smaller items into bigger objects (slotting), piling and balancing objects up, or lining up (ordering) objects. Hughes strongly believes that it is what the child does with an object that makes it heuristic play. They are actively engaged with the objects. This type of play is very reflective of the schematic play behaviours and processes highlighted by Piaget, and it supports the importance of sensory learning, and the active nature of learning. Both the treasure basket and heuristic play offer children choice, they choose the objects that interest them and what to do with them. It promotes concentration as they become deeply involved and interested in the objects and what they can do with them and it also facilitates their conceptual learning.

Hughes (2016) maintains that babies and toddlers who have had the experience of handling, mouthing, exploring and manipulating objects understand difficult concepts long before they have the language to express their understanding of these concepts. This mirrors the notion highlighted by Gopnik (2011) that babies are born with powerful causal learning mechanisms. It was very important from Goldschmied's perspective that none of the objects in the treasure basket or heuristic play were conventionally bought toys, but rather, a range of everyday objects, containers and natural. She believed that commercially available toys such as rattles, while they might be colourful and fun might not offer much to the young child. Because babies mainly use the sense of touch, smell and taste to explore and find out about objects, plastic toys such as rattles taste, smell and feel the same.

These views are also articulated by Tovey (2017), who in recent years claims that

> Much of our youngest learners' days can be spent in plasticised environments which can be bland static and sterile cut off from the real natural world or from authentic first-hand experiences. (:35)

Magda Gerber's (2002) philosophy correlates strongly with these thoughts especially on 'infant play' and proposes very specific types of play objects for children under 3 years. Her belief is that children need simple objects (such as a scarf, containers, balls, bottles, boxes, special gifts, wooden toys, blocks, knobbed toys) to encourage active engagement and opportunities to manipulate objects in a variety of ways. She recommends that young children be provided with objects that they can actively engage with, explore and manipulate. She implies that commercially available toys just entertain children and do not provide the opportunities they need to be deeply engaged. She insists that when an object or toy only does one thing (light up when you press a button or sing a song when you pull a lever) this limits their engagement and causes them to be passive or inactive. These ideas resonate with more recent theories on children's play and play materials such as from Nicholson's (1972) theory on 'loose parts', who proposes that the inclusion of loose parts into children's environment encourages more imaginative possibilities. Loose parts are described by Nicholson as material or objects that can be moved, carried, combined, redesigned, lined up, taken apart and put back together in multiple ways by the children, the possibilities are endless with imaginative children. They have no specific rules or instructions on their use, they can be used alone or combined and they can be natural, found, bought or upcycled. One crucial consideration when engaging children in loose parts play is the safety element of the materials (Daly and Beloglovsky 2016; Hargraves 2020).

One could ask what the learning value of exploring objects is for young children. Asmussen et al. (2018) highlight four competencies associated with children's future success. These are children's understanding of objects, their understanding of people, their understanding of number and their understanding of words. Asmussen et al. claim that these understandings are present at birth and that children contribute to their understanding of these objects through their own innate curiosity and interest with support from their individual cultural environment and adults. It is believed that it is during the first twelve months of life, that babies come to recognise that objects can be grouped into specific categories and that between the ages of 2 and 3, this understanding of objects becomes more refined. Gibson (1969) and Bremner (1998), as cited in Asmussen et al. (2018), claim that the strategies babies use are innate, for example, the ability they have to perceive the properties of objects in their environment and the fact that this perception and understanding of objects changes rapidly. Babies are also very skilful at being aware of what the form of the objects tells them they can do. Before babies are b able to concentrate on aspects of events that are most important to them This ability gradually changes in that they begin to focus more on the detail of the objects and can make discriminations (Asmussen et al. 2018).

The play experiences babies and toddlers engage in define what they actually learn and DeLoache, Simcok and Macari (2007) admit that it is the adults that play a huge part in supporting children's developing play interests and passions. Their research concluded that very young children's object play can develop into a fascination for various categories of objects by the age of 2. It is only when children's interests and passions are nurtured, that children can develop a level of expertise about object categories and this can often encourage learning of other cognitive skills. Babies and toddlers tend to be more deeply engaged when they are trusted with their own play interests. Similar results were highlighted in a more recent study in the United States (US) conducted by Bornstein, Hahn and Suwalsky (2013), in that babies who were more mature in the sense of their motor skills, and who explored more actively at 5 months of age, achieved higher academic levels at 14 years old. Studies such as Growing Up in Ireland (Williams, Murray, McCrory and McNally 2013) and Growing Up in Scotland (Melhuish 2010) found that providing infants with a variety of exploratory experiences and rich play objects had a very positive impact on their understanding of objects and their knowledge of object names throughout their pre-school development. Play is what children do, it is innate and a very natural sequence of development from infancy right into childhood. Specific types of play such as pretend and dramatic play are great incentives for the development of flexibility, working memory and children staying in roles, all of which are core self-regulation skills.

> ## Key Signposts: Cognitive and Constructivist Learning Theories
>
> - While children are born with a set of competencies, which facilitate their early learning, children's learning is also shaped by family, community, culture and society.
> - Babies and toddlers accomplish mastery by endless repetition, continuing the same activity over and over again.
> - Object play is important for babies and toddlers for many reasons and the types of objects that support sensory-rich engagement rather than passivity are very important.
> - During the first twelve months of life, babies increasingly come to recognise that objects can be grouped into categories. Between the ages of 2 and 3, their understanding of objects becomes increasingly more sophisticated as their language and motor skills continue to develop.
> - Recent studies from Scotland (2010), the United States (2013) and Ireland (2013) claim that providing babies and toddlers with a variety of exploratory experiences and rich play objects has a very positive impact on children's understanding of objects and their knowledge of object names throughout their pre-school development (Melhuish 2010; Bornstein, Hahn and Suwalsky 2013; Williams, Murray, McCrory and McNally 2013).

Bruner (1915–2016) referred to all humans, including babies and young children, as makers of meaning, active learners rather than passive learners (Bruner 1960). This mirrors elements of Piaget's theory where babies, according to Maguire-Fong (2015), are making sensorimotor meanings all the time and even without language and symbols, this meaning making is robust. Bruner did challenge a lot of the educational practice of his time, he argued that young children should always be encouraged to be active participants in their own learning, as opposed to being mainly receivers of facts and information from adults (Bruner 1960). More particularly, he proposed that greater importance should be given to understanding the processes by which children learn and the unique qualities each child brings to every new learning experience. Bruner had a key interest in the strategies younger children use when they are learning new tasks, especially problem-solving tasks. He was also interested in the important role adults have in supporting children's learning. This led him to develop the concept of scaffolding, where the adult works alongside children, guiding and directing them to build on the knowledge they have already mastered, while all the time avoiding being overly controlling (MacBlain 2018).

Bruner saw language as the central means by which younger children could develop their thinking and learning; and he stressed the crucial role of adults in giving babies, toddlers and young children opportunities to interact with, and observe interactions between others in their environment (Bruner 1974–1975). It is really important that adults make eye-contact with babies when they interact with them; engage them in dialogue; and are responsive to babies' reactions such as kicking, waving arms, smiling and grimacing. This according to Bruner is laying ad supporting the foundations of conversations for children. The term 'innate intersubjectivity' is explored by Trevarthen and Delafield (2016), who propose that babies are biologically wired to co-ordinate their actions with others and this ability to co-ordinate with others is crucial to assisting their cognitive and emotional learning while engaging socially. Additionally, Trevarthen and Dellafield claim that the most socially productive relationship between children and adults is bidirectional This echoes strongly with Bruner's (1975) concept of 'joint attention' Stenberg's (2009) and the concept of 'social referencing' where the baby learns to take into account the other person (Featherstone 2017).

Dewey (1859–1952), similar to Bruner, stressed the crucial communicative process between adults and young children and the continuous process of making meaning (Dewey 1902; 1915; 1916). He advocated for education that was based on first-hand experiences; and following children's interests, he placed a high value on a responsive curriculum and meaningful activity in children's learning, where children have to be participants in their learning. He also argued that curriculum should be relevant to young children's lives with a strong focus on learning by doing and the development of practical life skills (Featherstone 2017). Dewey stressed the importance of seeing all learning experiences as unique to each child and espoused, a theory of child-centred education (MacBlain 2018).

Key Signposts: Cognitive and Constructivist Learning Theories Continued

- Bruner stressed the importance of giving babies and young children opportunities to interact with and observe interactions between others. He put a high value on a responsive curriculum where children are involved in meaningful activity (Bruner 1960; 1974–1975).
- Bruner stressed the importance of giving babies and young children opportunities to interact with and observe interactions between others, while allocating adults an important role in supporting children to develop effective strategies for learning (Bruner 1974–1975).
- Frequent joint attention episodes need to be facilitated for babies and toddlers by adults. This happens through using verbal and visual cues to attract and maintain their attention and by leading and directing children's attention towards objects and actions, which according to Carpenter (2014) can begin after twelve months.
- Dewey argued that curriculum should be relevant to children's lives and should rely on learning by doing with the development of practical life skills (Dewey 1902; 1915; 1916; Featherstone 2017).

Behaviourist Approaches to Learning

Pavlov (1849–1936) is best known for his work in exploring conditioning and conditioned responses. His work and experiments have influenced methods in education such as behaviour modification therapies, which have become a key element in behaviourist approaches. Skinner (1904–1990), on the other hand, hypothesised that children's repeated actions, which were positively reinforced (e.g. praised or rewarded) became established, and then undesirable behaviour could be corrected by punishment (Brodie, 2018: 28). Skinner is regarded by many as the main figure in the field of behaviourism, which arose from the earlier work of Pavlov and John Watson (1878–1954). The behaviourist approach views young children as passive learners. This is in stark contrast to the majority of more up-to-date learning theories that view children as active agents in their own learning. Behaviourist approaches have also underpinned many of the intervention programmes devised for children identified as having additional needs. A number of these approaches such as those of Bereiter and Engelman in the 1960s were criticised for not taking into account the rich natural experiences that can arise for children during play and for not using children's current and emergent interests and passions to help them learn (David et al. 2003).

Behaviourist theories have also been criticised by motivational and mindset theories proposed by Dweck (2000; 2016) and Csikszentmihalyi (2015) who suggest that most of our conscious actions require motivation. This research indicates that motivation is really key to successful learning, in that it is impossible to learn if we do not want to learn, and that to gain expertise we have to see these skills and knowledge as valuable. Learning is in essence a matter of making sense of something and creating meaning rather than just a process where displays of behaviour are modified by an experience. Intrinsic motivation is the experience of wanting to engage in an activity for its own sake because the activity itself fulfils this inner need and feelings of satisfaction. This progression is really important according to Gray and MacBlain (2017) for all future learning in the early years because it lays the foundations for the way in which children will approach learning tasks in more formal settings as they get older. Engagement and intrinsic motivation develop and change over time and they are strongly influenced by cultural and individual developmental processes. Extrinsic motivation, however, refers to behaviour that is driven by external rewards. This type of motivation comes from outside sources as opposed to intrinsic motivation, which comes from within the individual person (Dweck 2000). Greenspan and Wieder (2006) caution that the continual use of rewards and reinforcers, often used in behaviour modification programmes, impedes children's intrinsic motivation to learn. It is important to keep in mind that children's motivation to learn is fostered when they see their learning environment as a place where they belong and when their sense of agency and purpose is supported. The National Academies of Science, Engineering and Medicine (2018) highlight the importance of being attentive to young children's engagement and persistence along with supporting their sense of control. Young children need an emotionally supportive and nonthreatening learning environment in which they feel safe and valued.

Key Signposts: Behaviourist Approaches to Learning

- Behaviourist approaches have underpinned many of the intervention programmes devised for children identified as having additional needs.
- Skinner believed that if children's actions were positively reinforced (e.g. praised or rewarded), they would become regular and that undesirable behaviour could be amended by punishment (Brodie 2018).
- It is crucial that intrinsic motivation is fostered in young children. The continual use of rewards can impede intrinsic motivation (Greenspan and Wieder 2006).
- Contrary to the majority of more contemporary learning theories, the behaviourist approach to learning views children as passive learners.
- It is important that adults take account of the rich natural experiences that can arise for young children during play and be attentive to using children's current and emergent interests and passions to help them learn (David et al. 2003).
- Activities and experiences need to be relevant, meaningful and intrinsically rewarding for babies and toddlers.

Social Learning Theories

It is important to note that social learning theorists oppose behaviourist theories because they believe that children can learn without getting direct rewards. Bandura (1925-present) proposed a social learning theory, which placed a greater emphasis upon children's cognitive development (Bandura 1976). He emphasised that young children learn by imitating what they see others doing in their environment and that adults are models of actions and models of thinking for babies, toddlers and young children. Bandura argues that much of children's early learning comes from the child actively imitating or observing modelling by others in their family or cultural group (Bandura 1976). Bronfenbrenner (1917–2005) had similar ideas to Bandura on how children learn but placed an even greater emphasis upon direct influences such as family, environment and the cultural community on children's learning and development along with the wider factors of society such as the economic and political climate (Bronfenbrenner and Morris 1998). A central principle of this bioecological model is that all genetic and biological elements of the child interact vigorously within the structures in which the child's development and learning take place (Asmussen et al. 2018). Bronfenbrenner's framework or model explains the factors that shape and determine children's learning and development; family and community contexts, the quality of the children's learning environment, the pedagogical practices and the relationship the children have with others (Melhuish et al. 2015). This mirrors many of the tenets of the concept 'co-constructing knowledge', where collaboration with others is used to construct knowledge, and which takes due account of the emotional aspects of learning, the dynamics of learning with others and the individual context of the child.

Tremblay, Boivin and Peters (2011), claim that emotional development in infancy and early childhood is important for the development of several inter-connected dispositions. Children with a developed emotional competence are more likely to engage in sustained learning, empathic and prosocial behaviours, express their emotions appropriately in various contexts, and use strategies to deal with negative or upsetting emotions.

Taken together, these abilities predict children's early school success and positive interpersonal relationships with peers and family members (Tremblay et al. 2011). Gray and MacBlain 2017 highlight similarities between Bandura and Bronfenbrenner in that they both acknowledge how societal influences impact on how social interactions with others is viewed as being a crucial element to learning and development. Additionally they reflect elements of a sociocultural view of learning, which includes the social, emotional, motivational, cognitive, developmental, biological and temporal contexts in which learning occurs for children.

> **Key Signposts: Social Learning Theories**
>
> - Social learning theorists oppose behaviourist theories because they believe that children can learn without getting direct rewards.
> - Each child is unique and has varied strengths, passions and interests.
> - Much of children's early learning comes from the child actively imitating or observing modelling by others in the family or group.
> - Parents/carers, family and society have a key role in children's learning.
> - Children's social interactions with others are central to their learning and development.
> - Learning is social and learning experiences needs to reflect children's lives.

Attachment Theories

Bowlby (1907–1990) is considered the pioneer of Attachment Theory. He emphasised the significance of attachment between babies and young children and the adults who care for them (Bowlby 1969; 1988). The attachment of babies and young children affects almost every other aspect of development (Brodie 2018). Attachment is defined in the literature as a deep and enduring emotional bond that connects one person to another across time and space) and that we are all born with attachment-seeking behaviours such as crying, clinging, imitation and smiling (Bowlby 1969; 1988; Ainsworth 1989). These behaviours, according to Ainsworth who expanded on Bowlby's work, are designed to keep carers close, ensuring that these innate needs for survival, safety and sensitive care are met. Attachment is really a process where a baby provides signals through crying or smiling. Parents/carers and early childhood teachers become tuned into these unique signals over time as they get to know the child or children in their setting. This ongoing attachment process in the first few years of life is crucial in shaping how we as humans grow and develop through childhood and into adulthood – neurologically, physically, emotionally, socially and psychologically. Research informs us that a child's first attachments are vitally important, all children whose needs have been met in a sensitive, loving and timely way by their primary carer have a sense of trust and confidence in themselves. Securely attached children do better at school and are likely to be good at making friends. Their early attachments help them to form close relationships later in life. They grow up knowing that when they need something someone will help them. Children whose early experiences of attachment have not been positive can be more susceptible in coping with future relationships and life events (Brodie 2018).

Many small children spend substantial parts of their lives in ELC settings, often from babyhood and this period of life is fundamental to every aspect of a child's future development. Many emotional, social and cognitive developmental tasks are accomplished in the context of children having secure attachment to a reliable, sensitive caregiver. Early childhood teachers are suitably placed to become additional attachment figures for children and it is crucial that they have an understanding of attachment to inform their daily practice and support them in identifying potential difficulties for children and families. Gerhardt's (2004) work in the United Kingdom (UK) highlighted how these earliest relationships shape the baby's nervous system, which can have lasting consequences for adult life. Furnivall et al. (2012) declare that having an attachment-informed approach is very important in practice as this can help children to manage those transitions and separations in a supportive way.

One such example of an attachment-informed approach in ELC settings is the 'key person' approach. Featherstone (2017) claims that this approach was introduced into the UK by Elinor Goldschmied to support very young children attending out-of-home care and the possible stress this might trigger. This approach proposes that each individual child is assigned a specific key person in the ELC setting who spends time getting to know them, their unique needs and daily rhythms and becomes the main contact person for their family. This approach is now a key feature of all high-quality ELC settings in the UK and is mandatory for all children (Department for Education (DfE) 2017). Having a key person approach is considered crucial to the child's wellbeing, sense of safety and belonging. The relationship that develops between the key person, the child and the parent/carer, shapes the foundation for all children's current and future learning experiences. This relationship provides a secure base for the child to explore from and a safe haven to return to. The child benefits by having a replacement primary caregiver who is stable and consistent, and scaffolds and guides the child's learning. The key person gets to know each of their respective children, by observing, playing with them and planning appropriately challenging learning experiences to support their development and learning.

A 'primary caregiving approach' was introduced in Singapore for very similar reasons to the key person approach in the UK. This approach involves a practice that requires the caregiver or early childhood teacher to assume responsibility for a small group of young children, becoming the main contact person between the child and the home, particularly those under the age of 3 (Ebbeck et al. 2015). The primary caregiver has the responsibility of meeting the care and educational needs of a small group of children, implementing child-centred activities and experiences and engaging in responsive and sensitive care for a small group of children. Page, Clare and Nutbrown (2013) advise that high-quality caregiver relationships are central to babies' and toddlers' emotional development and secondly, that interactions are the drivers for development (Melhuish et al. 2015). Relationships take time to develop, so the key person must be given that time and opportunity to become attuned and attached to their key baby or key toddler. Featherstone (2017) points out that well-attuned adults are very important to young children in that they are able to detect what babies are feeling or thinking and respond appropriately. A person who is well attuned responds in a timely and appropriate way using language and behaviours that reflect the other person's emotional state. They make every effort to understand the moods and emotions of the other person, and can change their response accordingly.

Terminology such as 'relational pedagogy' is cited in much of the recent literature and studies, which have expanded on the notion that, for optimal development, very young children need sensitive, responsive caregiving from attuned affectionate adults (Dalli et al. 2011; Melhuish et al. 2015). Noddings (1929-present) is best known for her educational position on the ethics of care (Noddings 2005). She introduced the concept of relational caring into educational contexts; this offered early childhood teachers a relevant means of understanding the importance of care in the lives of babies, toddlers and young children. This concept of relational pedagogy correlates with many scientific discoveries as cited by MacBlain (2018), which affirm the importance of attunement, touch and responsiveness as necessary elements for children's learning, wellbeing and development. Leong, Scarpate and Laverty (2018) stress the importance of parents/carers and early childhood teachers understanding that even little moments of play and interaction with babies contribute to positive development. Leong and colleagues suggest that a few simple signals such as eye-contact, using the baby's name, using infant-directed speech and pointing can help adults tune into young children during play. They also recommend making routine care times (changing nappies, bath time or feeding the child) playful moments. They also advocate reading books with the child and utilising those nap or bedtime routines as an opportunity for gentle play by singing songs or saying nursery rhymes. Respectful caring practice was introduced into the USA in the 1960s by Magda Gerber (1912–2012). Gerber was a pioneering infant specialist and educator, born in Hungary and moving to the USA in 1957. Gerber's philosophy or practice when working with children under 3 years had been influenced by a renowned Hungarian paediatric doctor, Emmi Picker, and has influenced early childhood teachers' practice in Europe, Australia and New Zealand (Gerber 2002). The basis of her philosophy is respect for and trust in the baby to be an initiator, explorer and a self-learner.

> Respect, means treating even the youngest child as a unique human being and trusting the baby to be an initiator, to be an explorer eager to learn what he or she is ready for. If people would trust nature's plan for how babies are created, they could relax and enjoy the daily miracles of natural development. (Gerber 2002: 11)

Gerber stresses that during caregiving times children should always be supported to be active participants rather than passive receivers. According to Geber, young children will be interested in exploring their environment without needing too many interventions when they have experienced that undivided and unhurried attention from their carer during those caregiving routines. Gerber clearly illustrates the importance of creating a safe, challenging, predictable environment in which children can do all the things they would do naturally; the more predictable an environment is, the easier it is for babies to learn, because predictability brings about security. She also proposes that babies and toddlers need to have lots of uninterrupted time to play, with freedom to explore and interact with other infants and toddlers. Gerber emphasises the importance of consistency, that is, the importance of establishing clearly defined limits for children while communicating appropriate expectations. Gerber provides very specific guidelines on the types and value of materials young children need such as natural open-ended materials which respond when the child activates them, rather than toys designed just to entertain, such as mobiles and wind-up toys. Fundamentally, she claims that babies and toddlers are self-learners, they don't need to be entertained but need to be trusted with their own play agendas, with time and freedom to reach, grasp, touch, explore, move their bodies and think.

Key Signposts: Attachment Theories

- Research confirms the central importance of attachment for young children's early development, wellbeing and learning.
- Responsive care requires attentive interactions from significant adults who can interpret the child's needs, interests and dispositions, as well as understanding and supporting children's self-directed or self-initiated play.

- In early learning and care (ELC) settings, a carefully thought out, clearly defined key person approach can beneficially support children's learning and development.
- Using talk, word games and singing with babies and toddlers effectively supports their language and communication skills.
- Babies and Toddlers need lots of open-ended materials and natural textures. They need to manipulate and engage with passive objects rather than toys designed to entertain, such as mobiles and wind-up toys (Gerber 2002).
- Babies and Toddlers are self–learners, they don't need to be entertained but need to be trusted with their own play agendas, they need time and freedom to reach, grasp, touch, move their bodies and think (Gerber 2002).

Neuroscience

MacBlain (2018) claims that the brain is essentially what controls and regulates learning for all children. It was once believed that children's brains were complete at birth but we now know that following birth, learning continues at a hastened pace and involves the strengthening of connections between neurons, which continues throughout a person's life. Babies and toddlers create their own brain function by using their senses, moving about and responding to affection and communication received from adults in their life. These sensory, emotional and physical activities young children experience, change the electrical activity in their brains, which in turn creates vital neural connections. Hughes (2010) claims that neuroscience and new technologies have validated what developmental, cognitive and evolutionary specialists have known and shared for years about what young children need in order to learn and develop. Attachment, responsive adults, attunement, touch, sensory experiences, social and emotional supports, language, movement, motivation and play.

Feuerstein (1921–2014) contested the belief that intellect was fixed from birth and argued that all children, despite their degree of challenge can, with the correct support, become effective learners (Feuerstein, Falik and Feuerstein 2014). This correlates with Gopnik's (2010; 2011) thinking in confronting the evolutionary psychology principle that we all have fixed and distinctive abilities from birth. Fundamentally, she claims that human beings have the capacity to change and are in a constant cycle of change throughout our lives. Neuroscientists refer to this capacity as plasticity, which is the ability to change in light of the experiences we have. Gopnik believes that this human capacity to change is why human beings have a much more extended period of dependence and a much longer childhood than other species. The most significant findings from neuroscience is that the brain of a baby is still largely undeveloped at birth and reliant on experiences for how it will be built. Neuroscience also confirms that learning, in the form of experience-dependent processes, continues through the entirety of child and adult development (Bornstein 2014).

Developmental psychologists and neuroscientists (National Scientific Council on the Developing Child 2004; 2007; 2010) suggest that the main influences on brain development are intentional, encouraging interactions from caring interested adults. The most important human relationship is that close positive relationship between children and the people who care for them. Strong synaptic connections in children's brains are stimulated by those secure affectionate and interested caregivers, these in turn shape the developing brain and influence lifelong learning. Gopnik (2011) believes that childhood is for learning and because of this, adults and children have a special relationship. Our brains are essentially shaped by social relationships, and the information we gather through these relationships supports our emotions, factual knowledge, and our motivation and interests. Babies need adults to nurture and care for them and Eliot (2000) believes that it is those warm, positive, close relationships and social interactions young children experience after they are born that essentially switch on those neuro-endocrine pathways in the brain. Studies of children raised in Romanian institutions reveal the effects of social and emotional deprivation on brain and cognitive function. While the children are believed to have had enough food, clothing and bedding, they had little opportunity to develop meaningful, stable relationship with loving, committed adults due to the rotation of staff. It is recorded that both their brains and bodies were abnormally small and the lack of a consistent nurturing relationship early in their lives had a key impact on this (The National Academies of Science, Engineering and Medicine 2018).

The evolutional theorist Eva Jablonka, as cited in Gopnik, positions reciprocal relationships and the adults in a child's life as crucial to children's learning.

> The mind of a human child working in concert with the minds of the people caring for him or her is the most flexible and powerful learning device in the known universe. Nurturing care is necessary for the experiences-expectant and experience-dependent brain to develop. (Gopnik 2016.52)

Finnegan and Lawton (2016) outline how the early years are critical for brain development, when most of the connections in the brain are formed. Brain development from birth to age 2 is greatly influenced by quality interactions with others and the home learning environment; which has a lasting impact throughout life. Findings from the neuropsychological and neuroimaging literature (Rosselli et al. 2014) demonstrate that the relationship of language changes during human development; in early life there is a rise in operational brain variability for language, and this changes over time. Two major dimensions of language development are highlighted: naming which is considered to be a major measure of children's lexical knowledge and verbal fluency, which is viewed as a key measure of language production ability. Rosselli claims that parents/carers and early childhood teachers can scaffold and support children's language and communication skills by talking, naming objects, having conversations with children, playing word games and singing (Rosselli et al. 2014).

A number of writers such as Farah (2010) and Yang and Gotlieb (2017), cited in Pound (2017), claim that the brain structures essential for all social, cognitive, emotional and cultural functioning are identical to the brain structures that support learning and academic skills. The relationship between brain development and learning is mutual: learning and development involve this continuous creation of neural connections in response to various stimulus and demands. Younger children's preference for human interactions continues as they develop which is actively supported by parents/carers and early childhood teachers. A specific behaviour that occurs universally across cultures is 'motherese', or infant-directed speech (IDS). This is where adults exaggerate their language when interacting with babies and babies appear to be attuned to this kind of speech intuitively. The development of the human brain has a big influence on behaviour and learning. Fundamentally, the absence of experience (i.e. a lack of opportunity to learn) has an impact on brain development and therefore on learning. Researchers have studied the effects of early deprivation experienced by children and demonstrate using neuroimaging that a lack of learning opportunities specifically psychosocial, linguistic and sensory reveal a dramatic decrease in overall brain volume.

The brain develops throughout life, and those moment-to-moment experiences that shape the architecture of a young child's developing brain are literally in the hands of those who care and educate them. The everyday experiences that babies and toddlers experience influence how structures form in the brain (Pound 2017).

Key Signposts: Neuroscience

- The most significant findings from neuroscience is that the brain of a baby is still largely undeveloped at birth and reliant on experiences for how it will be built.
- Babies' brains are more highly connected than adults' brains, they have more neural pathways available to them than adults (Gopnik 2010).
- Brain development from birth to age 2 is greatly influenced by the quality of the interaction with others and the home learning environment.
- Nurturing care is necessary for the experiences-expectant and experience-dependent brain to develop (Gopnik 2016: 52).
- Babies are wired to learn about their world and seem to have special qualities that make them especially well-suited for imagination and learning (Gopnik 2016).
- The everyday experiences that babies have impact the developing architecture of the brain (The National Academies of Science, Engineering and Medicine 2018).

Hierarchy of Needs

Maslow (1908–1970) hierarchy of needs theory, is used to support and determine children's development towards self-actualisation, the highest level of human development (Maslow 1943; 1954). This hierarchy of needs was an exploration of the innate human needs that we all should satisfy if we are to get to the level of self-actualisation. The five-tier hierarchical model includes basic physiological needs (water, air, food, sleep, safety and security), psychological needs (belongingness, love and affection) and self-fulfilment needs (esteem, personal worth, social recognition, accomplishment and self-actualisation). Each level of need builds on the one below and cannot be fully achieved until the level below has been fulfilled. However, the levels of the pyramid are not meant to be regarded as a fixed, rigid sequence. Ring et al. (2018) point out that while Maslow's pyramid has been criticised as being over-simplistic, it has been very influential in education and has prompted extensive research on the role of motivation in learning. Featherstone (2017) also concludes that it provides a useful tool for understanding the factors that impede or progress learning and the importance of always recognising and responding to individual children's needs in education.

Mia Kellmer Pringle (1920–1983) was an educational and clinical psychologist and an academic. She believed that all human needs are interdependent in a subtle, complex and continuous way rather than hierarchal as suggested by Maslow (Kellmer Pringle, 1974). She agreed with Maslow that children need love and security, however, she believed that this is probably the most important need as it provides the basis for all later relationships. She strongly advocated for children to have new experiences, which in her opinion are a fundamental requirement for mental growth. Young children need praise and recognition because, according to Kellmer Pringle, growing up requires a tremendous amount of learning; emotional, social and intellectual and strong incentives are necessary for children to continue through the difficulties and conflicts they will inevitably encounter. She also claims that the most effective incentives are praise and recognition sustained over time. Children also need responsibility, which is met by allowing children to gain personal independence, firstly through learning to look after themselves in matters of everyday care and then through a gradual extension of responsibility over other areas until they have the freedom and ability to decide on their own actions and accept responsibility for others. Maslow's theory is often referred to as a motivation theory because our underlying psychological needs impact on our intrinsic motivation to learn. Children are much more inclined to engage in activities or experiences if their interests, needs and goals are being met. Intrinsic motivation is the experience of wanting to engage in an activity for its own sake because the task itself fulfils a psychological need. This mirrors Csikszentmihalyi's (2002) flow theory which claims that children act freely, for the sake of the action itself rather than for ulterior motives.

> Key Signposts: Maslow's Hierarchy of Needs
>
> - Maslow's hierarchy of needs was an exploration of the innate human needs that we all should satisfy if we are to get to the level of self-actualisation (Maslow 1943; 1954).
> - Maslow's theory is often referred to as a motivation theory because our underlying psychological needs impact on our intrinsic motivation to learn. Children are more inclined to engage if their interests, needs and goals are being met.
> - Young children from birth need love and security, praise and recognition, new experiences and responsibility. These should be explicitly articulated in curriculum experiences for children under 3 years (Kellmer Pringle 1975).

Conclusion

Developments at policy level, both globally and nationally, indicate a concern to value and support all children from birth to 3 years during this critically important phase of their educational journey. Providing high-quality research-informed experiences for babies and toddlers yields significant benefits for children's learning and development. The research explored in this chapter reinforces the concept of the existence of a powerful urge to learn, which is there from birth and the unique learning capacity of children from birth to 3 years, which can and should be supported and nurtured by adults. Utilising a theoretical lens to examine how children (birth-3 years) learn reveals the critical importance of seeing children as active learners, constructing their own knowledge of the world around them from birth and the crucial role parents/carers and early childhood teachers have in supporting children throughout this pivotal phase of development. It is clear that while children are born with a set of competencies, which facilitate early learning, their development in this context is also shaped by the family, community, culture and society. Children need consistent, emotionally and physically present, responsive adults who connect positively with them and their families. Providing children with a range of opportunities to engage in rich, meaningful play and active exploration is a powerful incentive for the development of flexibility, working memory and staying in roles, all of which support the development of core self-regulation skills. It is essential that babies and toddlers have sensory-rich new experiences (novelty) to support their innate need to explore, to be curious and to make new discoveries in addition to experiences for exploration in natural spaces with natural objects. Babies and toddlers can beneficially participate in the daily routines such as nappy changing, feeding and tidying. Most importantly children's learning, wellbeing and development flourishes when they are supported by sensitive, responsive caregiving from attuned affectionate adults (Dalli et al. 2011; Melhuish et al. 2015).

Bibliography

Ainsworth, M. S. (1989). 'Attachments beyond Infancy', *American Psychologist*, 44(4), 709–716.

Arnold, C. (2010). *Understanding Schemas and Emotion in Early Childhood*. London: Sage.

Asmussen, K., Law, J., Charlton, J., Acquah, D., Brims, L., Pote, I., and Mc Bride, T. (2018). *Key Competencies in Early Cognitive Development: Things, People, Numbers and Words.* London: Early Intervention Foundation, <https://www.eif.org.uk/report/key-competencies-in-early-cognitive-development-things-people-numbers-and-words>, accessed 01 September 2020.

Athey, C. (2007). *Extending Thought in Young Children.* London: Paul Chapman.

Bandura, A. (1976.) *Social Learning Theory.* New Jersey, NJ: Prentice Hall Publishing.

Bernard van Leer Foundation. (2018). *Early Childhood Matters, Issue Number 127.* The Hague, Netherlands: Bernard van Leer Foundation, <https://bernardvanleer.org/app/uploads/2018/06/ECM18_ENG.pdf>, accessed 01 September 2020.

Bornstein, M. (2014). 'Human Infancy and the Rest of the Lifespan', *Annual Review of Psychology,* 65, 121–158.

Bornstein, M. H., Hahn, C. S., and Suwalsky, J. T. D. (2013). 'Physically Developed and Exploratory Young Infants Contribute to Their Own Long-Term Academic Achievement', *Psychological Science,* 24(10), 1906–1917.

Bowlby, J. (1969). *Attachment and loss: Vol. 1.* Loss. New York, NY: Basic Books.

Bowlby, J. (1988). *A Secure Base: Clinical Applications of Attachment Theory.* London: Routledge.

Brodie, K. (2018). *The Holistic Care and Development of Children from Birth to Three.* London: Routledge.

Bronfenbrenner, U., and Morris, P. A. (1998). 'The Ecology of Developmental Process'. In W. Damon and R. M. Lerner (eds), *Handbook of Child Psychology: Vol. 1. Theoretical Models for Human Development* (5th ed.), pp. 993–1028. New York, NY: John Wiley.

Bruce, T. (2004). *Developing Learning in Early Childhood.* London: Paul Chapman.

Bruner, J. S. (1960). *The Process of Education.* Cambridge, MA: Harvard University Press.

Bruner, J. S. (1974–1975). 'From Communication to Language – A Psychological Perspective', *Cognition,* 3(3), 255–287.

Carpenter, M. (2014). 'Social Cognition and Social Motivations in Infancy'. In U. Goswami (ed), *The Blackwell Handbook of Childhood Cognitive Development,* pp. 106–128. West Sussex: Blackwell Publishing.

Centre for Early Childhood Development and Education. (2006). *Síolta: The National Quality Framework for Early Childhood Education.* Dublin: Centre for Early Childhood Development and Education.

Csikszentmihalyi, M. (2002). *Flow: The Psychology of Happiness.* London: Rider.

Csikszentmihalyi, M. (2015). *Flow and the Foundations of Positive Psychology; The Collected Works of Mihaly Csikszentmihalyi.* New York, NY: Springer.

Dalli, C., White, E., Rockel, J., Duhn, I., Buchanan, E., Davidson, S., Ganly, S., Kus, L., and Wang, B. (2011). *Quality Early Childhood Education for Under-Two-Year-Olds: What Should It Look Like*? A Literature Review. Report to the Ministry of Education. Wellington, New Zealand: Ministry of Education.

Daly, L., and Beloglovsky, M. (2016). *Loose Parts: Inspiring Play in Young Children*. St. Paul, MA: Red Leaf Press.

David, T., Goouch, K., Powell, S., and Abbott, L. (2003). *Birth to Three Matters: A Review of the Literature Compiled to Inform the Framework to Support Children in Their Earliest Years*. London: Department for Education and Skills.

DeLoache, J. S., Simcock, G., and Macari, S. (Nov 2007). 'Planes, Trains, Automobiles – and Tea Sets: Extremely Intense Interests in Very Young Children', *Developmental Psychology*, 43(6), 1579–1586.

Department of Children and Youth Affairs. (2014). *Better Outcomes, Brighter Futures: The National Policy Framework for Children and Young People 2014–2020*. Dublin: Department of Children and Youth Affairs, <https://assets.gov.ie/23796/961bbf5d975f4c88adc01a6fc5b4a7c4.pdf>, accessed 04 July 2020.

Department for Education (DfE). (2017). *Statutory Framework for the Early Years Foundation Stage: Setting the Standards for Learning, Development and Care for Children from Birth to Five*. Manchester: Department for Education, <https://www.foundationyears.org.uk/files/2017/03/EYFS_STATUTORY_FRAMEWORK_2017.pdf>, accessed 02 September 2020.

Dewey, J. (1902). *The Child and the Curriculum*. Chicago, IL: University of Chicago Press.

Dewey, J. (1915). *The School and Society*. Chicago, IL: University of Chicago Press.

Dewey, J. (1916). *Democracy and Education: An Introduction to the Philosophy of Education*. New York, NY: Macmillan.

Dweck, C. (2000). *How You Can Fulfil Your Potential*. New York, NY: Ballantine Books.

Dweck, C. (2016). *Mindset: The New Psychology of Success*. New York, NY: Ballantine Books.

Ebbeck, M., Yong Phoon, D. M., Tan-Chong, E. C. K., Bee Tan, M. A., and Mui Goh, M. L. (2015). 'A Research Study on Secure Attachment Using the Primary Caregiving Approach', *Early Childhood Education Journal*, 43(3), 233–240.

Eliot, L. (2000). *What's Going on in There? How the Brain and Mind Develop in the First Five Years of Life*. New York, NY: Bantam Books.

Featherstone, S. (2017). *An Anthology of Educational Thinkers: Putting Theory into Practice in the Early Years*. Oxford: Bloomsbury.

Feuerstein, R., Falik, L. H., and Feuerstein, R. S. (2014). *Changing Minds & Brains: The Legacy of Reuven Feuerstein*. New York, NY: Teachers College Press.

Finnegan J., and Lawton, K. (2016). *Lighting Up Young Brains: How Parents, Carers and Nurseries support Children's Brain Development in the First Five Years.* London: Save the Children, <https://www.savethechildren.org.uk/content/dam/global/reports/education-and-child-protection/lighting-up-young-brains.pdf>, accessed 02 September 2020.

Furnivall, J., Mc Kenna, M., Mc Farlance, S., and Grant, E. (2012). *Attachment Matters for All: An Attachment Mapping Exercise for Children's Services in Scotland*, University of Strathclyde, Glasgow: Centre for Excellence for Looked After Children in Scotland, <https://pure.strath.ac.uk/portal/files/18198937/Attachment_mapping_FINAL_pdf>, accessed 02 September 2020.

Gerber, M. (2002). *Caring for Infants with Respect* (2nd ed.). Los Angeles, CA: Resources for Infant Educators.

Gerhardt, S. (2004). *Why Love Matters: How Affection Shapes a Baby's Brain.* Oxon: Routledge.

Goldschmied, E., and Jackson, S. (2004). *People under Three: Young Children in Day Care.* London: Psychology Press.

Gopnik, A. (2010). 'How Babies Think: Even the Youngest Children Know, Experience and Learn Far More Than Scientists Ever Thought Possible', *Scientific American* 303(1), 76–81.

Gopnik, A. (2011). *The Philosophical Baby: What Children's Minds Tell Us about Truth, Love and the Meaning of Life.* New York, NY: Harper Collins Publishers.

Gopnik, A. (2016). *The Gardener and the Carpenter: What the New Science of Child Development Tells Us about the Relationships between Parent and Children.* London: Random House Books.

Government of Ireland. (2018). *First Five: A Whole-of-Government Strategy for Babies, Young Children and their Families 2019–2028.* Dublin: The Government Publications Office, <https://assets.gov.ie/31184/62acc54f4bdf4405b74e53a4afb8e71b.pdf>, accessed 04 July 2020.

Gray, C., and MacBlain, S. (2017). *Learning Theories in Childhood* (2nd ed.). London: Sage.

Greenspan, S., and Wieder, S. (2006). *Engaging Autism: Using the Floortime Approach to Help Children Relate, Communicate, and Think.* Cambridge, MA: Da Capo.

Grenier, J. (2014). 'Understanding Schemas and Young Children from Birth to Three and Young Children Learning through Schemas: Deepening the Dialogue about Learning in the Home and in the Nursery', *Early Years*, 34(4), 437–439.

Hargraves, V. (2020). *Materials for Play: Why Open-ended Loose Parts are Important.* New Zealand: The Education Hub, <https://theeducationhub.

org.nz/materials-for-play-why-open-ended-loose-parts-are-important/>, accessed 01 September 2020.

Hughes, A. M. (2016). *Developing Play for the Under 3s: The Treasure Basket and Heuristic Play* (3rd ed.). Oxon: Routledge.

Kellmer Pringle, M. (1975). *The Needs of Children: A Personal Perspective.* London: Hutchinson.

Lagercrantz, H. (2016). *Infant Brain Development: Formation of the Mind and the Emergence of Consciousness.* Cham, Gewerbestrasse, Switzerland: Springer International Publishing.

Leong, V., Scarpate, M., and Laverty, V. (2018). *Play and Infant Interactions with Caregivers.* Cambridge: Play in Education Development and Learning, <https://www.pedalhub.org.uk/play-piece/play-and-infant-interactions-caregivers>, accessed 02 September 2020.

Lindon, J., and Brodie, K. (2016). *Understanding Child Development 0–8 Years* (4th ed.). London: Hodder Education.

MacBlain, S. (2018). *Learning Theories for Early Years Practice.* London: Sage.

Maguire-Fong, M. (2015). *Teaching and Learning with Infants and Toddlers: Where Meaning-Making Begins.* New York, NY: Teachers College Press.

Maslow, A. H. (1943). 'A Theory of Human Motivation', *Psychological Review*, 50(4), 370–396.

Maslow, A. (1954). *Motivation and Personality.* New York, NY: Harper.

Mathers, S., Eisenstaedt, N., Sylva, K., Soukakou, E., and Ereky-Stevens, K. (2014). *Sound Foundations, a Review of the Research Evidence on Quality of Early Childhood education and Care for Children under Three, Implications for Policy and Practice.* Oxford: The Sutton Trust.

Melhuish, E. (2010). *Growing Up in Scotland: The Impact of the Home Environment on Child Cognitive Development: Secondary Analysis of Data from 'Growing Up in Scotland'.* Edinburgh: Scottish Government.

Melhuish, E., Ereky-Stevens, K., Petrogiannis, K., Ariescu, A., Penderi, E., Rentzou, Tawell, A., Leseman, P., and Broekhuisen, M. (2015). *A Review of Research on the Effects of Early Childhood Education and Care (ECEC) upon Child Development*, CARE Project; Curriculum Quality Analysis and Impact Review of European Early Childhood Education and Care (ECEC), <http://ecec-care.org/fileadmin/careproject/Publications/reports/new_version_CARE_WP4_D4_1_Review_on_the_effects_of_ECEC.pdf>, accessed 04 July 2020.

National Academies of Science, Engineering and Medicine. (2018). *How People Learn II: Learners, Contexts and Cultures.* Washington, DC: The National Academies Press, <https://www.nap.edu/read/24783/chapter/1>, accessed 01 September 2020.

National Council for Curriculum and Assessment. (2009). *Aistear: The Early Childhood Curriculum Framework*. Dublin: National Council for Curriculum and Assessment, <https://www.ncca.ie/en/early-childhood/aistear>, accessed 04 July 2020.

National Scientific Council on the Developing Child. (2004). *Young Children Develop in an Environment of Relationships. Working Paper No.1*. Cambridge, MA: Center for the Developing Child, Harvard University, <https://developingchild.harvard.edu/wp-content/uploads/2004/04/Young-Children-Develop-in-an-Environment-of-Relationships.pdf>, accessed 02 September 2020.

National Scientific Council on the Developing Child. (2007). *The Science of Early Childhood Development: Closing the Gap between What We Know and What We Do*. Cambridge, MA: Center for the Developing Child, Harvard. Retrieve, <http://46y5eh11fhgw3ve3ytpwxt9r.wpengine.netdna-cdn.com/wp-content/uploads/2015/05/Science_Early_Childhood_Development.pdf>, accessed 02 September 2020.

National Scientific Council on the Developing Child. (2010). *Early Experiences Can Alter Gene Expression and Affect Long-Term Development: Working Paper No. 10*. Cambridge, MA: Center for the Developing Child, Harvard University, <https://developingchild.harvard.edu/resources/early-experiences-can-alter-gene-expression-and-affect-long-term-development/#:~:text=Early%20Experiences%20Can%20Alter%20Gene%20Expression%20and-%20Affect%20Long%2DTerm,healthy%2C%20productive%20members%20of%20society>, accessed 02 September 2020.

Nicholson, S. (1972). 'The Theory of Loose Parts: An Important Principle for Design Methodology. Studies in Design Education', *Craft and Technology*, 4(2), 5–14.

Noddings, N. (2005). *The Challenge to Care in Schools* (2nd ed.). New York, NY: Teachers College Press.

Nutbrown, C. (2013). *Understanding Schemas and Young Children*. London: Sage.

Page, J., Clare, A., and Nutbrown, C. (2013). *Working with Babies and Children from Birth to Three* (2nd ed.). London: Sage.

Piaget, J. (1956). *The Child's Conception of Space*. London: Routledge.

Pound, L. (2017). *How Children Learn-Book 3*. (How Children Learn Series) London: Practical Pre-school Books.

Rinaldi, C. (2005). *In Dialogue with Reggio Emilia: Listening, Researching and Learning*. New York, NY: Routledge.

Ring, E., O'Sullivan, L., Ryan, M., and Burke, P. (2018). *A Melange or a Mosaic of Theories? How Theoretical Perspectives on Children's Learning and Development Can Inform a Responsive Pedagogy in a Redeveloped Primary School Curriculum*. Dublin: National Council for Curriculum and Assessment, <https://

www.ncca.ie/media/3863/seminar_four_er_los_mr_pb_paper.pdf>, accessed 16 January 2020.

Robinson, M. (2003). *From Birth to One: The Year of Opportunity*. Buckingham: Open University Press.

Rosselli, M., Ardila, A., Matute, E., and Velez-Uribe, I. (2014). 'Language Development Across the Life Span: A Neuropsychological/Neuroimaging Perspective', *Neuroscience Journal*, 2014, <https://doi.org/10.1155/2014/585237>, accessed 02 September 2020.

Shonkoff, J. P., Richter, L., van der Gaag, J., and Bhutta, Z. A. (2012). 'An Integrated Scientific Framework for Child Survival and Early Childhood Development', *Paediatrics*, 129(2), 460–472.

Stenberg, G. (2009). 'Selectivity in Infant Social Referencing', *Infancy* 14(4), 457–473.

Tovey, H. (2017). *Bringing the Froebel Approach to Your Early Years Practice* (2nd ed.). Oxon: Routledge.

Tremblay, R. E., Boivin, M., and Peters RDeV. (2011). 'Emotions: Synthesis'. In R. E. Tremblay, M. Boivin, RDeV Peters, and M. Lewis (eds), *Encyclopaedia on Early Childhood Development*, Center of Excellence for Early Childhood Development and Strategic Knowledge Cluster on Early Child Development. Montréal: Center of Excellence for Early Childhood Development, <http://www.child-encyclopedia.com/emotions/synthesis>, accessed 01 September 2020.

Trevarthen, C., and Delafield-Butt, J. (2016). 'Intersubjectivity in the Imagination and Feelings of the Infant: Implications for Education in the Early Years'. In E. J. White and C. Dalli (eds), *Under Three Year Olds in Policy and Practice*, pp. 17–39. London: Springer.

United Nations. (1989). *Convention on the Rights of the Child*. New York, NY: United Nations, <http://www.ohchr.org/EN/ProfessionalInterest/Pages/CRC.aspx>, accessed 29 October 2019, accessed 12 January 2020.

United Nations. (2006). *General Comment No. 7 (2005) Implementing Child Rights in Early Childhood*. New York, NY: United Nations, <https://www2.ohchr.org/english/bodies/crc/docs/AdvanceVersions/GeneralComment7Rev1.pdf>, accessed 01 September 2020.

Vygotsky, L. S. (1980). *Mind in Society: The Development of Higher Psychological Processes*. Cambridge, MA: Harvard University Press.

Williams, J., Murray, A., Mc Crory, C., and Mc Nally, S. (2013). *Growing Up in Ireland-Development from Birth to Three Years. Report No 5 from the infant Cohort*. Dublin: The Stationary Office.

MARIE RYAN

Chapter 4 Interactions Drive Development: What Does This Actually Mean for Practice?

ABSTRACT
This chapter explores the potential of pedagogical interactions for enhancing learning and development with particular focus on cognitive development, learning and thinking. The chapter positions the notion that interactions drive development as an inclusive concept, which empowers both teachers and learners. An analysis of the work of seminal theorists and thinkers such as Piaget, Vygotsky and Pestalozzi provides a theoretical backdrop for the pedagogical approaches discussed. The role of the adult in the learning process is considered in the context of these theories. The chapter supports the notion that high-quality interactions develop and enhance children's thinking. Observational classroom research is cited, which notes that not all teacher-child interactions are created equally and that some do not enhance children's thinking and learning to the extent of others. Various approaches to interactional pedagogy, which supports children's thinking are discussed with particular emphasis on dialogic teaching, scaffolding, sustained shared thinking and guided-play. Peer interactions are discussed and suggestions for supporting high-quality peer interactions are proposed. The chapter also considers the role of pedagogical documentation as an inclusive strategy for building sustained learning interactions. Signposts to support, parents/cares, early childhood and primary teachers in supporting all children are threaded throughout the chapter.

Introduction – An Inclusive Concept?

Interactions drive development – a powerful reminder for inclusive educators of the potential influence that we can have on children's learning and development. Implicit within the notion that interactions drive development is an acknowledgement that developmental progress or delay is influenced by social-environmental factors. As such, the concept can be construed as falling within the social-model of disability as opposed to the medical-model, rejecting deterministic notions of ability and recognising an interactive understanding of how all children learn differently. Considering the social influences on development while attending to individual differences presents a much more positive, solution-focussed approach to learning differences. A child's developmental progress is not determined solely by innate capacities or deficiencies but rather is dependent on the interplay between external forces and internal resources. On a philosophical level, this perspective can be interpreted as a commitment to the education of all children; the simple message behind this notion is that teachers can make a difference depending on the quality of the interactions that the child experiences.

High-Quality Pedagogy = Interactional Pedagogy

In response to the question of 'what matters in the quality of ECCE (Early Childhood Care and Education)', Edward Melhuish (2015: 1) gave a simple and direct response: 'interactions drive development'. Melhuish was one of the principal investigators on the Effective Provision of Pre-school Education (EPPE) project (Sylva et al. 2004). This large-scale study, conducted in the United Kingdom (UK) context across a range of different types of pre-schools, and including 3,000 children from differing social backgrounds, was focused on determining what high-quality practice looked like in early childhood settings and how the quality of practice influenced children's outcomes. The researchers found that the quality of the interactions between children and staff were of particular importance; where staff showed warmth and were responsive to the individual needs of children, children made more progress. One of the primary conclusions of the EPPE study was that quality early years' education and care has a profound effect on children's learning and development and that one of the foremost indicators of quality was adult-child interactions. Particular attention was drawn to the ways in which the adults engaged with the children cognitively.

Adult-child interactions are not only associated with high-quality early years' education but also high-quality teaching in primary and post-primary settings. In the context of the primary curriculum, Ring et al. (2018) emphasised the importance of interactions in supporting children's development and learning. Bridget Hamre, Robert Pianta and their colleagues (2013) promote teaching through interactions (TTI) and adopt a definition of teacher quality, which focuses almost exclusively on teacher-child interactions, that is, the primary indicator for determining quality is how the teacher interacts with the children. They present a conceptual model that organises teacher-child interactions into three broad domains; (i) emotional interaction, (ii) organisational interaction and (iii) instructional interaction. Emotional interaction relates to relationship development, organisational interaction is concerned with behavioural supports and instructional interaction refers primarily to supporting children's cognitive development. According to Goble, Sandilos and Pianta (2019), in order to create emotionally supportive environments, teachers should use a warm tone and positive affect when communicating with children, incorporate children's interests into lessons and allow for autonomy, while being sensitive to children's needs and emotions. Teachers who create a supportive instructional environment foster a deep understanding of concepts and ideas through open-ended questioning, problem-solving, making real-world links, and encouraging language development through conversation, repetition and elaboration. Goble and colleagues (2019) demonstrated that improving teachers' interaction quality, particularly in the area of instructional interaction, has positive outcomes for children's learning and self-regulation. Throughout this publication, the importance of interactions for children's learning and development are highlighted, the emphasis in this chapter however will be on instructional interactions/ cognitive interactions; examining the theoretical underpinnings of this approach, the evidence supporting this approach, the types of instructional interactions evident in classrooms across the educational continuum and the complexity of teaching through interactions.

> **Key Signposts: Inclusive Pedagogy and Quality Interactions**
>
> - The contention that interactions drive development is an inclusive one which implies that children's learning and development can be supported by high-quality interactions with adults.
> - High-quality practice in early childhood education settings is associated with high-quality interactions.
> - Researchers on the Effective Provision of Preschool Education (EPPE) project found that the quality of the interactions between children and staff were of particular importance for children's learning and development; where staff showed warmth and were responsive to the individual needs of children, children made more progress (Sylva et al. 2004).
> - The EPPE study researchers noted that the highest quality interactions were when the early childhood teachers engaged with the children cognitively (Sylva et al. 2004).
> - Bridget Hamre and her colleagues present a conceptual model for teaching through interactions that organises teacher-child interactions into three broad domains; emotional interaction, organisational interaction and instructional interaction (Hamre et al. 2013).
> - Goble et al. (2019) demonstrated that improving teachers' interaction quality, particularly in the area of instructional interaction, has positive outcomes for children's learning and self-regulation.

Theoretical Backdrop – Interactions and Inter-thinking

One of the earliest most influential theorists on cognitive development was Jean Piaget (1952; 1956). Central to Piaget's work was the idea that child development is the product of the child's interaction with the world around them. He argued that through physical interactions with the environment the child learns about how the world works and makes sense of it. Piaget saw this an individual endeavour; that knowledge was something constructed by children's own exploration and discovery and that any attempt to impart knowledge on the part of an adult could be quite detrimental to a child's learning. For Piaget, adult intervention in children's thinking and learning was something to be avoided and he was vehemently opposed to transmission models of education. In his view the role of the adult in children's development was much like that of a gardener; provide the appropriate conditions, resources and experiences for the child, then step back and let nature take its course. According to Piaget, children must construct meaning for themselves, through first-hand experiences rather than relying on adults to tell them about the world.

While Piaget cautioned against instructional interactions between adults and children, he was much more positive about the potential for peer interactions to support children's development. His rationale was based around the concept of centration, meaning that young children, when attempting to solve a problem, will focus in on the first possible solution they encounter and that it is very difficult for them to consider other possible perspectives. If alternative suggestions are offered by an adult, who would have greater status and power than a child, then the child may adhere to what the adult advises, but will not actually develop their own understanding of the problem. According to Piaget, in order for children to develop cognitively, they must be called to question their own thinking. Piaget describes this as cognitive conflict. Cognitive conflict is what leads to the development of knowledge according to Piaget, who argues that if a peer, rather than an adult, presents an alternative solution, the child will be forced to consider this viewpoint. This cognitive conflict necessitates resolution, and in seeking resolution cognitive growth takes place. Doise, Mugny (1984) and Perret-Clermont (1980) examined this idea of sociocognitive conflict empirically and found strong evidence that children demonstrated greater understanding when working with peers who presented opposing viewpoints to their own. This finding held even if the alternatives proposed were incorrect. Contemporary researchers (e.g. Mercer and Littleton 2007) have reservations about the extent of the influence of cognitive conflict, suggesting it is more likely that the significance of peer interaction for learning and development should be accredited to the dialogue between the children, characterised by negotiation and argumentation, rather than the conflict per se. Although Piaget's work, for the most part, underplayed the importance of adult-child interactions for development, it did highlight the role of peer interaction in cognitive development and drew subsequent researchers' attention to the importance of peer learning and collaborative learning.

'The true direction of the development of thinking is not from the individual to the social, but from the social to the individual' (Vygotsky 1962: 10). While Piaget deemed adult-child interactions to be interfering, the Russian psychologist, Lev Vygotsky, considered them to be essential to children's development. Vygotsky suggested that development goes through a two-step process, firstly thinking is shared on the social level and then it is internalised by the individual. Vygotsky (1978) considered social interactions to be core to the developmental process, positing that children's understanding of the world develops through their interactions with others. Referring specifically to children with learning differences, he stated that 'the developmental path lies in relationships and collaborative activity with other humans' (Rieber and Carton 2003: 218). According to Vygotsky intellectual development is dependent on interaction. Alexander (2008) argues that this Vygotskian perspective challenges the view of the educator as a hands-off 'facilitator' of learning but does not call us back towards traditionalist transmission approaches either. Vygotsky's work suggests that both child involvement and teacher intervention, that is, child-teacher interaction, are essential for development.

Vygotsky presented a dynamic model of cognitive development, central to which was the concept of the 'Zone of Proximal Development' (ZPD). The ZPD is the gap between what a child can do independently and what they can achieve with help; the central role of the teacher is to help the child to bridge that gap. The ZPD is not the 'property of the child' but is an 'indication of the presence of certain maturing functions, which can be a target for meaningful interventive actions' (Chaiklin 2003: 43). Working within the ZPD means that attention should be focused on bringing a child to the next level of individual understanding, that is, developing their current ideas, rather than working towards the development of a prescribed set of specific skills. This is what differentiates an interactive model of ZPD from traditional, transmission, direct teaching approaches.

Vygotsky recognised a role for peer learning, but unlike Piaget, suggested that learning was more likely when lower performing children were paired with higher performing children (a more knowledgeable other). This interactive model of cognitive development emphasises the social guidance and value that a more knowledgeable other (MKO) brings to the learning process. According to Vygotsky, the interactions between the child and others, which occur at the inter-mental level, become the basis for the child's own internalisation of the learning (intra-mental). Discussion and negotiation with others are reprocessed by the individual child in a manner similar to that which Piaget would have described as constructing individual meaning. Both theorists subscribe to the theory that knowledge is constructed, dismissing transmission models of teaching, but Vygotsky places much more emphasis the role of the adult in priming the child for individual understanding, while Piaget is cautious about adults guiding children's thinking. Piaget does acknowledge a role for social interaction in learning however.

Both Piaget and Vygotsky agreed that knowledge was constructed and that social interaction could support learning and development; be it interactions between learners of similar ability, or interactions between learners and MKOs. Both types of interactions involve some kind of negotiation or dialogue. Mercer (2000), building on Vygotsky's concept of the ZPD, proposes an alternative concept – the Intermental Development Zone (IDZ). While the ZPD can sometimes present dialogue as a static concept, the IDZ takes account of the evolving states of knowledge and understanding between both partners in the learning activity (Mercer and Littleton 2007). This concept draws attention to the iterative and fluid nature of the interactive process and focuses on the quality of the dialogue to a greater degree than the concept of ZPD. An extension of this idea is *inter-thinking* which describes how cognition can be socially shared. Inter-thinking is the idea that thinking together or collaborative reasoning, helps children to think better than thinking on their own. In many regards inter-thinking reflects what effective interactions should strive to be and to achieve.

Social constructivist principles, suggest that language and particularly talk, could be the most powerful teaching tool at our disposal as educators. Talk is an often undervalued tool that can be used in highly sophisticated ways if in the hands of a skilled professional; a professional who has honed their skills over time. Skilled teachers use talk to move beyond interaction; to move towards inter-thinking. It is now generally accepted that language is an integrated component of human intellect, rather than a separate and discrete competency (Pinker 2007). The capacity to jointly plan actions and review them collaboratively is a uniquely human skill. Language enables this process of 'inter-thinking': the 'everyday process whereby people collectively and creatively use talk to solve problems and make joint sense of the world' (Littleton and Mercer 2013: 115). The message from social constructivist theorists is that there is an inherent relationship between talk and thinking. The role of talk is to uncover thinking, make thinking visible and then use talk to further develop and guide thinking. Interactions are common in educational settings but what distinguishes quality in settings is the extent to which those interactions promote inter-thinking. The contention behind inter-thinking suggests that children learn to reason alone through first reasoning collectively.

Ideas around teaching for thinking, while based on contemporary empirical research, are by no means new or revolutionary. In fact, just over 200 years ago, Johann Henrich Pestalozzi articulated a very similar message in one of his many letters to a colleague;

> It is well done to make a child read and write and learn and repeat, - but it is still better to make a child think. (Pestalozzi 1819: 125)

'The mode of doing this is not by any means to talk much to a child but to enter into conversation with a child; not to address to him many words, however familiar or well chosen, but to bring him to express himself on the subject; not to exhaust the subject but to question the child about it and to let him find out and correct the answers. It would be so ridiculous to expect that the volatile spirits of an infant could be brought to follow any lengthy explanations. The attention of a child is deadened by long expositions but roused by animated questions' (Pestalozzi 1819: 128).

Pestalozzi is calling educators to enter into conversations with children and to prompt children's thinking about subject areas. It is clear that Pestalozzi has an intimate knowledge of children, no doubt gleaned in his own personal dedication to supporting children's learning and development as a teacher. Illustrations of Pestalozzi depict him embracing children, comforting children, enthralling children; ultimately interacting with children to support their physical, cognitive and emotional development (hand, head, heart). His own experience and deep reflection on his work as an educator led him to conclude that excellent teaching is not an act of telling or transmission of information but rather an act of cognitive engagement between the teacher and learner. Conversing with a child in a manner in which one can find out what a child is thinking, and help that child to move that thinking forward, to advance their ideas and reasoning skills.

Key Signposts: Theoretical Backdrop

- According to Piaget, children must construct meaning for themselves, through first-hand experiences rather than relying on adults to tell them about the world.
- Piaget was cautious about adults guiding children's thinking but did acknowledge a role for peer interaction in learning and development. Piaget believed that if children worked in groups with similar peers who had opposing views to themselves this would result in cognitive conflict, which would ultimately lead to learning and development.
- Vygotsky (1978) considered social interactions to be core to the developmental process, and suggested that children's understanding of the world develops through their interactions with others.
- Inter-thinking (Mercer 2000) is the idea that thinking together or collaborative reasoning, helps children to think better on their own.
- Skilled teachers use talk to move beyond interaction; to move towards inter-thinking.
- Over 200 years ago Pestalozzi called on educators to enter into conversations with children and to prompt their thinking.

Classroom Interaction – Research on Talk in Practice

Observational research conducted in classrooms has found that while classrooms are characterised by numerous verbal interactions between peers and between teachers and learners, there is little evidence of inter-thinking. Maurice Galton and his colleagues conducted a large study examining talk in primary classrooms from 1976–1986, known as the ORACLE (Observational Research and Classroom *Learning* Evaluation) study, and found that classrooms were dominated by teacher talk (two-thirds of talk in the classrooms was teacher dominated) (Galton, Simon and Croll 1980; Galton 1987). When Galton replicated this study over a decade later, teacher talk had increased to three-quarters; classrooms were characterised by teachers talking at through statements, factual questions and closed questions, but not talking with them by asking open questions and building on their answers (Galton et al. 1999). Alexander, Willcocks and Nelson (1996) observed a similar imbalance and found very few examples of children initiating questions. More recent studies, (Smith et al. 2004; Smith, Hardman and Higgins 2006) have demonstrated that despite greater emphasis on more interactive teaching approaches in curriculum initiatives, teacher-led, closed-questioning continues to dominate the classroom talk. Smith and colleagues, (2004) found that only ten per cent of teacher-child exchanges could be characterised as open-ended and that fifteen per cent of teachers did not ask any open-ended questions at all. Sustained, extended dialogue between teachers and learners, occurred in just over eleven per cent of the questioning exchanges. Children's elaboration, argumentation and reasoning were rarely witnessed. For the most part, child exchanges were very short, (approx. five seconds), and were limited to three words or less. This lack of open-ended questions and sustained dialogue between teachers and children has also been a feature of early childhood classrooms as evidenced in the EPPE study (Sylva et al. 2004) mentioned earlier. Sylva and her colleagues (2004) found open-ended questioning to be quite a rare practice even in settings that were classified as 'good' or 'excellent'. Open-ended questions made up only 5.1 per cent of the questions asked in 'excellent' settings.

The dominant sequence of interactions between teachers and children in most classrooms appears to be initiation, response, follow-up. Initiation is usually a teacher question; response, involves a child answering the question and follow-up describes how the teacher provides some sort of feedback (Sinclair and Coulthard 1975). This is referred to as the IRF sequence of interaction or the IRE (initiation, response, evaluation). These IRF/E exchanges are particularly prevalent in directive forms of teaching and generally consist of closed teacher questions, brief child answers and some superficial praise or criticism, rather than any sort of informative or diagnostic feedback (Alexander 2001). The sequence reflects an emphasis on recall and lower-level questioning rather than more exploratory questions.

Key Signposts: Observing Interactions

- Classroom interactions are dominated by teacher talk.
- Classrooms are often characterised by teachers talking at children through statements, factual questions and closed questions, but not talking *with* them by asking open-ended questions and building on their answers (Galton et al. 1999).
- Lack of open-ended questions and sustained dialogue between teachers and children is also a feature of early childhood classrooms as evidenced in the EPPE study (Sylva et al. 2004).
- The dominant sequence of interactions between teachers and children in most classrooms appears to be initiation, response, follow-up/evaluation (IRF/E).
- The sequence reflects an emphasis on recall and lower-level questioning rather than more exploratory questions.

Dialogic Teaching – Teaching for Thinking

The IRF/IRE sequences reflect the majority of interactions that take place in classrooms. These types of sequences are reflective of direct teaching and behaviourist models of learning and in most cases fail to stimulate deeper thinking and learning. The IRF sequence involves the teacher interacting with the children but this type of interaction is unlikely to lead to significant cognitive development according to sociocultural theorists. High-quality interactions must provide children with opportunities to think for themselves. Contemporary researchers have examined the potential of careful crafting of understanding through dialogue and have found strong evidence for using dialogue as an effective pedagogical tool for all children. Various iterations of this approach have been described over the past number of decades; joint productive activity (Tharp and Gallimore 1988), dialogic teaching (Alexander 2008), exploratory talk (Barnes 1992) and sustained shared thinking (Sylva et al. 2004). These interactive approaches to learning and teaching were identified and specified in an effort to replace previous terminology and to draw attention away from particular organisational issues to what matters most: 'the quality, dynamics and content of talk, regardless of the way classrooms and lessons are organised' (Alexander 2008: 23). These approaches are underpinned by the principle that a child's answer should never be the end of a learning exchange but should form the basis for further discussion.

Within the EPPE study, quality interaction was characterised as shared cognitive engagement. The term coined to capture this type of interaction was 'sustained shared thinking' (SST). Sustained shared thinking is defined as 'an episode in which, two or more individuals "work together" in an intellectual way to solve a problem, clarify a concept, evaluate activities, extend a narrative, etc. Both parties must contribute to the thinking and it must develop and extend thinking' (Sylva et al. 2004: 36). In many regards SST is about tapping into children's thinking, finding out what ideas they are playing with, understanding what their level of understanding is, and then working from there to develop and extend that thinking. In the 'good' and 'excellent' settings where SST was observed in the EPPE project a number of key practices were observed. There was a strong relationship between adult intervention in child-initiated activities and intellectual challenge, that is, child-initiated activities became more cognitively engaging when adults joined them to extend their thinking. Adult modelling was also found to be related to periods of SST, as was open-ended questioning.

Child-initiated and adult-directed activities are often polarised in discussions with people arguing for one side or the other. The strong recommendation from the EPPE study was that both are essential for excellent practice and that there should be a balance between them. The findings highlight that a key role for educators in both child-initiated and adult-directed activities is to extend children's thinking.

Dialogic teaching involves encouraging children to engage in the reasoning, questioning, evidence use and collaborative building of ideas that can lead to a genuine understanding of new content. It is through dialogues that children develop their own thinking and reasoning capacities – how they make sense of the world. Alexander (2008) identifies a series of contexts and conditions, which facilitate dialogic approaches; using a variety of organisational approaches (group-work, whole-class, individual, etc.); creating an environment which is flexible to the learning needs of the task; ensuring a structure to learning units (introduction, transitions, conclusions); emphasising ideas rather than procedures; moving from interactions which are brief and random to those which are longer and sustained; and supporting children to develop their ability to communicate with confidence and competence. He went on to outline forty-eight characteristics of dialogic teaching which are valuable signposts for practice (Alexander 2008). In terms of teacher-child interaction, he advises that questions should be structured so as to provide thoughtful answers and that answers should provoke further questions and be seen as building blocks of dialogue. He encourages a balance between the social and cognitive purposes of talk and urges teachers to link teacher-child and child-child exchanges into coherent lines of enquiry rather than disconnected ideas (Alexander 2008: 42).

It is important to note that dialogical teaching approaches are not the panacea for all learning and development goals; depending on the learning goal and the individual child, alternative approaches may be more appropriate. Nystrand and colleagues (1997: 72, 73) report on the findings from a number of projects in which teachers were given professional development and support in relation to dialogic teaching approaches. They concluded that authentic questions, group-work and discussion do not always lead to learning and that there are times when IR/E sequences do lead to learning; but the ultimate indicator, or 'bottom-line' for learning through classroom interaction was the extent to which the interaction 'requires the student to think, not just report someone else's thinking' (Nystrand et al. 1997: 72, 73). The what of the interaction is just as important as the how; the content of the talk is just as important as the type of talk.

> **Key Signposts: Dialogic Teaching – Teaching for Thinking**
>
> - A child's answer should never be the end of a learning exchange but should form the basis for further discussion.
> - Child-initiated activities can became more cognitively engaging when adults join them to extend their thinking.
> - The strong recommendation from the EPPE study was that both child-initiated activities and adult-directed activities are essential for excellent practice and that there should be a balance between them.
> - Contexts and conditions to facilitate dialogic approaches (Alexander 2004) include: using a variety of organisational approaches (groupwork, whole-class, individual, etc.); creating an environment which is flexible to the learning needs of the task, ensuring a structure to learning units (introduction, transitions, conclusions); emphasising ideas rather than procedures; moving from interactions which are brief and random to those which are longer and sustained; and supporting children to develop their ability to communicate with confidence and competence.
> - Questions should be structured so as to provide thoughtful answers.
> - The 'bottom-line' for learning through classroom interaction is the extent to which the interaction 'requires the student to think, not just report someone else's thinking' (Nystrand et al. 1997: 72, 73).

Scaffolding: Supporting Children's Thinking

Extending and supporting children's thinking is quite a technical process. Scaffolding, a concept first introduced by Wood, Bruner and Ross (1976), further explains the ways in which interactions should guide learning. Scaffolding is a process of providing a temporary cognitive support, that is, reducing the cognitive burden of the task, such that children have an opportunity to focus on those aspects of the task that are within their capacity. Gradually these supports are reduced as the child masters each step of the process until ultimately, the child can complete the task independently. Supports must be contingently applied (i.e. based on the child's current level of competence), they must be faded out gradually, and there should be eventual transfer of responsibility (Van de Pol, Volman and Buishuizen 2010). These key criteria are what distinguish scaffolding from other forms of teacher support or assistance. Scaffolding is a common phrase in educational parlance but not always a common practice. True scaffolding can be seen as good teaching; sensitive, flexible guidance that is tailored, tapered and ultimately taken away once children have mastered the learning task.

Recent evidence suggests that this is much easier said than done however. Van de Pol, Mercer and Volman (2019) examined all interactions (between groups of children and teachers and children) across thirty-five classes in which the teachers had received professional development in scaffolding children's learning. They found that in many cases where teachers had given support contingently, children did not take this support on board and their level of understanding did not improve. More in-depth analysis of their data suggested that premature fading of support hampered its value. Further, they found that gradual fading of support was the most effective in supporting children's learning (Van de Pol et al. 2019). Evidently, there is a delicate balance to be found in providing support; just as it should be applied contingently, it should also be removed contingently, that is, we don't remove the mould until we know that the plaster has set.

Playful Interactions

While a more detailed exploration of play can be found in Chapter 7 of this book, this chapter considers play as an interactional pedagogy. Guided-play (Weisberg et al. 2016: 177) 'refers to learning experiences that combine the child-directed nature of free-play with a focus on learning outcomes and adult mentorship'. Guided-play requires a balance between child autonomy and adult scaffolding. The approach emphasises the importance of playful interaction in children's learning and development. Fisher et al. (2013) investigated three different strategies for teaching pre-schoolers the properties of triangles; (i) direct instruction, (ii) free-play or (iii) guided-play. Children were exposed to materials that could be used to construct triangles and sets of cards illustrating the shapes in one of three conditions. In the free-play condition the children could do whatever they wished with the materials. In the direct-instruction condition, the experimenter acted as an explorer discovering the properties of each shape while the children watched passively. While in the guided-play condition, the experimenter invited the child to explore alongside her in order to discover the shapes' properties. In post-experiment assessments children in both the guided-play and direct-instruction conditions showed greater learning gains than the children in the free-play condition. However, children in the guided-play condition were found to perform significantly better when transferring their knowledge to atypical shapes when compared to children in the didactic-instruction condition. The conclusion drawn by the researchers was that children's participation in discovery process, combined with appropriate scaffolding from an adult, allowed them to better understand the important features of the shapes (Fisher et al. 2013).

Evidence cited in Ring et al. (2018) and Chapter 7 of this publication indicate that interactions that are more playful better support children's learning. Laura Schultz and her team conducted a series of experiments, which indicate that if an adult demonstrates a particular function of a multi-functional toy, the observing child will only engage with that one function. However, if the adult happens upon the demonstrated function by 'accident', that is, in a playful manner, the child is likely to continue exploring themselves as they deem the adult to be a co-explorer rather than an expert (Schultz 2012). Schultz concludes that a balance should be sought and that playful, rather than directive, adult interactions are most likely to support young children's learning without curtailing their creativity.

Ultimately, it would appear that the message from the research is that adult-child interactions should reflect a balance between a learning focus and child autonomy. The content of the interactions is important; clear coherent lines of thinking that link together, forming the building blocks of understanding. Each interactional turn should build on the previous one. Adults should be respectful of children as active meaning makers and their interactions should be playful, guided and exploratory.

> ### Key Signposts: Playful Interactions
>
> - Guided-play emphasises the importance of playful interaction in children's learning and development.
> - Children in the guided-play condition outperformed those in the free-play condition and the direct-instruction condition in relation to generalisation of knowledge (Weisberg et al. 2016).
> - Interactions that are more playful better support children's learning.
> - Playful, rather than directive, adult interactions are most likely to support young children's learning without curtailing their creativity.
> - The content of the interactions is important; clear coherent lines of thinking that link together, forming the building blocks of understanding. Each interactional turn should build on the previous one.
> - Adults should be respectful of children as active meaning makers and their interactions should be playful, guided and exploratory.

Peer Interactions

Research in classrooms has found that interactions between children are often found to be unproductive. The ORACLE team of researchers, along with their analysis of teacher talk, examined peer interactions in British primary schools. They found that just because children were placed in groups or told to work together did not necessarily mean that they worked collaboratively as groups (Galton et al. 1980). Children were observed working in parallel on individual tasks and the tasks themselves were found to rarely require them to work together. More recent studies by Blatchford and Kutnick, (2003) and Robin Alexander (2008) have shown that even when children are assigned collaborative learning activities, the talk that characterises their interactions, is rarely productive. Group-work interactions regularly dissolve into arguments, can be very unbalanced with one child dominating, and they often go off-task. When friends are grouped together discussions tend to be quite uncritical, bland and are unlikely to present any opportunities for what Piaget would describe as cognitive conflict. Many groups can become highly competitive and disagreements can descend into hurtful personal criticism. Given such findings, it is probably unsurprising then that group-work and pair-work approaches are regarded with much scepticism by teachers (Fisher and Larkin 2008).

While it is all very well to place children in groups and to tell them to 'work together', the evidence outlined suggests that this will not happen without specific, targeted attempts to teach children to talk together. Researchers refer to this as 'oracy'; the direct teaching of speaking and listening skills. When children are taught the skills and given the opportunities to listen, think and reason together they demonstrate significant cognitive advancements. Researchers also emphasise the importance of task design when trying to ensure productive talk amongst peers. The tasks should be designed such that children need to work together to complete them. The tasks need to provide sufficient challenge to ensure that children will not be capable of solving them on their own. Research suggests that open-ended, challenging tasks are more effective for stimulating productive conversations than closed, single-answer tasks. Group or pair-work tasks should require children to work interdependently and reciprocally (Mercer and Littleton, 2007). Researchers also point to relational considerations in promoting collaboration between learners and suggest that training should be implemented to foster trust and mutual respect between the children (Blatchford et al. 2003). Children need to do more than just interact positively and cooperatively, they also need to learn to build constructively and critically on each other's ideas. Neil Mercer and his colleagues in Cambridge University developed the Thinking Together project, which explicitly taught children to use talk to think and reason together in groups

(Mercer, Wegerif and Dawes 1999; Mercer and Littleton 2007). Children were taught 'ground-rules' for talk and were allocated roles that emphasised reasoning and thinking skills (e.g. the questioner, the clarifier, etc.) rather than the generic roles which are often applied (e.g. time-keeper, recorder, etc.). Children were taught how to enact these roles and were given opportunities to practice collaboration skills. Children were encouraged to give reasons, seek clarification, ask questions and listen to each other's ideas. Teachers had a central role in the Thinking Together project, introducing the activity in a teacher-led whole-class session, intervening in a timely manner to support children's conversations and reviewing and consolidating learning at the end of the lesson with a whole-class, teacher-led plenary review (Mercer and Littleton 2007). Empirical research conducted on the project measured children's individual non-verbal cognitive reasoning skills following engagement with the project. Children who participated in the project significantly outperformed control groups (Mercer and Littleton 2007). These findings were replicated across groups of children aged 6–14 in the English school system. Mercer and Littleton (2007) argue that these findings support the sociocultural hypothesis that collective reasoning can influence the development of individual thinking and learning.

 Key Signposts: Peer Interactions

- Even when children are assigned collaborative learning activities, the talk that characterises their interactions, is rarely productive.
- Group-work interactions regularly dissolve into arguments, can be very unbalanced with one child dominating and often go off-task.
- 'Oracy' is the direct teaching of speaking and listening skills.
- When children are taught the skills and given the opportunities to listen, think and reason together they demonstrate significant cognitive advancements.
- Evidence suggests that collective reasoning can influence the development of individual thinking and learning.

Quality Interactions through Pedagogical Documentation

The chapter thus far has focussed on live, verbal interactions between teachers and children and between children themselves. It has been established that interactions need to involve SST together in order to advance children's learning and development. Making children's thinking visible is central to this and the chapter has thus far outlined how talk and questioning can uncover children's theories and ideas. The Reggio Emilia approach (discussed in detail in Chapter 8) also recognises the importance of making children's thinking visible but encourages teachers to listen to and use the 'hundred languages of children' to understand and develop children's theories about the world around them (Edwards, Gandini and Forman 2012). The important message here is that children's thinking can be just as evident in what they do, or what they create as it is in what they say; young children can often think with their hands. Recognising the multiple means in which children express themselves is an important concept in providing for the education for all.

'By asking a child questions about his drawing, I could understand what the picture represents in his mind – something that I would not see by just looking at his drawing' – this quote from a teacher who was using a pedagogical documentation approach cited by Buldu (2010: 144) highlights the way in which children's thinking becomes visible through dialogue mediated by the child's written expression. Teachers in this study noted that pedagogical documentation helped provide insights into children's thought processes. The tools of talk can only be used to develop thinking once thinking has become visible. Pedagogical documentation supposes that by recording activity we can open it up to discussion, reflection, meaning making and further construction (Ferraris 2013). Pedagogical documentation is a means of engaging in a pedagogy of listening, which Rinaldi (2005) argues is central to the search for meaning. Photographs, video clips, children's drawings, mark-marking, music-making, transcripts or records of teacher-child conversations and child-child conversations can all be used as tools to simulate cognitive interaction. Documentation when used in this way is not about finding answers and evidencing learning achievements but rather is about generating questions which will guide future planning and learning experiences. Documentation allows teachers the space and time to think about children's thinking, to find out about children's interpretations and to think about ways to develop these. Documentation allows for continuity and sustained learning experiences as children are prompted to revisit previous learning by looking at previous records through displays, portfolios, etc. Such practice aligns with best evidence in learning and development as regards beginning with children's prior knowledge (Ring et al. 2018). Learning interactions with parents can also be stimulated by pedagogical documentation approaches, with evidence suggesting that it increases dialogue between teachers and parents, and also encourages learning conversations between children and their parents (Buldu 2010).

> **Key Signposts: Quality Interactions through Pedagogical Documentation**
>
> - Children's thinking can be just as evident in what they do, or what they create as it is in what they say; young children can often think with their hands.
> - Recognising the multiple means in which children express themselves is an important inclusive concept.
> - Pedagogical documentation helps provide insights into children's thought processes.
> - Pedagogical documentation supposes that by recording activity we can open it up to discussion, reflection, meaning making and further construction (Ferraris 2013).
> - Documentation allows early childhood and primary teachers the space and time to think about children's thinking, to find out children's interpretations and to think about ways to develop these.
> - Documentation allows for continuity and sustained learning experiences as children are prompted to revisit previous learning by looking at previous records through displays, portfolios, etc.

Conclusion

The evidence for the importance of high-quality interactions in supporting development and providing for the inclusion of all learners is overwhelming, but unfortunately much of the interactions that take place in our classrooms and early learning and care (ELC) settings are not of high quality. This chapter sought to illustrate what high-quality interactions look like in practice and offered guidance for primary and early childhood teachers in terms of extending children's thinking. Strategies to support talking for thinking in classrooms and ELC settings, such as dialogic teaching and SST were described and explored. Guidance for practice was shared in relation of scaffolding and playful interactions. Research was cited in relation to the importance of teaching children talking and listening skills and which highlighted the potential of children reasoning collaboratively for individual cognitive growth. Finally, pedagogical documentation was explored in terms of its potential to make children's thinking visible and to sustain long-term thinking together interactions.

Bibliography

Alexander, R. J. (2001). *Culture and Pedagogy: International Comparisons in Primary Education*. Oxford: Blackwell.

Alexander, R. J. (2008). *Towards Dialogic Teaching: Rethinking Classroom Talk* (4th ed.). Cambridge, MA: Dialogos.

Alexander, R., Willcocks, J., and Nelson, N. (1996). 'Discourse, Pedagogy and the National Curriculum: Change and Continuity in Primary Schools', *Research Papers in Education*, 11(1), 81–120.

Barnes, D. (1992). *From Communication to Curriculum*. Harmondsworth: Penguin Books.

Blatchford, P., and Kutnick, P. (2003). 'Developing Group Work in Everyday Classrooms: An Introduction to the Special Issue', *International Journal of Educational Research*, 1(39), 1–7.

Blatchford, P., Kutnick, P., Baines, E., and Galton, M. (2003). 'Toward a Social Pedagogy of Classroom Group Work', *International Journal of Educational Research*, 39(1–2), 153–172.

Buldu, M. (2010). 'Making Learning Visible in Kindergarten Classrooms: Pedagogical Documentation as a Formative Assessment Technique', *Teaching and Teacher Education*, 26(7), 1439–1449.

Chaiklin, S. (2003). 'The Zone of Proximal Development in Vygotsky's Analysis of Learning and Instruction', *Vygotsky's Educational Theory in Cultural Context*, 1, 39–64.

Doise, W., and Mugny, G. (1984). *The Social Development of the Intellect*. Oxford: Pergamon Press.

Edwards, C., Gandini, L., and Forman, G. (eds) (2012). *The Hundred Languages of Children* (3rd ed.). Santa Barbara, CA: Praeger.

Ferraris, M. (2013). *Documentality: Why It Is Necessary to Leave Traces*. Translated by R. Davies. New York, NY: Fordham University Press.

Fisher, K. R., Hirsh-Pasek, K., Newcombe, N. S., and Golinkoff, R. M. (2013). 'Taking Shape: Supporting Preschoolers' Acquisition of Geometric Knowledge through Guided Play', *Child Development*, 84, 1872–1878.

Fisher, R., and Larkin, S. (2008). 'Pedagogy or Ideological Struggle? An Examination of Pupils' and Teachers' Expectations for Talk in the Classroom', *Language and Education*, 22(1), 1–16.

Galton, M. (1987). 'An ORACLE Chronicle: A Decade of Classroom Research', *Teaching and Teacher Education*, 3(4), 299–313.

Galton, M., Hargreaves, L., Comber, C., Wall, D., and Pell, T. (1999). 'Changes in Patterns of Teacher Interaction in Primary Classrooms: 1976-96', *British Educational Research Journal*, 25(1), 23–37.

Galton, M., Simon, B., and Croll, P. (1980). *Inside the Primary Classroom*. London: Routledge and Kegan Paul.

Goble, P., Sandilos, L. E., and Pianta, R. C. (2019). 'Gains in Teacher-Child Interaction Quality and Children's School Readiness Skills: Does It Matter where Teachers Start?', *Journal of School Psychology*, 73, 101–113.

Hamre, B. K., Pianta, R. C., Downer, J. T., DeCoster, J., Mashburn, A. J., Jones, S. M., and Brackett, M. A. (2013). 'Teaching through Interactions: Testing a Developmental Framework of Teacher Effectiveness in over 4,000 Classrooms', *The Elementary School Journal*, 113(4), 461–487.

Littleton, K., and Mercer, N. (2013). *Interthinking: Putting Talk to Work*. London: Routledge.

Melhuish, E. (2015). 'What Matters in the Quality of ECCE? Answer: Interactions Drive Development', Organisation for Economic Development and Co-Operation Meeting (OECD), Early Childhood Education and Care

International Policy Event, 28 October 2015, Chartered Accountants House, Pearse Street, Dublin 2: Pobal, <https://www.youtube.com/watch?v=2U1z0 C6EUbw>, accessed 5 January 2019.

Mercer, N. (2000). *Words and Minds: How We Use Language to Think Together*. London: Routledge.

Mercer, N., and Littleton, K. (2007). *Dialogue and the Development of Children's Thinking: A Sociocultural Approach*. Oxon: Routledge.

Mercer, N., Wegerif, R., and Dawes, L. (1999). 'Children's Talk and the Development of Reasoning in the Classroom', *British Educational Research Journal*, 25(1), 95–111.

Nystrand, M., Gamoran, A., Kachur, R., and Prendergast, C. (1997). *Opening Nialogue*. New York: Teachers College Press.

Perret-Clermont, A.-N. (1980). *Social Interaction and Cognitive Development in Children*. London: Academic Press.

Pestalozzi, J. H. (1819). *Letters on Early Education Addressed to J.P. Greaves ESQ.* London: Sherwood, Gilberg and Piper, <https://archive.org/details/lettersonearlyed00pestiala/page/n7/mode/2up>, accessed on 10 January 2020.

Piaget, J. (1952). *The Origins of Intelligence in Children*. New York, NY: International Universities Press.

Piaget, J. (1956). *The Child's Conception of Space*. London: Routledge.

Pinker, S. (2007). *The Language Instinct (1994/2007)*. New York, NY: Harper Perennial Modern Classics.

Rieber, R. W., and Carton, A. S. (eds). (1993). *The Collected Works of LS Vygotsky: The Fundamentals of Defectology (Abnormal Psychology and Learning Disabilities)*. New York, NY: Plenum.

Rinaldi, C. (2005). 'Documentation and Assessment: What Is the Relationship?'. In A. Clark, A. Kjørholt, and P. Moss (eds), *Beyond Listening: Children's Perspectives on Early Childhood Services*, pp. 17–28. Bristol: Policy Press.

Ring, E., O'Sullivan, L., Ryan, M., and Burke, P. (2018). *A Melange or a Mosaic of Theories? How Theoretical Perspectives on Children's Learning and Development can Inform a Responsive Pedagogy in a Redeveloped Primary School Curriculum*. Dublin: National Council for Curriculum and Assessment, <https://www.ncca.ie/media/3863/seminar_four_er_los_mr_pb_paper.pdf>, accessed 16 January 2020.

Schultz, L. (2012). 'The Origins of Inquiry: Inductive Inference and Exploration in Early Childhood', *Trends in Cognitive Sciences*, 16(7), 382–389.

Sinclair, J. M., and Coulthard, M. (1975). *Towards an Analysis of Discourse: The English Used by Teachers and Pupils*. Oxford: Oxford University Press.

Smith, F., Hardman, F., and Higgins, S. (2006). 'The Impact of Interactive Whiteboards on Teacher – Pupil Interaction in the National Literacy and Numeracy Strategies', *British Educational Research Journal*, 32(3), 443–457.

Smith, F., Hardman, F., Wall, K., and Mroz, M. (2004). 'Interactive Whole Class Teaching in the National Literacy and Numercy Strategies', *British Educational Research Journal*, 30(3), 395–411.

Sylva, K., Melhuish, E., Sammons, P., Siraj-Blatchford, I., and Taggart, B. (2004). *The Effective Provision of Pre-school Education (EPPE) Project: Findings from Pre-school to End of Key Stage 1*. Nottingham: Department for Education and Skills.

Tharp, R. G., and Gallimore, R. (1988). *Rousing Minds to Life: Teaching, Learning and Schooling in Social Context*. Cambridge: Cambridge University Press.

Van de Pol, J., Mercer, N., and Volman, M. (2019). 'Scaffolding Student Understanding in Small-Group Work: Students' Uptake of Teacher Support in Subsequent Small-Group interaction', *Journal of the Learning Sciences*, 28(2), 206–239.

Van de Pol, J., Volman, M., and Beishuizen, J. (2010). 'Scaffolding in Teacher–Student Interaction: A Decade of Research', *Educational Psychology Review*, 22(3), 271–296.

Vygotsky, L. S. (1962). *Thought and Language*. Cambridge, MA: MIT Press.

Vygotsky, L. S. (1978). *Mind in Society*. Cambridge, MA: Harvard University Press.

Weisberg, D. S., Hirsh-Pasek, K., Golinkoff, R. M., Kittredge, A. K., and Klahr, D. (2016). 'Guided Play: Principles and Practices', *Current Directions in Psychological Science*, 25(3), 177–182.

Wood, D., Bruner, J., and Ross G. (1976). 'The Role of Tutoring in Problem Solving', *Journal of Child Psychology and Psychiatry*, 17, 89–100.

Realising Inclusive Culture, Pedagogy and Practice

ANNA BARR AND PAULA HILLIARD

Chapter 5   Realising and Building Partnership with Parents and Families

ABSTRACT

Parents and families are the experts on the children in their care with the Irish Constitution (Bunreacht na hÉireann) recognising parents as the child's primary educators (Ireland 1937). Consequently, we have a responsibility to realise and build partnerships with parents and families in our educational settings. In this chapter, a child-centred model provides a focus and purpose for realising and building partnership with parents. High-quality practice is explored and guidance, legislation and policy in early learning and care (ELC) are considered. Parental involvement is conceptualised as a continuum, with the ultimate aim being to develop meaningful engagement in children's early learning (Goodall and Montgomery 2014). The chapter will suggest a number of strategies that can enhance: communication with parents and families; parental involvement in decision-making; and parental engagement in children's learning (Epstein 2011; European Agency for Special Needs and Inclusive Education (EASNIE) 2017a; 2017b). The importance of a seamless connection between the home and the education setting for all children is discussed with reference to the competencies associated with providing early childhood education for all children developed by the Leadership for INClusion in the Early Years (LINC) Consortium (LINC Consortium 2016–2020; Ring et al. 2019). These competencies are located in the significance of providing for an inclusive culture, practice and pedagogy to support high-quality early learning programmes for all children.

Introduction

There have been many legislative developments over the past twenty years such as the Education Act, 1998 and the Education for Persons with Special Educational Needs (EPSEN) Act 2004 that have clearly signalled a commitment at policy level to cementing the crucial role of parents in their children's education (Ireland 1998; 2004). Building partnership with parents and families is also promoted through the Primary School Curriculum; Síolta: The National Quality Framework for Early

Childhood Education; Aistear: The Early Childhood Curriculum Framework; First Five: A Whole-of-Government Strategy for Babies, Young Children and their Families 2019–2028 and more recently in the Draft Primary Curriculum Framework (National Council for Curriculum and Assessment (NCCA) 1999; Centre for Early Childhood Development and Education (CECDE) 2006; NCCA 2009; Government of Ireland (GoI) 2018; NCCA 2020a). In 2015, the Aistear/Síolta Practice Guide was introduced to support early childhood teachers using Aistear and Síolta together to better support children's learning and development (NCCA 2015). The practice guide pillar 'Parent Partnerships' incorporates guidelines on building and sustaining partnership with parents and families. These guidelines for good practice emphasise the importance of parents and early childhood teachers working together to enhance children's wellbeing and learning, in the early years. The guidelines identify what partnership looks like in action: from sharing information with parents; to engaging parents in decision-making about their child's learning; to encouraging active parental contribution to life in the setting (NCCA 2015).

It is now appreciated that the relationship between parents and early childhood teachers can work on multiple levels and can have a powerful impact on individual children's learning journey (Goodall and Montgomery 2014). Increasing parental involvement in children's overall learning, rather than solely with the early childhood setting, enhances children's lifelong wellbeing and learning achievement (CECDE 2007; Goodall and Montgomery 2014). Greater parental involvement in children's learning and engagement in early learning and care (ELC) early primary settings is included as a key strategic action in First Five: A Whole-of-Government Strategy for Babies, Young Children and their Families 2019–2028 (GoI 2018).

We will begin this chapter by identifying the impact a positive relationship between parents and early childhood teachers can have for the child as part of a child-centred model. Bronfenbrenner's bioecological systems theory (1979), which was referred to previously in Chapter 1, provides a framework that gives both the setting and parents and families, a role in building partnerships. The importance of partnership between parents and early childhood teachers will be discussed in relation to the provision of high-quality early childhood experiences. National and international legislation and policy, which promote the development of high-quality services for parents and families will be reviewed. This chapter will go on to explore a continuum of parental involvement in children's early learning, which can be used to build effective partnerships with parents and families (Goodall and Montgomery 2014). We will explore a number of strategies to enhance: communication with parents and families; parental involvement in decision-making; and parental engagement in children's learning (Epstein 2011; European Agency for Special Needs and Inclusive Education (EASNIE) 2017a; 2017b). The importance of a seamless connection between the home and the educational setting for all children is discussed with reference to the competencies associated with providing early childhood education for all children developed by the LINC Consortium (2016–2020). Realising and building effective partnerships with parents and families can support all those invested in the education of all children and ultimately ensures each child is enabled to reach his/her potential.

Key Signposts: Introduction

- Key legislative and policy documents signal a commitment at policy level to cement the crucial role of parents in their children's education.
- The Aistear/Síolta Practice Guide (National Council for Special Education (NCCA) 2015) recognises the importance of partnership with parents and includes a set of guidelines for good practice in developing partnership with parents.
- Parental engagement, in children's early learning, benefits long-term wellbeing and learning achievement.
- There are many levels of parental engagement. Engagement where parents are actively involved in their child's early learning, not just in the educational setting, is associated with positive child outcomes.

A Child-Centred Model

It is important to acknowledge and understand that partnership with parents and family can only grow when the setting and the parents understand that each has a responsibility for partnership to happen. Respecting that both have a valuable position and a common purpose through their commitment to the child will encourage and ensure collaboration between the setting and parents and families (French 2018). Having this common purpose means that everyone will be working from a child-centred model. Bronfenbrenner's bioecological systems theory (1979) provides a model that can be used to understand the importance of relationships in the child's life and can be directly applied to how we view the role of parents/families in children's early education experiences. In essence, the quality of the relationships the child has with individuals in his/her microsystem such as siblings, parents, grandparents and early childhood teachers has a direct effect on the child, and the relationships that those people have with each other (mesosystem) can have a positive or negative impact on the child's learning, development and wellbeing (see Figure 5.1).

Partnership with Parents and Families

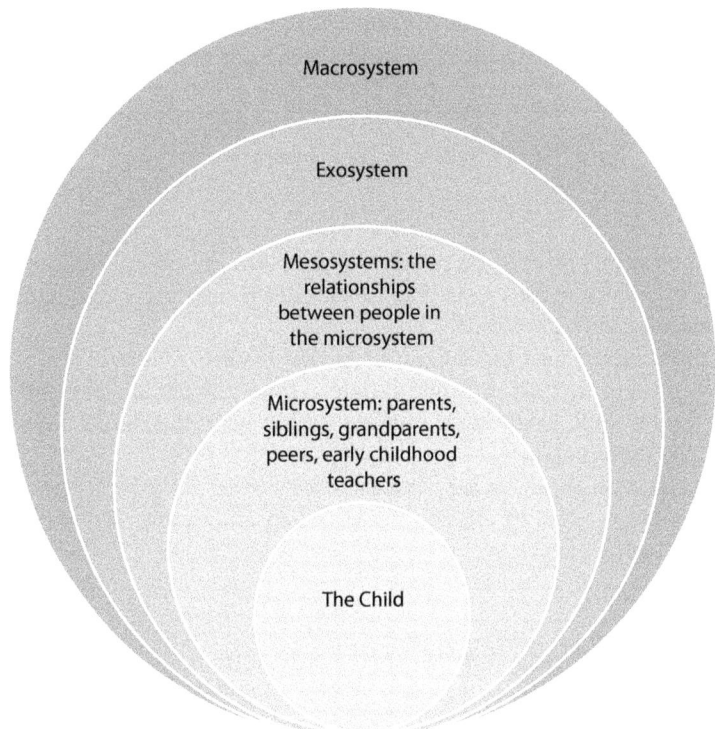

Figure 5.1. The Application of Bronfenbrenner's Bioecological Model of Development to Realising and Building Partnerships with Parents and Families

Time spent on nurturing these relationships to a place of trust and mutual respect supports the development of high-quality partnerships that have a direct impact on the child. These relationships are part of the everyday experiences that influence children's learning experiences and the impact everyday experiences have on the child's learning and development must never be underestimated (Hayes, O'Toole and Halpenny 2017). There is incontrovertible evidence that children benefit from having their family included in their setting and from parents being invited to share their unique insight into their child with early childhood teachers (King et al. 2002; Moyles et al. 2002). The model of parent partnership being advocated by the authors in the chapter recognises parents as the primary educator of the child, while appreciating the important role that early childhood teachers have in each child's microsystem.

> ### Key Signposts: Child-Centred Model
>
> - The early childhood setting and parents, as the primary educators of the child, have a shared responsibility in nurturing each child's learning and development.
> - Bronfenbrenner's bioecological model of development (1979) can be used to support early childhood settings and parents understand why building partnership impacts positively on the child's learning and development.
> - Relationships are part of the important everyday experiences that impact on children's learning experiences (Hayes, O'Toole and Halpenny 2017).

High-Quality Early Childhood Experiences

High-quality early childhood experiences have been identified as having a positive impact on children's present and long-term outcomes in terms of wellbeing, learning and development (Melhuish et al. 2015). Internationally the complex task of being in a position to evaluate the quality of early childhood provision is increasingly a priority for governments. A common theme across all quality evaluation frameworks is the extent to which building meaningful and reciprocal relationships and partnerships with parents and families is acknowledged. The EASNIE, citing the European Commission's (EC) proposed Quality Framework for Early Childhood Education and Care (ECEC) (2014), observes that early education settings should foster close partnerships with the family and recognise that the family should be involved in all dimensions of children's early learning experiences. Concurring with the EC, EASNIE identifies a discernible link between high-quality early childhood experiences and parent and family involvement, noting in this respect that 'quality cannot be left to chance' (EASNIE 2017a: 20).

In Ireland, Síolta: The National Quality Framework for Early Childhood Education, in the United Kingdom (UK), the Extension to the Early Childhood Environment Rating Scale (ECERS-E) and in the United States (US), The Early Childhood Environment Rating Scale – Revised (ECERS-R) all consider partnership with parents and adults working together to be significant contributors to high-quality provision (CECDE 2006; Siraj-Blatchford and Taggart 2010; Harms, Clifford and Cryer 2014; Taggart et al. 2015). The Tusla Quality and Regulatory Frameworks (QRFs) supports ELC settings in meeting their responsibilities in relation to the Child Care Act 1991 (Early Years Services) Regulations 2016 (Ireland 2016; Tusla 2020). The QRFs provides advice on how to implement Regulation 17: Information for Parents (Ireland 2016). They guide ELC settings in relation to what information they should be sharing with parents such as policies and curriculum and how they might share this, for example, through parent meetings, one-to-one contact and through the use of leaflets (Tusla 2020).

At primary level, Looking at Our School 2016; A Quality Framework for Primary Schools, published by the Department of Education and Skills (DES) Inspectorate, indicates a clear expectation that schools cultivate a commitment to building and maintaining relationships with parents (DES 2016). The DES commenced the development of an inspection process, early years education-focused Inspection (EYEI) for ELC settings in Ireland in 2015, which has evolved to the current quality framework detailed in A Guide to Early Years Education Inspection (EYEI) (Ring 2015; DES 2018). Informed by the principles in Aistear: The Early Childhood Curriculum Framework (NCCA 2009) and Síolta: The National Quality Framework for Early Childhood Education (CECDE 2006) together with evidence from international research, the quality framework includes the four areas delineated in Figure 5.2 (DES 2018). Area 1: observes the context within the setting to support children's learning and development and does this by looking at three outcomes. Area 2: observes the processes to support children's learning and development and focuses on eight outcomes. Area 3: observes children's learning experiences and achievements with a focus on five outcomes and lastly Area 4: observes management and leadership for learning with four outcomes (DES 2018).

The third outcome in Area 4 includes the criteria 'clear two-way channels of communication are fostered between the early-years setting, parents, families and children' (DES 2018: 16). This outcome provides signposts to

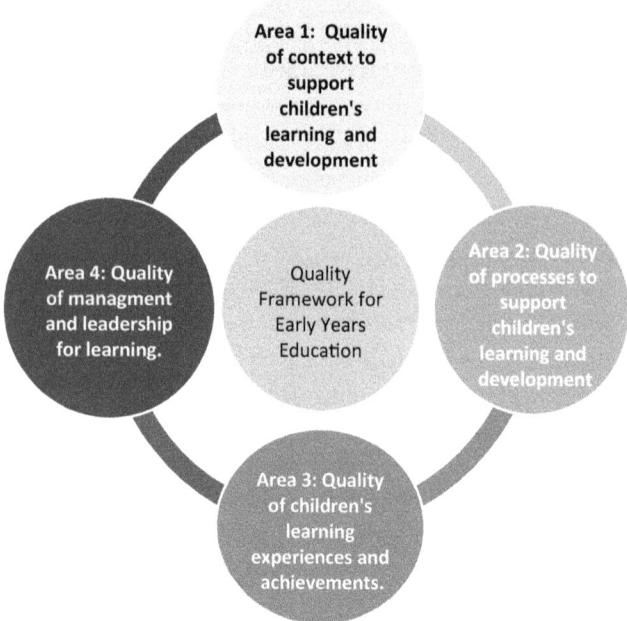

Figure 5.2. Quality Framework for Early Years Education (DES 2018: 16)

consider early childhood teachers' engagement in this two-way communication with parents. For example, are early childhood teachers being proactive in recognising parents as the primary educators and consulting with them about their child's learning? Are parents aware of the policies and procedures in the setting? How is the child's learning shared with the parents? Are there formal and informal opportunities to exchange information with the parents? Is the child's voice respected in this communication? Finally, is attention directed to engaging with families for whom English is not their first language? (DES 2018).

First Five: A Whole-of-Government Strategy for Babies, Young Children and their Families 2019–2028 recognises that 'parents and families are the single biggest influence on children's early learning' (GoI 2018: 80). The strategy reminds us that while children may spend a lot of their day in ELC, primary and special school settings, parents still have the most significant influence on children's lives. Another aspect of high quality is to

Partnership with Parents and Families 131

consider how the environment supports and nurtures relationships with parents and to do that we need to consider parents within the physical space of the setting (CECDE 2006). The Universal Design Guidelines for Early Learning and Care Settings utilises the principles underpinning Síolta: The National Quality Framework for Early Childhood Education in addition to a range of research evidence to provide guidance on creating accessible and accommodating environments for parents and families that help build relationships (Grey et al. 2019), Figure 5.3 provides a summary of these key principles to support the creation of environments that facilitate building relationships with parents and families, which are inextricably linked, rather than being mutually exclusive

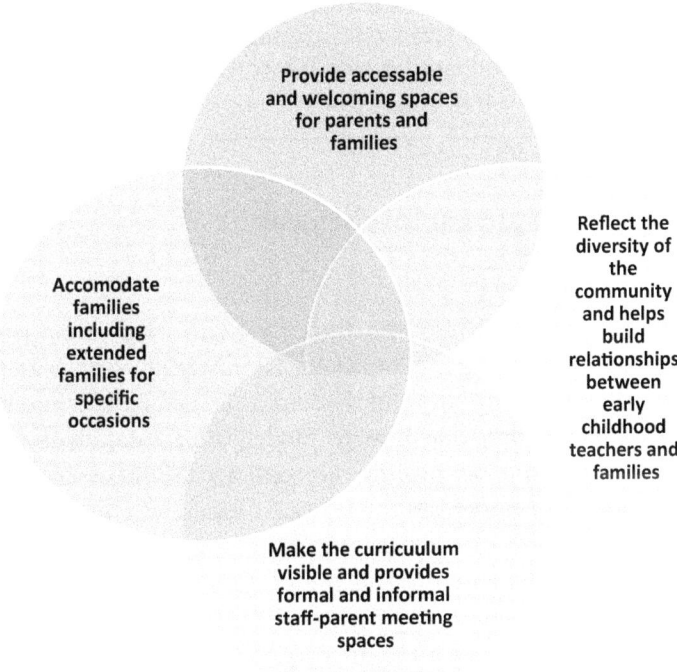

Figure 5.3. A Summary of Key Principles to Support the Creation of Environments that Facilitate Building Relationships with Parents and Families (Grey et al. 2019)

> **Key Signposts: High-Quality Early Childhood Experiences**
>
> - Realising and building partnership with parents are recognised internationally as being central to delivering high-quality early childhood experiences.
> - Legislation, policy both nationally and internationally, guides and informs early childhood teachers in relation to realising high-quality early childhood provision.
> - While children may spend a lot of their day in ELC, primary and special school settings, parents still have the most significant influence on children's lives.
> - The environment can effectively support and nurture relationships with parents through focusing on creating accessible and welcome spaces for parents and families that reflect the plurality of families and make children's learning visible.

A Continuum of Parental Involvement

As mentioned in the previous section, there is a wealth of legislation, policy and frameworks promoting the importance of fostering positive and reciprocal relations between early childhood settings and parents and families. Now we will explore one of many models of parental involvement that can be used to support practice. Goodall and Montgomery (2014) present a model that recognises the transient nature of children's early learning journey, which can be used in part, or as a whole to realise and build partnership with parents. This model, summarised in Figure 5.4 identifies three dimensions: (1) parental involvement with the setting; (2) parental involvement with children's learning; and (3) parental engagement with children's learning (see Figure 5.4) and is described as a continuum: it's not a 'straight pathway' that moves from one stage to the other, instead it is an ongoing, ever-changing and evolving process

Partnership with Parents and Families 133

(Goodall and Montgomery 2014: 400). At any time, a setting could be in different places on the continuum with different parents, depending on factors such as: families leaving and new families joining; how long the families have been coming to the setting; parents own confidence to get involved; time constraints due to other work or family commitments; and other barriers such as parents having English as a second language. Other factors to be considered are parents own aspirations for their child, their attitude to learning in the home and their interest in their children's learning (Goodall and Montgomery 2014).

Figure 5.4. A Continuum to Support Partnerships with Parents (Goodall and Montgomery 2014)

Parental Involvement with the Setting

Point one on the continuum is parental involvement with the setting which tends to involve one-way communication from the setting, where the setting controls the flow of information (Goodall and Montgomery 2014). Parents are informed of what is happening or what has happened through written communication such as newsletters or email updates, which provides a great start to building the foundation of partnership with parents (Goodall and Montgomery 2014; Tusla 2020). Verbally, the flow of one-way communication tends to happen during events such as a parent orientation for new parents at the beginning of the ELC or school year, or a parent's information evening on transition to primary school, as a way of providing guidance and support, however, at this point there is little opportunity created to listen or respond to parents (Goodall and Montgomery 2014). While these situations do provide parents with valuable ideas on supporting their child's learning, it can leave them in the position of being passive recipients with no opportunities for follow-on discussions to understand how this information can be used to make choices or decisions in relation to their child's learning. O'Kane (2016) draws attention to the need for two-sided dialogue between parents and early childhood teachers when supporting the transition to primary school. Edwards, Gandini and Foreman (2012) also emphasise the importance of collective discussion and decision-making between parents and early childhood teachers, explaining that the exchanging ideas is central to valuing the wisdom and expertise both parents and teachers can bring to supporting children's learning.

Parental Involvement with Children's Learning

This second point on the continuum involves a progression to parents becoming involved with their child's learning within the setting, which is an important part of partnership with parents, as it has the benefit of leading to better outcomes for children (O'Kane 2016; EASNIE 2017a). This involvement can happen in a variety of ways and in this section, the use of one-to-one parent-teacher meetings for discussing and planning children's progress, along with following a strengths-based approach to supporting each child's learning and development. Specific strategies such as 'all about me' forms and communication diaries as a way to encourage parental involvement with their child's learning are also discussed.

While at Point One on the continuum in Figure 5.4, parents might attend a meeting organised by the setting, at Point Two the focus moves to developing the relationship between the early childhood teacher and the parent through opportunities such as planned one-to-one meetings, which are organised to suit both the parent and early childhood teacher and where parents can ask questions and vice versa (Goodall and Montgomery 2014; EASNIE 2017a; Tusla 2020). What is important at Point Two is that parents are not passive in this meeting, it is more a sharing of ideas and it is appreciated that both parents and teacher can build a rich picture of the child as a learner, informed by knowledge from the seamless connection between home and ELC or school setting (Goodall and Montgomery 2014; EASNIE 2016). This creates a forum to share and exchange valuable knowledge on how the child learns best, while also building a mutually trusting relationship between parents and teachers. Communicating, as suggested in Joyce Epstein's model of parental involvement, promotes effective setting-to-home and home-to-setting communication, recognising how valuable this is for all children's early learning and development (Epstein 2011).

Adopting a strengths-based approach in the setting can be a starting point for two-way communication between parents and teachers. It is a way to look for opportunities to complement and support existing strengths and abilities of each child (State of Victoria (Department of Education and Early Childhood Development) 2012). A strengths-based approach provides a positive way to make decisions and plans to support the child, as it involves the exchange of knowledge from both directions, allowing parents to share what they know about their child's strengths, interests and needs from home, and allowing the teacher to share what s/he know from observing and getting to know the child in the setting (Department of Education and Early Childhood Development – State Government Victoria 2012; EASNIE 2017a; French 2018). It is also useful, during this communication, to invite parents to identify the aspirations and goals they have for their child. Understanding parent's aspirations and goals can help teachers to direct and advise parents, as they make and agree on decisions together. This is especially valuable when planning individual learning goals for children, as, importantly, both setting and parent will be similarly focused on supporting the child's learning, development and wellbeing (EASNIE 2017a).

Involving parents in the sharing of knowledge, goals and decision-making for their child can start with completing an 'all about me' form during initial enrolment in the setting, or more formally through the Access and Inclusion Profile as part of the Access and Inclusion Model (AIM) (Better Start 2018; Barnardos 2019). The AIM was launched by the government in 2016 to ensure that all children could fully participate in the Early Childhood Care and Education (ECCE) programme and the model endorses a strengths-based approach, while locating partnership with parents as central to its implementation (Inter-Departmental Group (IDG) 2015). Both the Access and Inclusion Profile and the Access and Inclusion Plan feature collaboration and parental involvement in both the planning and implementing of goals and actions to support all children fully participating in the pre-school setting (Better Start 2017; 2018). Similarly at primary level, an inclusive-whole-school framework includes promoting positive collaborative relations between schools and parents in identifying children's needs, providing effective teaching and learning for all children; maintaining a focus on prevention and early intervention and ensuring children's outcomes and achievements are monitored, recorded and regularly reviewed (DES 2017a; 2017b). According to Epstein's model of parental involvement, encouraging parents to be involved in decision-making about their child's learning and collaborating with community resources and interventions such as AIM, supports both parents and the setting and positively impacts their child's learning (Epstein 2011).

The Síolta standard Parents and Families 3.1 highlights that regular formal and informal two-way communication is important, and should be used to promote a seamless connection between home and the early childhood setting (CECDE 2006; Hayes et al. 2017). For the parents, it is important to highlight positives and achievements rather than only relaying the challenging incidents of that day 'so as to identify what works for the child and how it works so that those strategies can be continued and developed to match the child's abilities' (State of Victoria (Department of Education and Early Childhood Development) 2012: 6). This can be done verbally at the end of each day, or through a communication diary (Barnardos 2019). A communication diary can simply be a copy book used to jot down anecdotal or significant moments for a child during the day, and becomes a valuable tool when parents use it to comment back or add their own anecdotal moments from home. The process of using the diary for two-way communication supports parents to feel involved and builds a sense of trust and commitment to the same goals (EASNIE 2017a; Hayes et al. 2017)

Parental Engagement with Children's Learning

Involving parents in their children's learning within the early ELC can be extended and is located at Point Three on Goodall and Montgomery's (2014) continuum in Figure 5.4. The Síolta Standard: Parents and Families 3.2 guides early childhood teachers in providing a welcoming environment, where parents are invited to be involved in activities within the setting, but can also initiate an activity based on their area of interest or expertise (CECDE 2006). We are reminded by Goodall and Montgomery (2014) that parents should be encouraged and welcomed to take on an active, rather than passive role, where they see themselves as contributors to the learning rather than just helpers to the setting. This can be achieved through inviting parents to come and talk about their own occupation, a cultural aspect of their life, or to read a story, for example (Barnardos 2019). This affords parents the opportunity to support the learning of their own child as well as the learning of the whole cohort of children, in the room (EASNIE 2017a). This involves more ownership on the part of the parent in leading the process or activity, and is an important shift away from Point One on the continuum of partnership with parents, which as noted previously can often rely heavily on one-way communication from setting to home, along with some two-way involvement where parents might sometimes be invited into the setting.

Encouraging parental engagement within the setting encourages teachers to recognise that parents bring wisdom and expertise and are contributing positively to children's learning, rather than being a threat to how things are done in the setting (Edward et al. 2012). We are guided by Goodall and Montgomery (2014) that parental agency is at its strongest when parents are meaningfully engaged in their children's learning through their own choices and sense of their parental role, rather than from what the setting asks or tells them. When parents and the early childhood setting share responsibility for decisions and learning experiences, all children within the setting benefit. (EASNIE 2017a)

Achieving this level of parental engagement does not happen overnight, but instead starts with parents feeling welcome, valued and comfortable within the setting, and most importantly, invited to make a meaningful contribution to the educational setting (CECDE 2006; Barnardos 2019).

> **Key Signposts: An Effective Model of Parental Engagement**
>
> - Parents engagement with their children's learning is an ongoing, ever-changing and evolving process (Goodall and Montgomery 2014).
> - Keeping parents up-to-date provides a robust foundation for developing parental involvement in the setting (Goodall and Montgomery 2014).
> - Parental involvement with children's learning leads to better outcomes for children (European Agency for Special Needs and Inclusive Education (EASNIE) 2017a).
> - Regular formal and informal two-way communication promote a seamless connection between home and ELC setting (CECDE 2016; Hayes, O'Toole and Halpenny 2017).
> - Children benefit when parents and the early childhood setting share responsibility for decision-making and learning experiences (EASNIE 2017a).

Strategies for Realising and Building Partnership with Parents and Families: Inclusive Culture, Practice and Pedagogy

When developing strategies for realising and building partnership with parents and families, it is useful to consider the competencies associated with providing inclusive culture, practice and pedagogy developed by the LINC Consortium (LINC 2016–2020). While these competencies were 'designed to enhance the inclusion of children with additional needs in early years' settings' (Breen et al. 2018: 99), we suggest that they can equally be applied to supporting the learning, development and wellbeing of all children in the early years.

Inclusive Culture

The Diversity, Equality and Inclusion Charter and Guidelines for Early Childhood Care and Education (Department of Children and Youth Affairs (DCYA) 2016) identify the principles of an inclusive culture in ELC settings, which includes the early childhood teacher reflecting on his/her own attitudes and values, actively promoting equal opportunities for all families and children, working in partnership with parents and outside agencies, and underpinning practice with robust inclusive policies and procedures. These principles are also reflected in the competencies identified by the LINC Consortium and guide us to reflect on the importance of conveying a clear message to parents and families that they and their children are welcome for who they are, and that their unique differences are not only acknowledged, but also celebrated (LINC Consortium 2016–2020). Central to creating an inclusive culture is the active promotion of partnership with parents and ensuring that all policies are inclusive.

It is important not to assume that parents will automatically feel welcome in the early childhood setting, and also important that we work on building trust and communication from the outset with parents. At the heart of making parents feel welcome is valuing the identity and belonging of parents and their children (NCCA 2015). The Síolta Standard 14: Identity and Belonging, highlights that well-defined policies and procedures within ELC settings are needed to encourage that sense of belonging (CECDE 2006). Clearly worded policies and procedures should be living documents that guide and underpin what is said and done in practice, and all stakeholders including parents should be consulted when reviewing an existing policy or introducing a new policy (DES 2016; 2018; Tusla 2020). Some important policies for developing an inclusive culture for partnership with parents include a settling-in policy, inclusion policy and open-door policy. Barnardos (2019) suggest developing a specific policy in relation to parental engagement. When developing a settling-in policy, Tusla advises that it should contain the core elements mapped out in the QRF in terms of how children's transitions are supported and how parents are involved (2020). The EASNIE (2017a) highlights the value of an open-door policy in mapping out the setting's intentions and commitment to parents, allowing them to feel valued and respected and welcome to spend time and have a place within the setting. Including information on key policies in a parent handbook and signposts on where to access policies in full can provide reassurance for parents that they are viewed as equal and valued partners.

> **Key Signposts: Developing an Inclusive Culture**
>
> - The principles of an inclusive culture include the early childhood teacher reflecting on his/her own attitudes and values, actively promoting equal opportunities for all families and children, working in partnership with parents and outside agencies, and underpinning practice with robust inclusive policies and procedures (Department of Children and Youth Affairs (DCYA) 2016).
> - Developing policies in consultation with parents and other stakeholders creates living documents that guide and underpin what is said and done in practice.
> - All stakeholders, including parents, should be consulted when reviewing an existing policy or introducing a new policy.
> - Including information on key policies in a parent handbook and signposts on where to access policies in full can provide reassurance for parents that they are viewed as equal and valued partners.

Inclusive Practice

Inclusive practice involves the day to day running of the setting, putting into practice the policies and procedures that support the inclusion and active participation of all children. Inclusive practice involves the whole team being aware of their roles and responsibilities in promoting and identifying quality interactions and relationships as an important part of their everyday practice (EASNIE 2017a). These elements are represented in the competencies associated with cultivating inclusive practice developed by the LINC Consortium and guide early childhood teachers to reflect on how they actively partner with parents in creating positive transition experiences (LINC 2016–2020).

Creating positive transition experiences for parents and their children when they first join the setting is underpinned by the inclusive culture created through policies and procedures that support parents to feel welcome, valued and respected (NCCA 2015). Valuing that parents are experts on their child encourages parents to share their knowledge of their child and be involved in developing a settling-in plan to support a positive transition into the setting for the child (Barnardos 2019). We are reminded by the EASNIE (2017a) that part of this settling-in plan should involve working with parents to develop a personal profile of the child's strengths, interests and needs as well as their family life, for example, through an 'all about me' form (Barnardos 2019).

Another important aspect of supporting positive transitions is to create spaces within the setting for parents and their children to spend time, for example, providing seating in the shared central areas of the setting 'so parents can sit with their child as they prepare for the day or for going home' (Grey et al. 2019: 129), or providing adult-sized seating so parents can spend time in the in the room with their child during the daily transition or in the external spaces such as the lobby area where they can spend time as part of an open-door policy (Barnardos 2019). Introducing a key person approach is another strategy for supporting inclusive practice, as it identifies the child's primary contact within the ELC setting (NCCA 2015; Willoughby 2016; TUSLA 2020). A key person approach is discussed extensively by Doherty in Chapter 3. This approach supports partnership with parents as information is shared in both directions, informally through daily chats as well as formally through planned parent-teacher meetings or using a communication diary (EASNIE 2017a; Barnardos 2019). The EASNIE (2017a) identify that for parents to be able to make choices for their child they need to be well informed about their child's right to supports and an inclusive education. Early learning and care, primary and special school settings also have a central role in providing access to information and supports that empower parents to make decisions, for example, by providing information or links to relevant supports and agencies. The publication of Mo Scéal by the NCCA provides a range of resources to support parents, early childhood teachers in ELC and primary schools to support the transition from ELC setting to primary school (NCCA 2020).

Key Signposts: Engaging in Inclusive Practice

- Encouraging parents to get involved in completing an 'all about me' form and co-creating a settling-in plan for their child supports a positive transition for all (European Agency for Special Needs and Inclusive Education (EASNIE) 2017a; Barnardos 2019).
- Creating a space within the setting, incorporating adult-sized seating can encourage parents to feel welcome to spend time during the day and is part of an open-door policy (Barnardos 2019; Grey et al. 2019).
- A key person approach builds trust and supports two-way communication between home and the setting (NCCA 2015; Barnardos 2019).
- Encouraging communication through daily chats, a communication diary or parent-teacher meeting can support regular sharing of ideas between early childhood teachers and parents to support planning and decision-making in relation to their child' learning (EASNIE 2017a; Barnardos 2019).
- Providing information or links to relevant supports and agencies can be valuable for parents when making decisions about their child's learning, development and wellbeing (EASNIE 2017a; Barnardos 2019).
- The publication of Mo Scéal by the NCCA provides a range of resources to support parents, early childhood teachers in ELC and primary schools to support the transition from early learning and care (ELC) setting to primary school (NCCA 2020).

Inclusive Pedagogy

Síolta: The National Quality Framework for Early Childhood Education (CECDE 2006) identifies pedagogy in early childhood as the whole range of learning, teaching and relationships children experience that supports their holistic development. Inclusive pedagogy involves the learning experiences for the child that supports him/her to fully participate (Ring et al. 2018). According to Moyles et al. (2002: 5) this involves the child, teacher and family coming together to share ideas in 'a mutual learning encounter'. Inclusive pedagogy involves the child and the parents feeling included and consulted in the learning environment and curriculum (NCCA 2009; DES 2018). The competencies associated with providing inclusive pedagogy developed by the LINC Consortium (LINC 2016–2020) prompt us to reflect on how partnership with parents is used as part of planning, implementing and evaluating their child's learning (LINC Consortium 2016–2020). The EASNIE (2017a) highlights the use of children's learning journals to show their journey of growth and development while in an early childhood setting. This encourages early childhood teachers to focus on building the child's strengths rather than focusing on the challenges (EASNIE 2017a). Research indicates the benefits of including parents in the process of documenting and evaluating their child's experiences, which can be achieved by sending the learning journals home for parents to evaluate, to give feedback and share suggestions on planning and further learning experiences (EASNIE 2017a).

The quality framework for EYEI (DES 2018) outlines that the child's sense of identity and belonging is nurtured when there are opportunities that bring parents, child and early childhood teacher together within the ELC setting. For example, a parent might lead sports skills or children's yoga activities, or organise an activity to cook with the children in the setting (Barnardos 2019). For other parents, their engagement may involve leading a morning storytelling session as the children transition into the setting, this could include favourite books from home (Barnardos 2019). It is also important to recognise that there can be barriers to parental involvement in decision-making and to be aware and sensitive to parents' confidence and ability to contribute.

> **Key Signposts: Adopting an Inclusive Pedagogy**
>
> - Inclusive pedagogy involves learning experiences that support children to fully participate (Moyles, Adams and Musgrove 2002; Ring et al. 2018).
> - Inclusive pedagogy involves the child, parent and early childhood teacher coming together to share ideas, thus nurturing the child's sense of identity and belonging (Department of Education (DES) 2018).
> - Including parents in evaluating their child's learning journal supports planning for further learning experiences (European Agency for Special Needs and Inclusive Education (EASNIE) 2017a).
> - Inviting parents to read stories or get involved in activities based on their interests positive supports parental engagement (Barnardos 2019).

The EASNIE (2017c) provides a self-reflection tool in relation to realising and building partnership with parents through a family friendly early childhood environment that can be beneficially used to support practice. This self-reflective tool provides five prompts in Table 5.1 that relate to developing an inclusive culture, engaging in inclusive practice and adopting an inclusive pedagogy.

Table 5.1. Inclusive Early Childhood Education Environment Self-Reflection Tool (EASNIE 2017c: 25)

Family-friendly environment Questions	
1	Do parents feel welcome and are they invited to take part in the settings activities?
2	How is a trustful relationship with families developed?
3	Are parents well informed about everyday activities?
4	How are parents involved in decision-making about their child's learning, development and support needs?
5	How are parents involved in planning, implementing and monitoring their children's engagement and learning?

Conclusion

There is a range of legislation, policies and frameworks that promote the need for and benefit of building partnership with parents as part of high-quality early childhood provision in ELC, primary and special school settings. At the heart of partnership with parents is the child and the child's need for high-quality early childhood experiences that promote their wellbeing, learning and development. Research highlights the significant positive impact on the child's learning journey when both parents and early childhood settings collaborate effectively. The evidence reminds us that collaboration can take place in lots of different ways with many different levels of parental involvement and engagement. Encouraging meaningful parent engagement in a child's learning is powerful and significant for children in ELC, primary and special school settings, with the caveat that we are mindful, respectful, sensitive and flexible in relation to the level of engagement each parent is comfortable with, and acknowledge always that parents are the experts when it comes to their own children.

Bibliography

Barnardos. (2019). *Working in Partnership with Parents: A Guide for Early Childhood Professionals*. Dublin: Barnardos.

Better Start. (2017). *Guidelines for Completing an Individual Access and Inclusion Plan*. Dublin: Better Start, <https://aim.gov.ie/wp-content/uploads/2017/11/guidelines-for-completing-an-individual-access-and-inclusion-plan.pdf>, <https://aim.gov.ie/wp-content/uploads/2016/06/AIM-Level-4-Access-and-Inclusion-Profile.pdf>, accessed 06 September 2020.

Better Start. (2018). *Level 4 Supporting Access to the ECCE Programme for Children with a Disability: Access and Inclusion Profile, Published Update V2 September 2018*. Dublin: Better Start, <https://aim.gov.ie/wp-content/uploads/2016/06/AIM-Level-4-Access-and-Inclusion-Profile.pdf>, accessed 06 September 2020.

Breen, F., Kelleher, S., Ring, E., and Stapleton, S. (2018). 'LINC Programme: Enabling Leadership for Inclusion through an innovative Competency-Based Adult Continuing Professional Learning Programme', *The Irish Journal of Community and Adult Education: The Adult Learner*, 99–115, <https://files.eric.ed.gov/fulltext/EJ1197457.pdf>, accessed 06 September 2020.

Bronfenbrenner, U. (1979). *The Ecology of Human Development: Experiments by Nature and Design*. Cambridge, MA: Harvard University Press.

Centre for Early Childhood Development and Education. (2006). *Síolta: The National Quality Framework for Early Childhood Education*. Dublin: Centre for Early Childhood Development and Education, <http://siolta.ie/media/pdfs/final_handbook.pdf>, accessed 08 September 2020.

Centre for Early Childhood Development and Education. (2007). *Síolta: Research Digest: Standard 3 Parents and Families*. Dublin: Centre for Early Childhood Development and Education.

Department of Children and Youth Affairs. (2016). *Diversity, Equality and Inclusion Charter and Guidelines for Early Childhood Care and Education*. Dublin: Department of Children and Youth Affairs, <https://aim.gov.ie/wp-content/uploads/2016/06/Diversity-Equality-and-Inclusion-Charter-and-Guidelines-for-Early-Childhood-Care-Education.pdf>, accessed 06 September 2020.

Department of Education and Early Childhood Development – State Government Victoria. (2012). *Strength-Based Approach. A Guide to Writing Transition Learning and Development Statements*. Melbourne: Communications Division for Early Childhood Strategy Division, Department of Education and Early Childhood Development, <https://www.education.vic.gov.au/documents/childhood/professionals/learning/strengthbappr.pdf>, accessed 06 September 2020.

Department of Education and Skills. (2016). *Looking at our School 2016: A Quality Framework for Primary Schools*. Dublin: Department of Education and Skills, <https://www.education.ie/en/Publications/Inspection-Reports-Publications/Evaluation-Reports-Guidelines/Looking-at-Our-School-2016-A-Quality-Framework-for-Primary-Schools.pdf>, accessed 30 August 2020.

Department of Education and Skills. (2017a) *Circular No 0012/2017. Circular to the Management Authorities of All Mainstream Primary Schools Special Education Teaching Allocation*. Athlone: Department of Education and Skills, <https://www.education.ie/en/Circulars-and-Forms/Active-Circulars/cl0013_2017.pdf>, accessed 21 January 2020.

Department of Education and Skills. (2017b). *A New Model for Allocating Special Education Teachers to Mainstream Schools*. Dublin: Department of Education and Skills, <https://www.education.ie/en/The-Education-System/

Special-Education/a-new-model-for-allocating-special-education-teachers-to-mainstream-schools.pdf>, accessed 21 January 2020.

Department of Education and Skills. (2018). *A Guide to Early Years Education Inspection (EYEI)*. Dublin: Department of Education and Skills, <https://www.education.ie/en/Publications/Inspection-Reports-Publications/Evaluation-Reports-Guidelines/guide-to-early-years-education-inspections.pdf>, accessed 06 September 2020.

Edwards, C., Gandini, L., and Forman, G. (2012). *The Hundred Languages of Children* (3rd ed.). Oxford: Praeger.

Epstein, J. (2011). *School, Family and Community Partnerships: Preparing Educators and Improvising School* (2nd ed.). New York: Westview Press.

European Agency for Special Needs and Inclusive Education. (2017a). *Inclusive Early Childhood Education: New Insights and Tools – Contributions from a European Study*. (M. Kyriazopoulou, P. Bartolo, E. Björck-Åkesson, C. Giné, and F. Bellour, eds). Odense. Denmark: European Agency for Special Needs and Inclusive Education, <https://www.european-agency.org/resources/publications/inclusive-early-childhood-education-new-insights-and-tools-contributions>, accessed 21 January 2020.

European Agency for Special Needs and Inclusive Education. (2017b). *Inclusive Early Childhood Education: New Insights and Tools – Final Summary Report*. (M. Kyriazopoulou, P. Bartolo, E. Björck-Åkesson, C. Giné, and F. Bellour, eds). Odense, Denmark: European Agency for Special Needs and Inclusive Education, <https://www.european-agency.org/sites/default/files/IECE-Summary-ENelectronic.pdf>, accessed 21 January 2020.

European Agency for Special Needs and Inclusive Education. (2017c). *Inclusive Early Childhood Education Environment Self-Reflection Tool*. (M. Kyriazopoulou, P. Bartolo, E. Björck-Åkesson, C. Giné, and F. Bellour, eds). Odense, Denmark: European Agency for Special Needs and Inclusive Education, <https://www.european-agency.org/resources/publications/inclusive-early-childhood-education-environment-self-reflection-tool>, accessed 06 September 2020.

French, G. (2018). *The Time of Their Lives: Nurturing Babies' Learning and Development in Early Childhood Settings*. Dublin: Barnardos.

Goodall, J., and Montgomery, C. (2014). 'Parental Involvement to Parental Engagement: A Continuum', *Educational Review*, 66(4), 399–410.

Government of Ireland. (2018). *First Five: A Whole-of-Government Strategy for Babies, Young Children and Their Families 2019–2028*. Dublin: The Government Publications Office, <https://assets.gov.ie/31184/62acc54f4bdf4405b74e53a4afb8e71b.pdf>, accessed 04 July 2020.

Grey, T., Corbett, M., Sheerin, J., Heeney, T., Ring, E., and O'Sullivan, L. (2019). *Universal Design Guidelines for Early Learning and Care Settings*. Dublin: Department of Children and Youth Affairs in collaboration with the Centre for Universal Design, National Disability Authority, <https://aim.gov.ie/wp-content/uploads/2019/06/universal-design-guidelines-for-elc-settings-introduction-1.pdf>, accessed 6 January 2019.

Harms, T., Clifford, M., and Cryer, D. (2014). *Early Childhood Environment Rating Scale (ECERS-3)* (3rd ed.). New York, NY: Teachers College Press.

Hayes, N., O'Toole, L., and Halpenny, A. (2017). *Introducing Bronfenbrenner: A Guide for Practitioners and Students in Early Year Education*. Oxon: Routledge.

Inter-Departmental Group. (2015). *Supporting Access to the Early Childhood Care and Education Programme for Children with a Disability*. Dublin: Inter-Departmental Group, <http://nda.ie/nda-files/Supporting-Access-to-the-Early-Childhood-Care-and-Education-for-Children-with-a-Disability.pdf>, accessed 21 January 2020.

Ireland. (1937). *Bunreacht na hÉireann. Constitution of Ireland*. Dublin: Government Publications Office, <https://www.gov.ie/en/publication/d5bd8c-constitution-of-ireland/>, accessed 11 January 2020.

Ireland. (1998). *Education Act, 1998*. Dublin: The Government Publications Office.

Ireland. (2004). *Education for Persons with Special Educational Needs Act, 2004*. Dublin: The Government Publications Office.

Ireland. (2016). Child Care Act 1991 (Early Years Services) Regulations 2016. Dublin: The Government Publications Office.

King, C., King, S., Law, M., Kertoy, M., Rosenbaum, P., and Hurley, P. (2002). *Family-Centred Service in Ontario: A 'Best Practice' Approach for Children with Disabilities and Their Families*. Ontario: CanChild.

Leadership for INClusion in the Early Years Consortium. (2016–2020). *Competencies Associated with Providing for Inclusion in the Early Years*. Mary Immaculate College, Limerick: Leadership for INClusion in the Early Years Consortium.

Melhuish, E., Ereky-Stevens, K., Petrogiannis, K., Ariescu, A., Penderi, E., Rentzou, Tawell, A., Leseman, P., and Broekhuisen, M. (2015). *A Review of Research on the Effects of Early Childhood Education and Care (ECEC) upon Child Development*, CARE Project; Curriculum Quality Analysis and Impact Review of European Early Childhood Education and Care (ECEC), <http://ecec-care.org/fileadmin/careproject/Publications/reports/new_version_CARE_WP4_D4_1_Review_on_the_effects_of_ECEC.pdf>, accessed 04 July 2020.

Moyles, J., Adams, S., and Musgrove, A. (2002). *SPEEL Study of Pedagogical Effectiveness in Early Learning*. Norwich: Queens Printer (Department for Education and Skills), <https://dera.ioe.ac.uk/4591/1/RR363.pdf?e= 5305098/62475902>, accessed 06 September 2020.

National Council for Curriculum and Assessment. (1999). *Primary School Curriculum*. Dublin: The Stationery Office, <https://curriculumonline.ie/ getmedia/93de2707-f25e-4bee-9035-92b00613492e/Introduction-to-primary-curriculum.pdf>, accessed 04 July 2020.

National Council for Curriculum and Assessment. (2009). *Aistear: The Early Childhood Curriculum Framework*. Dublin: National Council for Curriculum and Assessment, <https://www.ncca.ie/en/early-childhood/aistear>, accessed 04 July 2020.

National Council for Curriculum and Assessment. (2015). *Aistear/Síolta Practice Guide*. Dublin: National Council for Curriculum and Assessment, <www.ncca.ie/en/Practice-Guide>, accessed 04 July 2020.

National Council for Curriculum and Assessment. (2020a). *Draft Primary Curriculum Framework. For Consultation*. Dublin: National Council for Curriculum and Assessment, <https://ncca.ie/media/4456/ncca-primary-curriculum-framework-2020.pdf>, accessed 06 September 2020.

National Council for Curriculum and Assessment. (2020a). *Mo Scéal*. Dublin: National Council for Curriculum and Assessment, <https://ncca.ie/en/early-childhood/mo-sc%C3%A9al> accessed 06 September 2020.

O'Kane, M. (2016). *Research Report No. 19. Transition from Preschool to Primary School*. Dublin: National Council for Curriculum and Assessment, <https://www.ncca.ie/media/3196/3754_ncca_researchreport19_lr.pdf>, accessed 06 September 2020.

Ring, E. (2015).'Early Years' Education-Focused Inspections: A Reason to Celebrate', *Children's Research Digest*, 2(2), 42–46.

Ring, E., Kelleher, S., Breen, F., Heeney, T., McLoughlin, M., Kearns, A., Stafford, P., Skehill, S., Campion, K., Comerford, D., and O'Sullivan, L. (2019). *Interim Evaluation of the Leadership for Inclusion in the Early Years (LINC) Programme*. Limerick: Mary Immaculate College, <https://documentcloud.adobe.com/link/track?uri=urn:aaid:scds:US:d8c95d7d-2d75-40a8-9f65-b6582908c08d>, accessed 6 January 2019.

Ring, E., O'Sullivan, L., Ryan, M., and Burke, P. (2018). *A Melange or a Mosaic of Theories? How Theoretical Perspectives on Children's Learning and Development can Inform a Responsive Pedagogy in a Redeveloped Primary School Curriculum*. Dublin: National Council for Curriculum and Assessment, <https://www.ncca.ie/media/3863/seminar_four_er_los_mr_pb_paper.pdf>, accessed 16 January 2020.

Sylva, K., Siraj-Blatchford, I., and Taggart, B. (2010). *ECERS-E: The Four Curricular Subscales Extension to the Early Childhood Environment Rating Scale (ECERS-E)* (4th ed.). New York, NY: Teachers College Press.

Taggart, B., Sylva, K., Melhuish, E., Sammons, P., and Siraj-Blatchford, I. (2015). *Effective Pre-school, Primary and Secondary Education Project (EPPSE 3–16.)*. London: Department for Education, <https://assets.publishing.service.gov.uk/government/uploads/system/uploads/attachment_data/file/455670/RB455_Effective_pre-school_primary_and_secondary_education_project.pdf.pdf>, accessed 06 September 2020.

Tusla – Child and Family Agency. (2020). *Early Years Quality and Regulatory Framework (QRF)*. Dublin: Early Years Inspectorate, Tusla, <https://www.tusla.ie/services/preschool-services/early-years-quality-and-regulatory-framework/>, accessed 06 September 2020.

Willoughby, M. (2016). *Quality Early Years Care and Education: What to Look for in an Early Years' Service*. Dublin: Barnardos.

SHIRLEY HEANEY AND SARAH FEENEY

Chapter 6   Wellbeing as Central to Including All Children in the Early Years

ABSTRACT
Wellbeing has been considered from multiple perspectives for centuries. Spanning the diverse domains of philosophy, history, psychology, health and literature, wellbeing has been brought to the forefront of education in recent years. While the search for an agreed definition of wellbeing continues, research consistently highlights the strong link between providing effectively for children's wellbeing and including all children in the early years. When children are supported in developing a strong sense of personal wellbeing and belonging, their learning and development is enhanced. A lens has been cast upon the importance of children's wellbeing in the context of education both nationally and internationally. Recent policy level developments in Ireland have articulated a commitment to supporting children's wellbeing in the early years, both at pre-school and primary school levels. In this chapter, the concept of wellbeing is explored in the context of the inclusion of all children. Practical strategies are suggested, which can promote children's wellbeing, while simultaneously enhancing the inclusive culture in children's early learning experiences. The role and responsibility of the adult in nurturing children's wellbeing are interrogated and signposts for practice identified.

Introduction: The Case for Wellbeing

Human wellbeing is referred to in the literature as 'an abstract, multi-dimensional, social and culturally constructed phenomenon' (Sandseter et al. 2018: 5). A universally agreed concept of wellbeing is not 'clearly identifiable and any definition is affected by the presence of additional needs, and the extent of those needs' (Daly 2018: 200). The complex nature of defining wellbeing originates from the philosophical contributions of Aristippus (c. 435–356 BCE) and Aristotle (384–322 B.C), who sought to conceptualise how a 'good life' can be realised (Niemiec and Ryan 2013: 215). Aristippus' theory of hedonic wellbeing has been defined as 'the presence of positive affect and the absence of negative affect' (Deci and Ryan 2008a: 1). This theory views wellbeing as subjective and is concerned with understanding one's happiness in terms of what makes life experiences 'pleasant and unpleasant' (Kahneman 1999: ix). Aristotle's theory of eudemonic wellbeing focuses on meaning and highlights that wellbeing encapsulates more than happiness, that the 'actualisation of human potential' is an integral element of wellbeing (Ryan and Deci 2001: 143). This theory proposes an objective view of wellbeing, defining it as the 'degree to which a person is fully functioning' (Ryan and Deci 2001: 141).

While considering the difficulties evident in the literature regarding the identification of a shared understanding of wellbeing, what is readily identifiable is that when children are supported in developing strong wellbeing, their learning and development is enhanced (Price and McCallum 2016). Furthermore, the complex nature of child wellbeing is influenced by the experiences that children encounter in all aspects of their lives and is inextricably linked to the bioecological approach discussed previously in Chapter 1. In supporting children's wellbeing in early learning and care (ELC) and school environments, it is essential that adults provide a stimulating environment where children are valued, welcomed and supported to flourish and realise their individual potential. A commitment to supporting wellbeing and promoting an inclusive culture for all children in ELC settings is represented in the Irish context with the introduction of the Access and Inclusion Model (AIM) in 2015 (Inter-departmental Group (IDG) 2015). Both the AIM model and the Leadership for INClusion in the Early Years (LINC) Programme advocate that when equal opportunities are provided for all children to attend ELC settings where an inclusive culture is realised, a positive impact on children's holistic development follows (IDG 2015; LINC Consortium 2016–2020; Ring et al. 2019).

In the primary school context, the publication of the Guidelines for Mental Health Promotion: Wellbeing in Primary Schools (National Educational Psychological Service (NEPS), Department of Health (DoH), Department of Education and Skills (DES) and Health Service Executive (HSE) 2015) signalled the way forward in valuing and developing child wellbeing throughout children's primary school years. In an opening statement, the guidelines confirm that while home is the primary environment for child development, 'mental health and wellbeing is everyone's concern and involves the whole school community, parents/guardians and relevant stakeholders' (NEPS, DoH, DES and HSE 2015: 8). More recently in the Wellbeing Policy Statement and Framework for Practice, the DES identifies the promotion of wellbeing as central to its mission in enabling children 'to achieve their full potential and contribute to Ireland's social, cultural and economic wellbeing' (DES 2019: 1). Wellbeing is now considered discreetly throughout the 'Primary School Curriculum' (PSC) and in particular within the Social Personal and Health Education (SPHE), where its aim is to foster the child's 'personal development, health and wellbeing' (National Council for Curriculum and Assessment (NCCA) 1999: 2). More recently wellbeing is identified as one of the key competencies for children in primary school in the Draft Primary Curriculum Framework (NCCA 2020).

This chapter explores the concept of wellbeing in an early childhood setting where all children are included, examining critical elements in the early years across ELC, primary and special school settings. The role of positive interactions in contributing to the development of wellbeing is examined, along with a discussion on the central importance of promoting wellbeing. Practical strategies are suggested for promoting children's social inclusion in the context of a child-centred approach. Adult roles and responsibilities will be explored. This chapter will conclude by outlining the positive benefits of teaching children to problem-solve.

Key Signposts: Introduction: The Case for Wellbeing

- A universally agreed concept of wellbeing is not 'clearly identifiable and any definition is affected by the presence of additional needs, and the extent of those needs' (Daly 2018: 200).

- Child wellbeing is influenced by the experiences that children encounter in all aspects of their lives and is inextricably linked to the bioecological framework discussed in Chapter 1.
- The literature clearly identifies that when children are supported in developing strong wellbeing, their learning and development is enhanced.
- It is essential that adults provide a stimulating environment where all children are valued, welcomed and supported to flourish and realise their individual potential.

The Role of Positive Interactions in Contributing to Children's Overall Development

Early childhood is now understood as a 'critical period' and a time of great opportunity for learning and development (Caldwell 2017: 73), as the learning and development that occurs in these formative years 'sets the foundation for lifelong learning, behaviour, health and well-being' (Organisation for Economic Co-operation and Development (OECD) 2015: 6). Research highlights that the experiences children encounter in the first six years of life are a driving force for their overall development (Melhuish et al. 2015). The quality of interactions a child has in these early years can have a significant impact on the physical development of the brain (Whitebread, Kuvalja and O'Connor 2015). As discussed previously by Doherty in Chapter 3, the first three years of life are referred to as 'the period of the most rapid growth', with 90 per cent of brain development occurring in this stage of development (Winter 2010: 10). Therefore, the experiences children encounter in these critical years can 'enhance or diminish innate potential, laying either a strong or a fragile platform on which all further development and learning are built' (Winter 2010: 5). The importance of children engaging in positive and nurturing ELC and school environments cannot be underestimated (NCCA 2009a; 2009b; Melhuish et al. 2015; Kearns 2017).

Children's development is influenced by several factors, including the quality of the interactions they experience with their parents, teachers and peers, in addition to their engagement in the home, community and educational environments (Melhuish et al. 2015; Moser et al. 2017). As previously discussed by Ryan in Chapter 4, when children experience a high-quality interactional environment, their learning, development and wellbeing are enhanced both for the present and future. In Ireland, Síolta, the National Quality Framework for Early Childhood Education (Centre for Early Childhood Development and Education (CECDE) 2006a) and Aistear, the Early Years Curriculum Framework (NCCA 2009a) were developed to support early childhood, primary school and special school teachers to provide high-quality early childhood experiences for children aged birth to 6 years. Both frameworks endorse the significant role positive interactions play in children's overall development and wellbeing (cognitive interactions are discussed in detail by Ryan in Chapter 4). Síolta highlights that 'positive, meaningful interactions within the wider context of child development are founded and complemented by the presence … of a responsive adult' (CECDE 2006a: 3). Under the theme of wellbeing, Aistear states that the interactions children experience influence their wellbeing and it is therefore essential that children engage in positive interactions and are supported to feel 'valued; respected; empowered; cared for and included' in all the environments that they engage in (NCCA 2009a: 16).

Key Signposts: The Role of Positive Interactions in Contributing to Children's Overall Development

- Early childhood is a critical period and a time of great opportunity for learning and development, as the learning that occurs in these formative years lays the foundation for lifelong learning.
- The quality of interactions a child experiences in the first six years have a significant impact on the physical development of the brain.
- Children's development is influenced by a number of factors, including the quality of the interactions children experience with their parents, teachers and peers, in addition to their engagement in the home, community and educational environments.

- Both Síolta: The National Quality Framework for Early Childhood Education (Centre for Early Childhood Development and Education (CECDE) 2006a) and Aistear: The Early Childhood Curriculum Framework (National Council for Curriculum and Assessment (NCCA) 2009a) were developed to support teachers to provide high-quality early childhood experiences for children aged birth to 6 years and endorse the significant role positive interactions play in children's overall development and wellbeing.

The Influence of Quality Early Childhood Experiences on Child Development and Wellbeing

A wealth of evidence has demonstrated the positive impact that engaging in quality early childhood education programmes has for children's overall development (Sylva et al. 2004; Hayes et al. 2013; Bradshaw, Lewis and Hughes 2014). Researchers agree that high-quality early childhood education 'impacts children's academic development and their emotional and social wellbeing more powerfully than any other phase of education' (Whitebread et al. 2015: 6). Moreover, from both a child development and an economic viewpoint, the earlier that children engage in high-quality early childhood education, the stronger the impact this has on their holistic development (Heckman 2000; Heckman, Pinto and Savey 2013; Harvey 2014). Therefore, it is essential that children are provided with equitable opportunities to engage in high-quality early childhood environments, where they experience interactions that are 'responsive; affectionate and readily available' (Melhuish et al. 2015: 5).

Theories on child development, in relation to what children need and how they learn continue to emerge and evolve. Regarding social and emotional development, theoretical perspectives are still largely rooted around the work of Maslow (1943), Piaget (Piaget and Inhelder 1947), Erikson (1965), Vygotsky (1978; 1886), Ainsworth (Ainsworth and Bell, 1970) and Bowlby (1988). Examination of such theories as part of early childhood teacher education has led to early childhood teachers being acutely aware of the central role mental health and wellbeing plays and the importance of facilitating and promoting wellbeing in both ELC settings and schools (NCCA 2009a; NEPS, DoH, DES and HSE 2015). The recently published Wellbeing Policy Statement and Framework for Practice (DES 2019: 9) highlights the 'best interests of our children and young people' as a 'central focus' for policy and practice. In order to fulfil this central focus, the policy states that stakeholders must value children's voice to ensure that a 'sound developmental base for present and future wellbeing, as well as academic achievement' (DES 2019: 9).

As discussed previously in Chapter 2, children are considered active agents in their learning and in Ireland, a child-centred approach to meeting children's needs is promoted. In considering what these 'needs' include we must first start with children's legal rights. Articles 3 and 12 of the United Nations Convention on the Rights of the Child (UNCRC), have particular relevance to early learning environments (United Nations (UN) 1989; CECDE 2006b). Article 3 states that the child's best interests are of 'paramount importance' and Article 12 explains that the child's voice must be considered in matters affecting her/him (UN 1989). Síolta: The National Quality Framework for Early Childhood Education expressly states that:

> ensuring that these rights are met puts a duty on practitioners to enable every child to exercise choice, and to use initiative as an active participant and partner in her/his own development It means moving beyond simply safeguarding children's rights, to actively promoting them. (CECDE 2006b: 2).

Due to the complex nature of child development and wellbeing, children are reliant on engaging in high-quality environments, where due consideration is given to both structural and process quality (Melhuish 2015; Whitebread et al. 2015) and to developing and maintaining a culture where all children are included and can meaningfully participate and flourish (Department of Children and Youth Affairs (DCYA) 2016). Inclusive environments support all children and positively contribute to the overall wellbeing of children with diverse needs and abilities (Dikens 2014). What constitutes a 'quality' early childhood education varies in the literature, however from extensive empirical research, structural and process quality have been identified as 'critical facilitators' in supporting children's learning and development in early childhood environments (Melhuish et al. 2015: 45). Structural quality refers to organisational and physical features such as adult-child ratios; teacher qualifications; availability of materials and the characteristics of the physical space. While process quality refers to the quality of children's experiences associated with the curriculum; pedagogical practices; and supportive positive interactions and relationships (Melhuish et al. 2015; Whitebread et al. 2015). From their research on the impact of high-quality early years' provision on children's development, Melhuish and colleagues found that there are seven key 'quality characteristics' which influence child development in early childhood education (2015: 5) as outlined in Table 6.1. When we consider the seven characteristics it is useful to do so in the context of structure and process quality.

Table 6.1. The Seven Key Quality Characteristics of Early Childhood Education (Melhuish et al. 2015: 5)

1	Adult-child interaction that is responsive, affectionate and readily available.
2	Well-trained staff who are committed to their work with children.
3	A developmentally appropriate curriculum with educational content.
4	Ratios and group sizes that allow staff to interact appropriately with children.
5	Supervision that maintains consistency in the quality of care.
6	Staff development that ensures continuity, stability and improving quality.
7	Facilities that are safe, sanitary and accessible to parents.

Key Signposts: The Influence of Quality Early Childhood Experiences on Child Development and Wellbeing

- Researchers agree that high-quality early childhood education 'impacts children's academic development and their emotional and social wellbeing more powerfully than any other phase of education' (Whitebread et al. 2015: 6).

- From both a child development and an economic viewpoint, the earlier that children engage in high-quality early childhood education the stronger the impact this has on their holistic development.
- Structural and process quality have been identified as critical facilitators in supporting children's learning and development in early childhood environments (Melhuish et al. 2015).
- Seven key 'quality characteristics' influence child development in early childhood education and are related to interactions; staff qualifications; curriculum; adult/child ratios; supervision; staff development; safe environment with accessibility for parents (Melhuish et al. 2015: 5).

The Central Importance of Providing Environments that Support Children's Social Interaction: Promoting children's social interaction is a key priority and best practice, from ELC settings and beyond. According to the European Agency for Special Needs and Inclusive Education (EASNIE), 'the development of inclusive practice is an essential feature of professional learning for all teachers and teacher educators' (EASNIE 2015: 26). Inclusive practices certainly require an understanding and commitment from all stakeholders. Creating an ethos where all children and staff, experience feelings of belonging and being valued is critical to being truly inclusive (NCCA 2009a; EASNIE 2015). Moving from a language of deficit towards celebrating difference and promoting the value of being different creates an atmosphere where inclusivity can thrive DCYA 2016). Consciously promoting initiatives underpinned by the principle of universality that can benefit all is the first step in this process.

In the Irish context, the National Council for Special Education's (NCSE) continuum of support framework depicted in Figure 6.1, is a useful scaffold for ELCs, primary and special school settings within which to locate a systematic approach to creating inclusive settings (NCSE 2018). This model highlights the importance of providing whole-setting, intensive and targeted supports (NCSE 2018), which align well with the AIM model and the concept of universal design for learning (UDL) (Hall et al. 2012; Inter-Departmental Group (IDG) 2015).

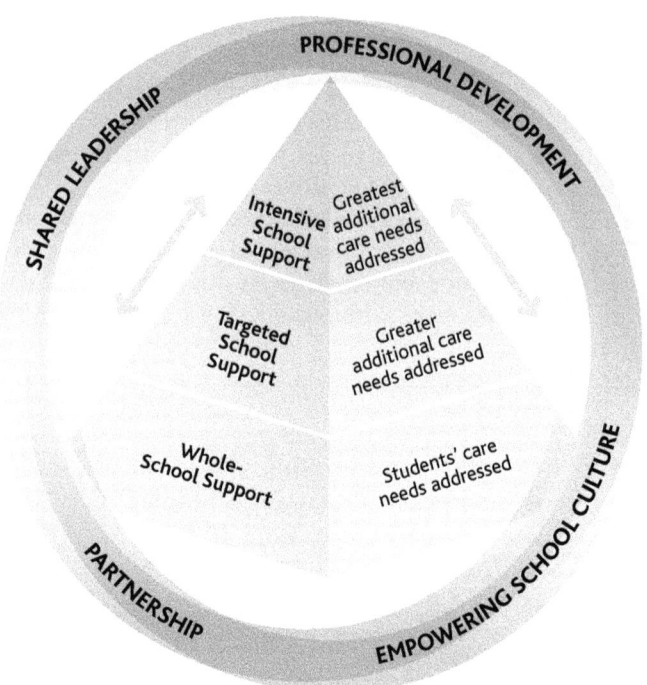

Figure 6.1. Continuum of Support within an Inclusive School Culture (NCSE 2018: 34)

UDL is highlighted as a best practice approach to supporting the inclusion of all children (Hall et al., 2012; Grey et al. 2019). UDL is 'the design and configuration of an environment so that it can be accessed, understood and used to the greatest extent possible by all people, regardless of their age, size, ability' or additional need (Grey et al. 2019: 7). These principles can equally be applied pedagogically to support all children's learning and development through designing learning opportunities that children can easily access and engage with, such an approach will aid all children in benefiting from the learning experiences available within the environment to the greatest extend possible. Within ELC and school settings therefore, employing principles from UDL theory can help all children engage in a way that suits them best (Burgstahler 2009; Meyer et al. 2012; Johnson-Harris and Mundschenk 2014; Grey et al. 2019).

Children's social interactions are promoted in environments that are easily understood and where children are comfortable and secure. Children learn best when they are 'calm and ready' (Yack et al. 2015: 125). Employing visual supports and clear signage around the setting can help all those in the setting navigate more effectively and contribute to children's sense of security, confidence and wellbeing (Grey et al. 2019). Every individual has sensory preferences, and these preferences impact on how we experience and engage within our environments. Creating inclusive learning environments that accommodate all sensory preferences through providing a variety of seating options and adapting light, temperature and background noise in accordance with children's observed responses further supports children's interactions with their environment (Feeney 2018). Providing an environment that facilitates movement breaks supports children in 'maintaining their levels of alertness' and fosters positive social interactions (National Behaviour Support Service (NBSS) 2017: 1). There is increasing evidence that movement breaks benefit all learners (Kwak et al. 2009; Donnelly and Lanbourne 2011; Webster et al. 2015; Feeney 2018). Movement breaks are, at the most basic level, where children are facilitated in taking a break from table-top activities and engaging in physical activity before returning to their previous activity.

Social interaction can further be promoted through adopting whole-setting specific strategies that promote peer support, as peer support is an 'effective and powerful tool' for promoting inclusion (Briggs 2004: 24). This can include implementing a buddy system (Briggs 2004); friendship benches/friendship bus stops (Lindon 2012) and creating peer-learning opportunities (NCCA 1999; 2009a; 2020). Buddy systems are where children are paired up by adults for some play sessions. Friendship benches/bus stops are physical playground spaces or seats where children can go to wait if they have no one to play with, all children are encouraged to invite those sitting on the 'buddy bench'/at the 'bus stop' to join their play. Peer learning opportunities are promoted by both Aistear: The Early Childhood Curriculum Framework (NCCA 2009a) and primary school curricula (NCCA 1999; 2020). These opportunities can be created in class situations when adults select pairs or groupings of children to work together; these groupings can be subtly chosen to encourage social mixing of children who do not tend to play or work together usually, or to promote and develop better peer interactions by including good social role models in the groups (NCCA 2009a). These peer mentoring practices may help to promote an overall sense of 'sameness' across different profiles of children, if we all understand that we are all different therefore all the same!

> **Key Signposts: The Central Importance of Providing Environments that Support Children's Social Interaction**
>
> - Creating early years' environments that promote children's social interaction and celebrate difference is a key priority of best practice in promoting high-quality early learning experiences for all children.
> - Employing Universal Design for Learning (UDL) theory can help all learners engage in a way that suits them best (Hally, Meyer and Rose 2012).
> - Use of visual supports and clear signage around the setting can help all children navigate more effectively and can contribute to children's sense of security, confidence and wellbeing (Grey et al. 2019).
> - Accommodating sensory preferences through providing a variety of seating options and adapting light, temperature and background noise in accordance with children's observed responses further supports children's interactions with their environment (Feeney 2018).
> - Facilitating movement breaks supports children in 'maintaining their levels of alertness' (National Behaviour Support Service (NBSS) 2017: 1)
> - Social interaction can be promoted through adopting specific strategies, such as buddy systems, friendship benches/friendship bus stops and peer-learning opportunities.

The Influence of Peer Interactions on Children's Learning and Development

Early learning and care settings and school environments provide children with opportunities to develop peer interactions and to form friendships (Guralnick, Connor and Clark Johnson 2011). Peer interactions are a central requirement of an inclusive culture and contribute positively to many aspects of development for all children (Chen et al. 2017; Syrjämäki et al. 2018), including wellbeing (Syrjämäki et al. 2018); self-regulation (Barnett et al. 2008); social and cognitive development (Chen et al. 2017). While inclusive educational environments can provide children with opportunities for developing social skills (Ozkubat and Ozdemir 2014), the literature highlights that some children can find peer interactions difficult (Guralnick et al. 2011; McCollow and Hoffman 2019). Research reminds us that in early childhood, play is the primary means through which the child learns and develops (NCCA 2009a; 2009b; Pellegrini 2009; Whitebread et al. 2015; O'Sullivan and Ring 2018; O'Sullivan, Ring and Horgan 2018). Play 'forms the context for peer interaction' (Syrjämäki et al. 2018: 419) and supports child wellbeing (Mainstone-Cotton 2017; Moore and Lynch 2017; Moser et al. 2017). However, Reunamo et al. (2013) found that low levels of peer interactions among young children can result from a difficulty in engaging in play with their peers due to limited play skills, with Suhonen et al. (2015) observing that some children tend to engage in more solitary play and less verbal social play than other children (Suhonen et al. 2015). Aistear; The Early Childhood Curriculum Framework (NCCA 2009a) reminds us that while all children have the potential to engage in playful experiences, some children may require support. Therefore, it is important that early childhood teachers are cognisant of the fact that children's play develops over time and is enriched in ELC settings that are structured to provide a variety of play experiences in the indoor and outdoor environment, which are based on observed individual children's strengths, interests and needs (NCCA 2009a).

Teachers have a fundamental role in supporting the peer interactions of all children, which can be achieved through engaging in pedagogical practice that guides interactions during play experiences (Syrjämäki et al. 2018). Pedagogical practice is an 'interactive process' that occurs between a child, teacher and the environment (Siraj-Blatchford 2004: 138) and has been referred to as the 'how' of teaching (McMongle 2012: 30). For pedagogical practice to be effective, the teacher must understand how children learn and develop and their role in supporting this process for each individual child. It is important to consider that our pedagogical practice is 'rooted in the values and beliefs' that we have for children and reinforced by 'knowledge, theory and practice' (Stephen and Pugh 2007 cited in Whalley and Allen 2011: 66). The positive impact of early childhood teachers using a wide repertoire of pedagogical interaction strategies and observation methods is well documented in the literature in relation to children's learning and development (Moyles, Adams and Musgrove 2002 and Mac Naughton and Williams 2008; NCCA 2009a; Neaum 2016).

Key Signposts: Supporting Peer Interaction Through Pedagogical Practice

- Early childhood teachers have a fundamental role in supporting the peer interactions of all children, which can be achieved through engaging in pedagogical practice that guides peer interactions during play experiences (Syrjämäki et al. 2018).
- When early childhood teachers scaffold children's play skills during peer interactions by utilising a repertoire of pedagogical strategies, a positive impact on both individual and group peer interactions can occur (Syrjämäki et al. 2018: 429).
- When early childhood teachers utilise observation methods to inform their practice, children's learning and developed is supported (National Council for Curriculum and Assessment (NCCA) 2009a)

The Responsibility of the Adult in Fostering Positive and Respectful Relationships

In the foreword to 'Guidelines for Mental Health Promotion: Well-Being in Primary Schools', Minister Jan O'Sullivan and Minister Kathleen Lynch state that:

> Schools play a vital role in the promotion of positive mental health in children ... Listening to the voice of the child and fostering healthy relationships with peers, teachers and school staff are essential to children's positive experience of school and their cognitive and emotional development. (NEPS, DoH, DES and HSE 2015: 2)

In ELC and school settings, learning environments can be as diverse as the staff and children within them. Establishing positive and respectful relationships for all our learners is a critical element in fostering wellbeing for young children and is the responsibility of the teacher and wider ELC and school community. Experiencing and engaging in positive relationships are crucial for all learners. It is well documented that some children can experience low self-esteem, poor self-concept and poor levels of wellbeing (Moreira et al. 2015; Daly 2018). Carlson, Hyunshik and Schroll (2004) found that 'teachers' attitudes and beliefs', along with positive classroom practices 'proved important in identifying attributes' in competent special education teachers. Teachers play a crucial role in developing children's wellbeing, their positive self-concept and their attitudes to learning (Tynan and Nohilly 2018). Teachers can elicit positive outcomes for children by providing activities that are attractive and appealing to them. If students perceive that their teachers support them and take an interest in their lives, it can encourage them and promote their wellbeing (Chong et al. 2018). Research conducted with older school children suggests that their interpretation of their teacher's support and interest in them, along with their own self-efficacy has a huge impact on their success (Mercer et al. 2011).

Young children 'experience their world as an environment of relationships, and these relationships affect virtually all aspects of their development' (National Scientific Council on the Developing Child 2004: 1). The Irish Diversity Equality and Inclusion Charter and Guidelines for Early Childhood Care and Education (DCYA 2016) were developed with the purpose of empowering children to reach their full potential through supporting the inclusive of all children in early childhood education settings. The guidelines state that:

> Young children enter the early childhood service with a general awareness of difference ... children learn and have their views reinforced by attitudes they experience primarily through relationships with adults and the wider community ... it is the early childhood practitioner's role to acknowledge this awareness, and to promote diversity and equality within their setting (DCYA 2016: 15)

Early childhood teachers who 'critically explore' their personal attitudes and practices regarding inclusive practice provide more inclusive environments for children than those who do not (DCYA 2016: 8). While critically reflecting upon our own attitudes and values in relation to facilitating the inclusion of all children may not be easy, such a reflective process may be necessary before we can support children in understanding and having positive attitudes towards difference (DCYA 2016). This is an important element in providing for the inclusion of all children, as research highlights that teacher attitudes are critical in ensuring the 'success of inclusive education' (Sari, Çeliköz and Sercer 2009: 31) and have a significant influence on the experiences that a child has within inclusive environments (Lee et al. 2015a). In a study which explored early childhood teachers' attitudes in relation to promoting successful inclusive early childhood education, Lee and colleagues (2015a) found that engaging in continuing professional development (CPD) which focused on inclusive practices was associated with developing positive attitudes towards inclusion. The correlation between engaging in CPD related towards inclusion and teacher attitudes towards inclusion has been positively demonstrated in the literature (Baker-Ericzen at al. 2009; Lee et al. 2015b; Ring et al. 2019).

Anti-bias education, developed by Derman-Sparks and the Anti-Bias Curriculum (ABC) Task Force (1989), is an active approach to challenging prejudice which has influenced practice in early childhood education internationally. It places 'diversity and equity goals at the centre of all aspects' of the curriculum (Derman-Sparks et al. 2015: 11) by 'supporting children in developing a fuller, truer understanding of themselves and the world, and strengthens their sense of themselves as capable, empowered people' (Derman-Sparks et al. 2015: 10). Implementing an anti-bias approach contributes to 'the creation of an inclusive culture and is an effective way of creating secure, respectful and reciprocal relationships that value diversity' (DCYA 2016: 70). The anti-bias approach, detailed in Table 6.2, aligns with the theoretical philosophy of Aistear: Early Childhood Curriculum Framework (NCCA 2009a) and Síolta: The National Quality Framework for Early Childhood Education (CECDE 2006a) frameworks in terms of advocating for inclusion; equality; diversity; positive self-identity and supporting all children's sense of belonging within their environment.

Table 6.2. Goals for an Anti-Bias Approach (Adapted from Derman-Sparks and the Anti-Bias Curriculum Task Force (1989) cited in DCYA 2016: 25)

1	Provide an inclusive education environment in which all children can succeed.
2	Enable children with additional needs to develop autonomy, independence, confidence and pride.
3	Provide all children with accurate, appropriate information about their own and others' additional needs, and foster understanding that a person with an additional need is different in one respect, but similar in many other respects.
4	Enable all children to develop the ability to interact knowledgeably, comfortably and fairly with people who have various additional needs.
5	Show children with additional needs how to handle and challenge name-calling, stereotypical attitudes and physical barriers.
6	Show children how to resist and challenge stereotyping, name-calling and physical barriers directed against children or adults with additional needs.

> **Key Signposts: The Responsibility of the Adult in Fostering Positive and Respectful Relationships**
>
> - Establishing positive and respectful relationships for all our learners in early childhood education is a critical element in fostering well-being for your young children, and is the responsibility of the teacher and wider early learning and care (ELC) and school community.
> - Early childhood teachers who 'critically explore' their personal attitudes and practices regarding inclusive practice provide more inclusive environments for children than those who do not (Department of Children and Youth Affairs (DCYA): 8).
> - Anti-bias education, developed by Derman-Sparks and the Anti-Bias Curriculum Task Force (1989), is an active approach to challenging prejudice which has influenced practice in early learning and care settings internationally.
> - Implementing an anti-bias approach in early childhood education contributes to 'the creation of an inclusive culture and is an effective way of creating secure, respectful and reciprocal relationships that value diversity' (DCYA 2016: 70).

Problem-Solving Approach to Conflict Resolution

Aistear: The Early Childhood Curriculum Framework's theme of Identity and Belonging advocates for children to be supported in developing a positive self-identity and feeling of belonging within their environment (NCCA 2009a). A sense of belonging is essential in supporting children's wellbeing (Woodhead and Brooker 2008), therefore for children to thrive their wellbeing must be supported (Bailey 2012). Central to children's wellbeing is their ability to problem-solve and resolve conflict in a positive manner. When considering how we can support young children to problem-solve and resolve conflicts, we need to consider the environment that children are interacting within. As discussed previously, how the environment is constructed impacts on children's interactions with their peers (Arthur et al. 2018). In addition, we need to consider how we view 'behaviour' as the behaviours in which a child engages are believed to have a communicative function therefore 'by recognising that all behaviour has meaning, we respect the child … through validating their experience, and go further in not only listening to them but also learning from their communication' (Schmidt-Neven 2010: 8). Consequently, when teachers view 'challenging behaviour' as actions that children employ to communicate their needs, such behaviour can then be reframed as 'skill learning' (Fox and Lentini 2006; Paciorek 2009; O'Neill 2014). Supporting the child should be the intent behind all responses towards a child's behaviour as children need the support of trusted adults who understand their needs and support them in developing strategies to regulate their emotions (Shonkoff and Phillips 2000) and to resolve conflicts with their peers (Arthur et al. 2018). A problem-solving approach to supporting conflicts for children in early childhood education in Ireland is recommended by Síolta: the National Quality Framework for Early Childhood Education in Ireland (CECDE 2006a).

HighScope has developed a problem-solving approach which can be implemented in ELC settings and infant classrooms to support children in resolving conflicts. Wiltshire (2012) highlights that when the problem-solving approach is facilitated by a supportive adult who guides children through the six steps of the process it can be used effectively with children of all ages. This approach highlights that conflict is a 'healthy normal part of human learning and human development' and advocates that early childhood teachers use the conflicts that arise as teachable moments to support children in negotiating and solving conflicts with their peers through teaching social and emotional skills (Wiltshire 2019: 72). In supporting children's engagement in the problem-solving process the teacher guides the child through six steps. The steps do not always follow in sequence and some of the steps may need to be repeated depending on the nature of the conflict (Wiltshire 2012). Table 6.3 summarises the six steps of the HighScope *Problem-Solving Approach* to Conflict Resolution (Holt 2007: 49).

Table 6.3. Six Steps of the HighScope Problem-Solving Approach to Conflict Resolution (Adapted from Holt 2007: 49)

Step One:	Approach calmly, stopping any hurtful actions.	Place yourself between the children Go down to the child's level Use a calm voice Remain neutral
Step Two:	Acknowledge children's feelings.	Use simple language such as: 'Sarah you sound angry' or 'Peter you look sad' 'Can you tell me what happened?'
Step Three:	Gather information.	Ask the child/children 'what's the problem?' Listen for the details of the problem.
Step Four:	Restate the problem.	'So the problem is ......' Substitute neutral words for hurtful or judgemental ones.
Step Five:	Ask for ideas for solutions and choose one together.	Ask the children 'What can we do to solve this problem?' Encourage the children to think of a solution but offer options if needed.
Step Six:	Be prepared to give follow-up support.	Acknowledge the children's accomplishments, for example, 'You solved the problem!' Stay nearby in case anyone is not happy with the solution and the process needs repeating.

Key Signposts: A Problem-Solving Approach to Conflict Resolution

- Conflict is a 'healthy normal part of human learning and human development'. A central element of children's wellbeing is their ability to problem-solve and resolve conflict in a positive manner (Wiltshire 2019: 72).
- HighScope has developed a problem-solving approach to support children in resolving conflicts. When the problem-solving approach is facilitated by a supportive adult who guides children through the six steps of the process, it can be used effectively with children of all ages (Wiltshire 2012).
- The six steps of the HighScope *Problem-Solving Approach* to Conflict Resolution include; approach calmly; stop any hurtful actions; acknowledge children's feelings; gather information; restate the problem; ask for ideas for solutions and choose one together and be prepared to give follow-up support (Holt 2007).

Conclusion

In today's society, it is important that all those directly involved in child development are committed to promoting children's positive mental health and wellbeing. As discussed in this chapter, the early years are critical in children's growth and development and those providing education to young children have a responsibility to foster all children's wellbeing, self-confidence and self-competence (NCCA 1999; CECDE 2006a; NCCA 2009a; NEPS, DoH, DES and HSE 2015). The role of adults is central in fostering positive and respectful relationships and this is achieved through adopting a child-centred approach, as advocated by Aistear: The Early Childhood Curriculum Framework (NCCA 2009a), Síolta: The National Quality Framework for Early Childhood Education(CECDE 2006a) and the Primary School Curriculum (NCCA 1999; 2020; Ring et al. 2018). In focusing intentionally on teaching young children, through multi-modal methods, how to interact successfully, how to be aware of their own strengths and celebrating individual differences, how to work together and problem-solve, all children's wellbeing is enhanced and early childhood education is making a valuable and significant contribution to the creation of an inclusive society.

Bibliography

Ainsworth, M. D., and Bell, S. M. (1970). 'Attachment, Exploration and Separation: Illustrated by the Behaviour of One-Year-Olds in a Strange Situation', *Child Development*, 41(1), 49–76.

Arthur, L., Beecher, B., Death, E., Dockett, S., and Farmer, S. (2018). *Programming and Planning in Early Childhood Settings* (7th ed.). South Melbourne: Cengage Learning Australia.

Bailey, G. (2012). *Emotional Well-Being for Children with Special Educational Needs and Disabilities: A Guide for Practitioners*. London: Sage.

Baker-Ericzén, M., Mueggenborg, M. G., and Shea, M. M. (2009). 'Impact of Trainings on Child Care Providers' Attitudes and Perceived Competence toward Inclusion: What Factors Are Associated with Change?', *Topics in Early Childhood Special Education*, 28(4), 196–208.

Barnett, W. S., Jung, K., Yarosz, D. J., Thomas, J., Hornbeck, A., Stechuk, R., and Burns, S. (2008). 'Educational Effects of the Tools of the Mind Curriculum: A Randomized Trial', *Early Childhood Research Quarterly*, 23(3), 299–313.

Bowlby, J. (1988). *A Secure Base: Clinical Applications of Attachment Theory*. London, England: Routledge.

Bradshaw, P., Lewis, G., and Hughes, T. (2014). *Growing Up in Scotland: Characteristics of Pre-School Provision and Their Association with Child Outcomes*. Edinburgh: Scottish Government, <https://dera.ioe.ac.uk/20322/2/00453130_Redacted.pdf>, accessed 25 August 2020.

Briggs, S. (2004). *Inclusion and How to Do It: Meeting SEN in Secondary Classrooms*. London: David Fulton Publishers Ltd.

Burgstahler, S. (2009). *Universal Design of Instruction (UDI): Definition, Principles, Guidelines (Report)*. Washington, DC: Do It.

Caldwell, B. M. (2017). 'The Fourth Dimension in Early Childhood Education'. In R. D. Hess and R. M. Bear (eds), *Early Formal Education: Current Theory, Research, and Practice*, pp. 71–82. London: Routledge.

Carlson, E., Hyunshik, L., and Schroll, K. (2004). 'Identifying Attributes of High Quality Special Education Teachers', *Teacher Education and Special Education*, 27(4), 350–359.

Centre for Early Childhood Development and Education. (2006a). *Síolta: The National Quality Framework for Early Childhood Education*. Dublin: Centre for Early Childhood Development and Education, <http://siolta.ie/media/pdfs/final_handbook.pdf>, accessed 29 October 2010.

Centre for Early Childhood Development and Education. (2006b). *Reader Digest Standard 1 The Rights of the Child*. Dublin: Centre for Early Childhood Development and Education, <http://siolta.ie/media/pdfs/Research%20Digest%20-%20Rights%20of%20the%20child.pdf>, accessed 20 October 2019.

Chen, J., Lin, T., Justice, L., and Sawyer, B. (2017). 'The Social Networks of Children with and without Disabilities in Early Childhood Special Education Classrooms', *Journal of Autism Developmental Disorders*, 49(7), 2779–2794.

Chong, W. H., Liem, G. A. D., Huan, V. S., Kit, P. L., and Ang, R. P. (2018). 'Student Perceptions of Self-Efficacy and Teacher Support for Learning in Fostering Youth Competencies: Roles of Affective and Cognitive Engagement', *Journal of Adolescence*, 68, 1–11.

Daly, P. (2018). 'Promoting Children's Wellbeing'. In E. Ring, P. Daly, and E. Wall (eds), *Autism from the Inside Out: Signposts for Parents, Early Childhood, Primary, Post-Primary and Special School Settings*, pp. 199–218. Oxford: Peter Lang.

Deci, E. L., and Ryan, R. M. (2008a). 'Hedonia, Eudaimonia, and Wellbeing: An Introduction', *Journal of Happiness Studies*, 9(1), 1–11.

Department of Children and Youth Affairs. (2016). *Diversity, Equality and Inclusion Charter and Guidelines for Early Childhood Care and Education*. Dublin: Department of Children and Youth Affairs, <http://www.preschoolaccess.ie/wpcontent/uploads/2016/06/Diversity-Equality-and-Inclusion-Charter-and-Guidelines-for-Early-Childhood-Care-Education.pdf>, accessed 20 October 2019.

Department of Education and Skills. (2019). *Wellbeing Policy Statement and Framework for Practice 2018–2023. Revised October 2019*. Dublin: Department of Education and Skills, <https://www.education.ie/en/Publications/Policy-Reports/wellbeing-policy-statement-and-framework-for-practice-2018%E2%80%932023.pdf>, accessed 20 October 2019.

Derman-Sparks, L., and Anti-Bias Curriculum Task Force. (1989) *Anti-Bias Curriculum: Tools for Empowering Young Children*. Washington, DC: National Association for the Education of Young Children.

Derman-Sparks, L., Lee-Keenan, D., and Nimmo, J. (2015). *Leading Anti-Bias Early Childhood Programs: A Guide for Change*. Washington, DC: National Association for the Education of Young Children.

Dikens, M. (2014). 'Supporting the Well-Being of Children with Disabilities and Their Families'. In J. Manning-Morton (ed), *Exploring Well-Being in the Early Years*, pp. 120–132. Maidenhead: Open University Press.

Donnelly, J. E., and Lanbourne, K. (2011). 'Classroom-Based Physical Activity, Cognition, and Academic Achievement', *Preventive Medicine*, 52 (supplement), 36–42.

Erikson, E. H. (1965). *Childhood and Society*. Harmondsworth: Penguin.

European Agency for Special Needs and Inclusive Education. (2015). *Empowering Teachers to Promote Inclusive Education. Literature Review*. Odense, Denmark: European Agency for Special Needs and Inclusive Education, <https://www.european-agency.org/sites/default/files/Empowering%20Teachers%20to%20Promote%20Inclusive%20Education.%20Literature%20Review.pdf>, accessed 08 September 2020.

Feeney, S. (2018). 'Addressing Children's Sensory Differences: Strategies for Practice'. In E. Ring, P. Daly, and E. Wall (eds), *Autism from the Inside Out: Signposts for Parents, Early Childhood, Primary, Post-Primary and Special School Settings*, pp. 67–96. Oxford: Peter Lang.

Fox, L., and Lentini, R. H. (2006). *"You Got It!" Teaching Social and Emotional Skills*. Washington, DC: National Association for the Education of Young Children, <https://challengingbehavior.cbcs.usf.edu/docs/YouGotIt_Teaching-Social-Emotional-Skills.pdf>, accessed 29 October 2019.

Grey, T., Corbett, M., Sheerin, J., Heeney, T., Ring, E., and O'Sullivan, L. (2019). *Universal Design Guidelines for Early Learning and Care Settings*. Dublin: Department of Children and Youth Affairs in collaboration with the Centre for Universal Design and the National Disability Authority, <https://aim.gov.ie/wp-content/uploads/2019/06/universal-design-guidelines-for-elc-settings-introduction-1.pdf>, accessed 6 January 2019.

Guralnick, M. J., Connor, R. T., and Clark Johnson, L. (2011). 'The Peer Social Networks of Young Children with Down Syndrome in Classroom Programmes', *Journal of Applied Research in Intellectual Disabilities*, 24(4), 310–321.

Hall, T., Meyer, A., and Rose, D. H. (2012). 'An Introduction to Universal Design for Learning'. In T. E. Hall, A. Meyer, and D. H. Rose (eds), *Universal Design for Learning in the Classroom*, pp. 1–8. New York, NY: The Guilford Press.

Harvey, B. (2014). *The Case for Prevention and Early Intervention: Promoting Positive Outcomes for Children, Families and Communities.* Dublin: Prevention and Early Intervention Network, <http://edepositireland.ie/bitstream/handle/2262/77306/PEIN_A4_Report_%28April_2014%29_11_4_14_%28Web_Version%29.pdf?sequence=1&isAllowed=y>, accessed 29 October 2019.

Hayes, N., Siraj-Blatchford, I., Keegan, S., and Goulding, E. (2013). *Evaluation of the Early Years Programme of the Childhood Development Initiative.* Dublin: Childhood Development Initiative (CDI), <https://www.parentsplus.ie/wp/wp-content/uploads/2015/06/hayes-PPEY-CDIReport_09.01.pdf>, accessed 29 October 2019.

Heckman, J. (2000). *Invest in the Very Young.* Chicago, IL: University of Chicago Press.

Heckman, H., Pinto, R., and Savey, P. (2013). 'Understanding the Mechanisms through Which an Influential Early Childhood Program Boosted Adult Outcomes', *American Economic Review*, 103(6), 2052–2086.

Holt, N. (2007). *Bringing the High Scope Approach to your Early Years Practice.* New York, NY: Routledge.

Inter-Departmental Group. (2015). *Supporting Access to the Early Childhood Care and Education Programme for Children with a Disability.* Dublin: Inter-Departmental Group, <https://aim.gov.ie/wp-content/uploads/2016/06/Inter-Departmental-Group-Report-launched-Nov-2015.pdf>, accessed 29 October 2019.

Johnson-Harris, K. M., and Mundschenk, N. A. (2014). 'Working Effectively with Students with BD in a General Education Classroom: The Case for Universal Design for Learning', *Clearing House*, 87(4), 168–174.

Kahneman, D. (1999). 'Objective Happiness'. In D. Kahneman, R. Diener, and N. Schwarz (eds), *Wellbeing: The Foundation of Hedonic Psychology*, pp. 3–25. New York, NY: Russell Stage Foundation.

Kearns, K. (2017). *Birth to Big School* (4th ed.). South Melbourne: Cengage Learning Australia.

Kwak, L., Kremers, S. P. J., Bergman, P., Ruiz, J. R., Rizzo, N. S., and Sjostrom, M. (2009). 'Associations between Physical Activity, Fitness and Academic Achievement', *The Journal of Paediatrics*, 155(6), 914–918.

Leadership for INClusion in the Early Years Consortium. (2016–2020). *A Competency Framework for Inclusion in Early Childhood Education and Care.* Mary Immaculate College, Limerick: Leadership for INClusion in the Early Years Consortium.

Lee, F. L. M., Yeung, A. S., Barker, K., Tracey, D., and Fan, J. C. M. (2015a). 'Teacher Perceptions of Factors for Successful Inclusive Early Childhood Education in Hong Kong', *Australasian Journal of Special Education*, 39(2), 97–112.

Lee, F. L. M., Yeung, A. S., Tracey, D., and Barker, K. (2015b). 'Inclusion of Children with Special Needs in Early Childhood Education: What Teacher Characteristics Matter', *Topics in Early Childhood Special Education*, 35(2), 79–88.

Lindon, J. (2012). *Understanding Children's Behaviour 0–11 Years: Linking Theory and Practice*. Oxon: Hodder Education.

Mainstone-Cotton, S. (2017). *Promoting Young Children's Emotional Health and Wellbeing: A Practical Guide for Practitioners and Parents*. London: Jessica Kingsley Publishers.

Maslow, A. H. (1943). 'A Theory of Human Motivation', *Psychological Review*, 50(4), 370–396.

McCollow, M. M., and Hoffman, H. H. (2019). 'Supporting Social Development in Young Children with Disabilities: Building a Practitioner's Toolkit', *Early Childhood Education Journal*, 47(3), 309–320.

McMongle, A. (2012). *Professinal Pedagogy Project: Professional Pedagogy for Early Childhood Education,* Dongel: Dongeal Childcare Committee, https://www.yumpu.com/en/document/read/45358595/eocp-professional-pedagogy-for-early-childhood-education-pobal, accessed 06 January 2021.

Mac Naughton, G., and Williams, G. (2008). *Teaching Young Children: Choices in Theory and Practice* (2nd ed.). Maidenhead: Open University Press.

Melhuish, E., Ereky-Stevens, K., Petrogiannis, K., Ariescu, A., Penderi, E., Rentzou, Tawell, A., Leseman, P., and Broekhuisen, M. (2015). *A Review of Research on the Effects of Early Childhood Education and Care (ECEC) upon Child Development*, CARE Project; Curriculum Quality Analysis and Impact Review of European Early Childhood Education and Care (ECEC), <http://ecec-care.org/fileadmin/careproject/Publications/reports/new_version_CARE_WP4_D4_1_Review_on_the_effects_of_ECEC.pdf>, accessed 29 October 2019.

Mercer, S. H., Nellis, L. M., Martinez, R. S., and Kirk, M. (2011). 'Supporting the Students Most in Need: Academic Self-Efficacy and Perceived Teacher Support in Relation to Within-Year Academic Growth', *Journal of School Psychology*, 49(3), 323–338.

Moore, A., and Lynch, H. (2017). 'Understanding a Child's Conceptualisation of Well-Being through an Exploration of Happiness: The Centrality of Play, People and Place', *Journal of Occupational Science*, 25(1), 124–141.

Moreira, P. A. S., Bilimoria, H., Alvez, P., Santos, M. A., Macedo, A. C., Maia, A., Figueiredo, F., and Miranda, M. J. (2015). 'Subjective Wellbeing in Students with Special Educational Needs', *Cognition, Brain and Behaviour. An Interdisciplinary Journal*, 19(1), 75–97.

Moser, T., Leseman, P., Melhuish, E., Broekhuizen, M., and Slot, P. (2017). *European Framework of Quality and Wellbeing Indicators*, CARE Project: Curriculum Quality Analysis and Impact Review of European Early Childhood Education and Care (ECEC), <https://dspace.library.uu.nl/handle/1874/352708>, accessed 29 October 2019.

Moyles, J., Adams, S., and Musgrove, A. (2002). *SPEEL Study of Pedagogical Effectiveness in Early Learning*. Norwich: Queens Printer (Department for Education and Skills), <https://dera.ioe.ac.uk/4591/1/RR363.pdf?e=5305098/62475902>, accessed 06 September 2020.

National Behaviour Support Service (NBSS). (2017). *Movement Breaks: Occupational Therapy Tips*, <https://www.nbss.ie/sites/default/files/publications/movement_breaks_tip_sheet_0.pdf>, accessed 08 September 2020.

National Council for Curriculum and Assessment. (1999). *Primary School Curriculum*. Dublin: The Stationery Office.

National Council for Curriculum and Assessment. (2009a). *Aistear: The Early Childhood Curriculum Framework*. Dublin: National Council for Curriculum and Assessment.

National Council for Curriculum and Assessment. (2009b). *Key Messages from the Research Papers*. Dublin: National Council for Curriculum and Assessment.

National Council for Curriculum and Assessment. (2020). *Draft Primary Curriculum Framework. for Consultation*. Dublin: National Council for Curriculum and Assessment, <https://ncca.ie/media/4456/ncca-primary-curriculum-framework-2020.pdf>, accessed 06 September 2020.

National Council for Special Education. (2018). *Comprehensive Review of the Special Needs Assistant Scheme. A New School Inclusion Model to Deliver the Right Supports at the Right Time to Students with Additional Care Needs*. Trim: National Council for Special Education, <http://ncse.ie/wp-content/uploads/2018/05/NCSE-PAP6-Comprehensive-Review-SNA-Scheme.pdf>, accessed 6 January 2020.

National Educational Psychological Service, Department of Health, Department of Education and Skills and the Health Service Executive. (2015). *Guidelines for Mental Health Promotion: Well-Being in Primary Schools*. Dublin: Department of Education and Department of Health, <https://www.education.ie/en/Publications/Education-Reports/Well-Being-in-Primary-Schools-Guidelines-for-Mental-Health-Promotion.pdf>, accessed 20 October 2019.

National Scientific Council on the Developing Child. (2004). *Young Children Develop in an Environment of Relationships*. Working Paper No.1. Harvard: Center for the Developing Child, Harvard University, <https://developingchild.harvard.edu/wp-content/uploads/2004/04/Young-Children-Develop-in-an-Environment-of-Relationships.pdf>, accessed 29 October 2019.

Neaum, S. (2016). *Child Development for Early Years Students and Practitioners* (3rd ed.). London: Sage.

Niemiec, P., and Ryan, R. M. (2013) 'What Makes a Life Well Lived? Autonomy and Its Relation to Full Functioning and Organismic Wellness', In S. A. David, I. Boniwell, and A. C. Ayres (eds), *The Oxford Handbook of Happiness*, pp. 214–226. Oxford: Oxford University Press.

O'Neill, B. E. (2014). 'Improving with Challenging Behaviour: Creating New Performances with Children in Early Childhood Special Education'. In E. Nwokah and J. A. Sutterby (eds), *Early Childhood and Special Education. Advances in Early Education and Day Care* (Vol 18), pp. 70–87. Bingley: Emerald Publishing Limited.

Organisation for Economic Co-operation and Development (OECD). (2015). *Early Learning and Development: Common Understandings*. France: OECD.

O'Sullivan, L., and Ring, E. (2018). 'Play as Learning: Implications for Educators and Parents from Findings of a National Evaluation of School Readiness in Ireland', *International Journal of Play*, 7(3), 266–289.

O'Sullivan, L., Ring, E., and Horgan, K. (2018). 'The Power of Play to Promote Wellbeing and Connections with Others in Children with Autism Spectrum Differences', *Children's Research Digest*, 5(2), 59–65.

Ozkubat, U., and Ozdemir. (2014). 'A Comparison of Social Skills in Turkish Children with Visual Impairments, Children with Intellectual Impairments and Typically Developing Children', *International Journal of Inclusive Education*, 18(5), 1464–5173.

Paciorek, K. M. (2009). *Annual Editions: Early Childhood Education*. New York, NY: McGraw Hill.

Pellegrini, A. (2009). *The Role of Play in Human Development*. Oxford: Oxford University Press.

Piaget, J., and Inhelder, B. (1947). 'Diagnosis of Mental Operations and Theory of the Intelligence', *American Journal of Mental Deficiency*, 51, 401–406.

Price, D., and McCallum, F. (2016). 'Wellbeing in Education'. In F. McCallum and D. Price (eds), *Nurturing Wellbeing Development in Education: From Little Things, Big Things Grow*, pp. 1–21. London: Routledge.

Reunamo, J., Lee, H.-C., Wu, R., Wang, L.-C., Mau, W.-Y., and Lin, C.-J. (2013). 'Perceiving Chance in Role Play', *European Early Childhood Research Journal*, 21(2), 292–305.

Ring, E., Kelleher, S., Breen, F., Heeney, T., McLoughlin, M., Kearns, A., Stafford, P., Skehill, S., Campion, K., Comerford, D., and O'Sullivan, L. (2019). *Interim Evaluation of the Leadership for Inclusion in the Early Years (LINC) Programme*. Limerick: Mary Immaculate College, <https://documentcloud.

adobe.com/link/track?uri=urn:aaid:scds:US:d8c95d7d-2d75-40a8-9f65-b6582908c08d>, accessed 6 January 2019.

Ring, E., O'Sullivan, L., Ryan, M., and Burke, P. (2018). *A Melange or a Mosaic of Theories? How Theoretical Perspectives on Children's Learning and Development can Inform a Responsive Pedagogy in a Redeveloped Primary School Curriculum.* Dublin: National Council for Curriculum and Assessment (NCCA), <https://www.ncca.ie/media/3863/seminar_four_er_los_mr_pb_paper.pdf>, accessed 25 August 2020.

Ryan, R. M., and Deci, E. L. (2001). 'On Happiness and Human Potentials: A Review of Research on Hedonic and Eudemonic Wellbeing', *Annual Review of Psychology*, 52(1), 141–166.

Sandseter, E., Hansen, B., Seland, M., Rimul, J., Venema, M., Van de Korput, J., Van Keulen, H., Van, W., Kernan, M., Cortellesi, G., Villa, A., Palazuelos, M., Koyuncu, L., Sharmahd, N., Kimpe, C., Vida, J., Zake, D., Liepina, K., and Z. Topalovic. (2018). *Social and Emotional Well-Being of Young Children in ECEC Settings: Research Report of the SEED Project: A Study Conducted in Five European countries.* Leiden: SEED Project, <https://icdi.nl/media/uploads/downloads/seed-research-report-21dec18-final.pdf>, accessed 29 October 2019.

Sari, H., Çeliköz, N., and Secer, Z. (2009). 'An Analysis of Pre-School Teachers' and Student Teachers' Attitudes to Inclusion and Their Self-Efficacy'. *International Journal of Special Education*, 24(3), 29–44.

Schmidt-Neven, R. (2010). *Core Principles of Assessment and Therapeutic Communication with Children, Parents and Families: Towards the Promotion of Child and Family Well-Being.* New York, NY: Routledge.

Shonkoff, J., and Phillips, D. (2000). *From Neurons to Neighbourhoods: The Science of Early Childhood Development.* Committee on Integrating the Early Childhood Development, National Research Council and Institute of Medicine. Washington, DC: National Academies Press.

Siraj-Blatchford, I. (2004) 'Quality Teaching in Early Years'. In A. Anning, J. Cullen, and M. Fleer (eds), *Early Childhood Education: Society and Culture*, pp. 137–148. London: Sage Publications.

Suhonen, E., Nislin, M. A., Alijoki, A., and Sajaniemi, N. K. (2015). 'Children's Play Behaviour and Social Communication in Integrated Special Day-Care Groups', *European Journal of Special Needs Education*, 30(3), 287–303.

Sylva, K., Melhuish, E. C., Sammons, P., Siraj-Blatchford, I., and Taggart, B. (2004). *The Effective Provision of Pre-School Education (EPPE) Project: Final Report.* London: Department for Education and Skills/Institute of Education, University of London, <https://discovery.ucl.ac.uk/id/eprint/10005309/1/sylva2004EPPEfinal.pdf>, accessed 29 October 2019.

Syrjämäki, M., Pihlaja, P., and Sajaniemi, N. (2018). 'Enhancing Peer Interaction During Guided Play in Finnish Integrated Special Groups', *European Early Childhood Education Research Journal*, 26(3), 418–431.
Tynan, F., and Nohilly, M. (2018). *WISE (Wellbeing in Schools Everyday)*. Mary Immaculate College, Limerick: Curriculum Development Unit.
United Nations. (1989). *Convention on the Rights of the Child*. New York, NY: United Nations, <http://www.ohchr.org/EN/ProfessionalInterest/Pages/CRC.aspx>, accessed 29 October 2019.
Vygotsky, L. S. (1978). *Mind in Society: The Development of Higher Psychological Processes*. Cambridge, MA: Harvard University Press.
Vygotsky, L. (1986). *Thoughts and Language*. Cambridge, MA: MIT Press.
Webster, C. A., Russ, L., Vasou, S., Goh, T. L., and Erwin, H. (2015). 'Integrating Movement in Academic Classrooms: Understanding, Applying and Advancing the Knowledge Base', *Obesity Reviews*, 16(8), 691–701.
Whalley, M. E., and Allen, S. (2011). *Leading Practice in Early Years Settings* (2nd ed.). Exeter: Learning Matters.
Whitebread, D., Kuvalja, M., and O'Connor, A. (2015). *Quality in Early Childhood Education: An International Review and Guide for Policy Makers. Report for the World Summit for Education*. Dohar, Qatar: WISE, <https://www.wise-qatar.org/app/uploads/2019/04/wise-research-7-cambridge-11_17.pdf>, accessed 29 October 2019.
Wiltshire, M. (2012). *Understanding the HighScope Approach: Early Years Education in Practice*. Oxon: Routledge.
Wiltshire, M. (2019). *Understanding the HighScope Approach: Early Years Education in Practice* (2nd ed.). Oxon: Routledge.
Winter, P. (2010). *Engaging Families in the Early Childhood Development Story: Neuroscience and Early Childhood Development: Summary of Selected Literature and Key Messages for Parenting*. Carlton South, Victoria: Ministerial Council for Education, Early Childhood Development and Youth Affairs, <http://www.educationcouncil.edu.au/site/DefaultSite/filesystem/documents/Reports%20and%20publications/Publications/Early%20childhood%20education/Engaging%20Families%20in%20the%20ECD%20Story-Neuroscience%20and%20ECD.pdf>, accessed 25 August 2020.
Woodhead, M., and Brooker, L. (2008). 'A Sense of Belonging', *Early Childhood Matters*, 111, 3–6.
Yack, E., Aquilla, P., and Sutton, S. (2015). *Building Bridges through Sensory Integration* (3rd ed.). Arlington, TX: Sensory World.

LISHA O'SULLIVAN

Chapter 7   Play as a Pedagogy for All Children

ABSTRACT

This chapter will discuss the role of play as a propeller for children's wellbeing, learning and development, during their early years inearly learning and care (ELC), primary and special school settings. It will be suggested that all children can engage in and benefit from all types of play. It will be argued that it is the responsibility of educators to provide opportunities to enable all children's participation in high-quality play through considering the challenges and affordances of different play types. The significance of clearly articulating what playful learning looks like, in practice, will be addressed, as will the contribution of play to children's wellbeing, self-regulation and social competence. Strategies for promoting inclusive play and for using Aistear: The Early Childhood Curriculum Framework (National Council for Curriculum and Assessment (NCCA 2009) as a tool to support the development of inclusive play provision, will be discussed. It will be recommended that developing a playful pedagogical approach can support all children to learn in a child-centred way that builds on individual interests and celebrates diverse ways of exploring, meaning making and knowing.

Introduction

As the evidence base in support of playful learning continues to grow, so does the emphasis on developing sustainable pedagogical approaches, which support learning through play (Saracho 2012; O'Sullivan and Ring 2018). While the growth of universal, inclusive early childhood education, in the Irish context, brings much welcomed diversity to our ELC settings, it also presents us with the challenge of ensuring that all children have unlimited opportunities to learn and develop through play (Ring and O'Sullivan 2019). For the purposes of the present discussion, children with additional needs include children whose capacity to fully participate in education is limited, in some way, as a consequence of physical, sensory, cognitive, social and/or communicative differences (Ireland 2004). There is evidence to suggest that, even when children with additional needs are included in mainstream educational settings, this does not automatically lead to inclusive, playful learning (Brown and Bergen 2002; Bray and Cooper 2007; Kemp et al. 2013). According to Odom and colleagues,

> inclusion has multiple meanings but is essentially about belonging, participating, and reaching one's full potential in a diverse society. (Odom, Buysse and Soukakou 2011:347)

This chapter will argue that a playful pedagogical approach can fulfil a central role in promoting this type of inclusion in ELC, primary and special school settings. Consideration will be given to how we conceptualise playful learning and the intersection between playful learning and optimal learning conditions. The primary benefits of playful learning will be addressed prior to considering the role of Aistear, the Early Childhood Curriculum Framework (NCCA 2009), in promoting an inclusive curriculum. The chapter will conclude by identifying effective pedagogical strategies for inclusive playful learning in the early years.

Playful Learning

Zosh and colleagues (2018), suggest that playful pedagogical approaches successfully harness the characteristics of optimal learning. Their review, of the research evidence, suggests that learning is optimised when the context is: joyful; meaningful; actively engaging; iterative; and socially interactive. These characteristics of optimal learning, while evident in contexts other than play, are clearly present when learning is playful (Zosh et al. 2018). Play, first and foremost, is a joyful experience for children. Moreover, the element of surprise or novelty that is present when learning is playful can contribute to curiosity and creativity (Zosh et al. 2018). Playful learning involves intrinsic motivation – players experience joy from simply engaging in the activity and no external rewards are required. This nurtures autonomy and feelings of competence, which in turn, improve overall wellbeing and performance (Deci and Ryan 2008; Gray 2013: King and Howard 2016). When children learn through play, they are exploring what is important to them in an authentic and meaningful context (Whitebread 2015). For play to be meaningful, children clearly need to have control over the content of their play and to have choice around themes and objects (Zosh et al. 2018). Meaningful experiences allow children to make connections with what is already known about events, people, places, objects and concepts. Through exploring what is known, in play, children are enabled to reach extended and deeper understandings (Whitebread 2015). Play is actively engaging and involves learning, which is minds-on, as well as hands-on (Mistry, Rogoff and Herman 2001). Hands-on learning involves using all the senses to interact with the world and to integrate the information gained, through explorations, to extend understanding (Blaustein 2005). Active engagement is also minds-on and involves children becoming deeply absorbed in experiences, concentrating and resisting distraction, as they play. Active engagement optimises learning due to what Whitebread (2015: 14), describes as the 'generation effect' – information which is generated or transformed is much more memorable, for young children, than information which is simply received from others.

Zosh and colleagues suggest that the idea of play being iterative is consistent with the Piagetian view of the child as a Little Scientist, constructing their own knowledge and understanding through:

> generating hypotheses, testing those hypotheses and then using the generated data to inform one's own understanding. (Zosh et al. 2018: 7)

As play can be repetitive, children have the opportunity to regularly revisit, revise and expand their hypotheses, which supports their growing competence to solve increasingly complex problems (Liu et al. 2017). Finally, play is also characterised by being socially interactive (Saracho 2012; Bodrova and Leong 2015; Zosh et al. 2018). While play can be solitary and solitary play is associated with many benefits, social play, with both adults and peers, makes a unique contribution to learning. While children learn from playing with a more competent other, according to Bodrova and Leong (2015: 376), social play with peers creates what Vygotsky (1978) originally referred to as a Zone of Proximal Development (ZPD). They propose that, in play, the peer group:

> may collectively act as a 'more knowledgeable other' even if individual children do not differ in their knowledge levels. (Bodrova and Leong 2015: 376)

The type of socially shared processes provoked in collaborative play supports learning through encouraging shared regulation of the play, reducing individual cognitive load, requiring the creation of a joint interpretation and the articulation of internal thoughts and feelings, through extended conversations (Elias and Berk 2002; Monighan Nourot 2015). Socially interactive experiences such as play also promote wellbeing through providing meaningful opportunities for children to develop reciprocal and lasting connections with others (Deci and Ryan 2008; Gray 2015).

Taken together, this evidence suggests that when children engage in playful learning they are happy and motivated and are developing a range of important lifelong learning skills. From an inclusive perspective, it is important that we acknowledge and support all children's capacity for playfulness. Some children, however, have been observed to demonstrate lower levels of engagement in play (Bray and Cooper 2007; Kemp et al. 2013). If we observe lower levels of engagement it is critical to consider how the child's individual needs, the environment and our pedagogical approach, might be inhibiting playful engagement. It is also important to remember that individual children have their own unique play interests, as is often noted in the case of autistic children, we should be careful not undermine any child's potential to thrive in playful learning contexts. A truly inclusive curriculum will enable all children to experience learning which is joyful, meaningful, actively engaging, iterative and socially interactive (Zosh et al. 2018). According to Buchanan and Giovacco Johnson (2009: 45), the play of children with additional needs can challenge the 'grand narratives' of development. Consequently, we need to reflect if all children have the same opportunities for playful learning as their peers and if our own grand narratives, of play, might inhibit the play of diverse learners.

> **Keynote Signposts: Defining Play**
>
> - The characteristics of optimal learning (joyful; meaningful; actively engaging; iterative; and socially interactive) are visible when learning is playful, illustrating the powerful interconnection between play and learning (Zosh et al. 2018).
> - When children engage in playful learning, they are happy and motivated and are developing a range of important lifelong learning skills.
> - It is important that we acknowledge and support all children's capacity for playfulness and provide all children with equal opportunities to learn and develop through play.

Many Ways to Play, Many Ways to Learn and Develop

Focusing on the specific types of play children engage in can also support high-quality inclusive play. It is important that we adopt a broad and balanced approach when attempting to categorise play, as research on play in diverse cultural contexts and on the play of children with additional needs, points to potential difficulties with taking a narrow approach to categorising play. Trawick-Smith (2010), in a study of play in Puerto Rico found that, in this cultural context, play with language was a particularly prevalent form of naturally occurring play, while Eisele and Howard (2012) have found evidence of the characteristics of playfulness in the ritual repetitive behaviours of autistic children. Whitebread (2012) proposes a model involving five main types of play. This model includes physical play (active play, rough and tumble play and fine-motor practice); object play (exploring and experimenting, constructing and making); pretend play; symbolic play (play with symbolic systems such as language, music and visual media) and games with rules. Providing for these five types of play ensures that children reap the benefits of each type of play and it also ensures that the play needs and interests of all children are accommodated. While children will enjoy engaging in different types of play, many will exhibit preferences for specific types of play. For all children, the quantity and quality of play will be influenced by their abilities and interests and each type of play can present its own unique affordances and challenges (Buchanan and Giovacco Johnson 2009).

Physical Play

Active play is the main context in which young children are physically active; and it is associated with many benefits including those for emotional wellbeing, health and fitness, co-ordination and balance, and self-regulation (Pellegrini 2009). Children with additional needs, however, can experience reduced opportunities for physical activity (Sit et al. 2017). This type of play can be particularly challenging for children with additional visual or physical needs and it is important to reflect on how the environment can be adapted or how assistive technology can be used to make active play more feasible (Johnson, Christie and Wardle 2005). Children with additional needs have been observed to enjoy participating in active play as it is not always as reliant on social interaction and communication, as some other types of play (Hestenes and Carroll 2000). Moreover, the sensory processing differences, which some children may experience, can make running, jumping, climbing, spinning and swinging very appealing as such experiences stimulate their proprioception and vestibular systems (Maude 2015; O'Sullivan 2018). Rough and tumble play is characterised by physically vigorous behaviours such as chasing and play-fighting and has similar benefits to physical play (Pellegrini 2009). Children with additional needs may be less likely to be engaged in this type of play, by adults, even though it is important for physical development and self-regulation (Orr 2000). In terms of benefits, the reciprocal role-taking which is a feature of rough and tumble (e.g. alternating between the chaser and the chased) provides opportunities to develop important social skills, in so far as it provides a predictable structure for engagement (Tremblay et al. 1981). Rough and tumble play can also appeal to some autistic children as it can meet their needs for sensory input (El-Ghoroury and Romanczyk 1999). Rough and tumble play opportunities require careful planning and support as adults endeavour to balance children's safety needs with their motivation to engage in this type of play (Pellegrini 2009; Carlson 2011). Fine-motor practice involves activities such as colouring, cutting and manipulating various materials (Whitebread 2012). This type of play supports fine-motor development and control in addition to self-regulation through fostering important concentration and perseverance skills (Whitebread 2012). While engaging in fine-motor practice might be challenging for some children, the provision of adaptive equipment (e.g. adapted scissors and crayons) and adequate adult scaffolding can support the engagement of all learners (Johnson et al. 2005).

Object Play

Play with objects involves using objects and materials to explore and experiment or to construct and make (O'Sullivan 2018). Exploring and experimenting opportunities allow children to find out about the physical world and its objects and materials. While this type of play is particularly attractive to babies and toddlers, young children throughout the early years remain motivated to explore and experiment in their environment and all it contains (Gascoyne 2019). This type of play supports fine-motor skills, self-regulation, language, problem-solving, collaboration and creativity (Goldschmied and Jackson 1994; Whitebread 2012; Gascoyne 2019). It is also a pre-requisite for more advanced play such as constructing and making and pretence. Children, for example, need to have a good understanding of object properties and functions in order to use them symbolically. Research suggests that the exploring and experimenting, of some children with additional needs, can be less sophisticated (Johnson et al. 2005; Kemp et al. 2013). This, however, is often due to lack of opportunity rather than ability or interest (Buchanan et al. 2009). For children with additional visual needs, for example, motivation to reach out and explore the environment can be reduced as they may have more limited awareness of what their environment has to offer (Snell 1997). Careful adult guidance can ensure that all children are given ample opportunity to explore their world.

Constructing and making provides a context through which children can use a range of materials, to create structures, which represent what they know about objects, buildings and so on (Whitebread 2012). This type of play encourages creativity, mathematical understanding, problem-solving, language and self-regulation (Wolfgang, Stannard and Jones 2003; Sarama and Clements 2009; Michnick Golinkoff and Hirsh Pasek 2016). It has been reported that some children can demonstrate less engagement in constructing and making and more stereotypical and less creative, use of objects (Hughes 2010). Children with additional visual needs, for example, may be less motivated to engage in this type of play due to limited visual input and non-visual feedback. For children with additional hearing needs, limited auditory input may reduce information available, from others, in relation to object possibilities (Lewis 2003; Hughes 2010). The tendency of autistic children to engage with objects in ritualistic and stereotypical ways is well documented (Tomchek and Dunn 2007; Eisele and Howard 2012). This is most likely a consequence of having less exploring and experimenting experience, limited joint engagement opportunities and differences with inhibitory control (O'Sullivan 2018). Where children demonstrate less engagement in object play, it is important, again, to consider if this represents a lack of interest and ability or alternatively if it suggests that the physical and social environments are not providing the necessary scaffolding.

Pretend Play

During pretend play, children create non-literal worlds where they assign their own meanings to objects, materials, people and behaviours (Barnett and Owens 2015). Pretend play is associated with a range of developmental accomplishments including emotional wellbeing, self-regulation, social skills, creativity and language and literacy (Smilansky 1990; Michnick Golinkoff and Hirsh Pasek 2016; Whitebread et al. 2017). Whitebread (2012), distinguishes pretend play, which involves using language to develop non-literal scenarios, from symbolic play which involves play with language itself. Children with additional cognitive, visual and hearing needs can experience delays in pretend play development (Lewis 2003; Hughes 2010). A number of factors, most likely, will influence any observable delay in developing pretend play. Firstly, children may have had more limited opportunities to learn through exploring and experimenting resulting in less information about the properties of objects (i.e. in order to transform a cardboard box into a car we need to know something of the properties of a car and cardboard box). Lack of visual or auditory input can also influence pretend play development as much of what children enact in pretence is based on what they see and hear. Children, consequently, may not have as much detail about familiar scripts such as cooking or shopping, for example. A lack of spontaneous pretend play is a recognised feature of autism spectrum differences (ASD) and when these children engage in pretence, it can be less frequent, less complex and more likely to occur under more structured conditions (Kasari, Chang and Patterson 2013). Rather than having a pretend play deficit, autistic children may find pretence less motivating, preferring the more sensory-motor features of play (i.e. spinning the wheels of a toy car is more rewarding than pretending the car is driving to the petrol station). Furthermore, as autistic children tend to engage less in cultural routines and interactions, they may have less social knowledge of roles or they simply may not be as interested in cultural reproduction (recreating roles, events, etc.) (Jarrold and Conn 2011). More limited engagement in exploring and experimenting and differences with joint engagement, can also affect the pretend play ability of autistic children (O'Sullivan 2018). Social pretence with peers can be a particular challenge for children with additional visual, hearing cognitive and language and communication needs due to its improvisational nature and the fact that many important play messages or 'metacommunications' can involve a mixture of verbal and non-verbal communication (Sawyer 1997; Douglas and Sterling 2012; Whitebread and O'Sullivan 2012). Clearly, social pretence is important for promoting pretend play skills and has the net effect of enhancing learning and development across domains (Kasari et al. 2013). Hestanes and Carroll (2005), for example, found that children with additional needs engaged in more talk when engaged in pretend play. It is therefore important that we consider the type of supports, that can foster communication between children with additional needs and their peers, during social pretend play.

Symbolic Play

Symbolic play includes play with language, music and various visual media, allowing children to use a variety of symbol systems to communicate meaning (Whitebread 2012). This type of play has benefits for communication; creativity and self-regulation (Whitebread 2012). Symbolic play can be particularly important for children who are non-verbal or experience language delays as it provides an alternative mechanism for the expression of thoughts and feelings. Buchanan and Giovacco Johnson (2009) provide a lovely illustration of a 32-month-old child, Corey, with cerebral palsy. While this child's capacity to engage in traditional pretend play was limited by significant motor challenges and a reliance on non-verbal communication and sign language, he demonstrated a wonderful interest and capacity to engage in symbolic play with music:

> Corey's play took on a unique form: instead of acting out his thinking in pretend play, he used sign language and gestures understood by his mother to request that she sing about things or events on his mind. (Buchanan and Giovacco Johnson 2009: 49)

Just as many children use pretend play to make meaning of everyday experiences, this little boy, with his mother's support, was able to use symbolic play with music as a mechanism to make sense of everyday events, such as going to the post office. While music may be challenging for children who are highly sensitive to auditory input, it can be highly beneficial for children who enjoy auditory stimulation (Tomchek and Dunn 2007).

Adapting auditory inputs to meet children's individual needs should support all children engaging in play with language and music. Young children are very interested in using media such as drawing, painting and collage to record, represent and communicate their internal feelings and thoughts (Whitebread 2012). This type of play is again invaluable for children with language and communication needs as it offers an important alternative mode of expression (Jolly 2010). This type of play may present challenges for children with additional physical needs but with careful planning and the use of assistive tools, all children should be enabled to enjoy this type of play.

Games with Rules

Games with rules can include simple chase games, physical games, fantasy games, board games, electronic games and more organised sports. Games with rules can vary in terms of how playful they are and they will be more playful when players have choice around playing or not (Baines and Blatchford 2011). Games with rules can support physical development (i.e. physical games), communication, social interaction, self-regulation and democratic values (Piaget 1962; Pellegrini 2009; McClelland and Tominey 2015; Michnick Golinkoff and Hirsh Pasek 2016). Games with rules can appeal to children with additional needs as they offer a level of structure and predictability, which can support engagement and social interaction (Hestanes and Carroll 2000). A lack of structure can often make engaging in more open-ended and improvisational forms of social play, such as pretence, difficult for children with additional cognitive, communication and social needs (Dewey, Lord and Magill 1988). Research by Dewey and colleagues (1988), for example, found that autistic children rated games highest in terms of preference over construction play, pretend play and object play. Game-playing becomes more dominant in school-age children and while games do offer structure, it is important that children, in the early years, are supported with the cognitive (i.e.

remembering rules) and social demands (i.e. turn-taking), of such play (Pellegrini 2009).

Creating Opportunities to Engage in All Types of Play

In a truly inclusive play environment, all learners are supported to engage in all types of play. Research on the play of children with additional needs suggests that, overall, these children demonstrate similar play preferences to their peers (Hestenes and Carroll 2000; Bray and Cooper 2007). Consequently, we have a responsibility to carefully observe the factors, which support or impede individual children's engagement in the different types of play so that we can create inclusive play opportunities where each child benefits from a broad and balanced play diet.

Keynote Signposts: Many Ways to Play: Many Ways to Learn and Develop

- Focusing on the broad types of play children engage in, can support the provision of play opportunities, which meet all children's play needs and interests.
- There are five types of play which support learning and development: physical play, object play, pretend play, symbolic play and games with rules (Whitebread 2012).
- Each type of play can present affordances and challenges for children with additional needs.
- Rather than assuming lack of interest or ability to engage in certain types of play, adults should carefully consider what supports or hinders children's engagement in all play types.

The Potential of Play to Propel Learning and Development

Play is associated with a range of benefits including benefits for wellbeing, self-regulation and social competence (Saracho 2012; Michnick Golinkoff and Hirsh Pasek 2016). It is associated with positive affect and contributes to children's long-term emotional and psychological wellbeing (Gray 2015; King and Howard 2016). As an intrinsically motivating endeavour, play is associated with positive feelings and not with rewards or external evaluation (Gray 2013; 2015). Free-play, in particular, provides an important break from adult-led activities, which can sometimes be emotionally, socially, physically and cognitively demanding for children with additional needs (Mastrangelo 2009). For autistic children, for example, opportunities to engage in preferred activities (even if these are viewed as ritualistic and stereotypical) can support self-regulation, which can then increase feelings of competence when engaging in subsequent adult-led activities (O'Sullivan, Ring and Horgan 2018). Play ultimately promotes wellbeing through providing a low-risk context to learn and develop in, to experience autonomy and a sense of success (Johnson et al. 2005; Pellegrini 2009; Gray 2013; Howard and McInnes 2013; King and Howard 2016; Michnick Golinkoff and Hirsh Pasek 2016). Play also provides the type of collaborative learning context through which children can develop emotionally warm and secure relationships with significant others (Michnick Golinkoff and Hirsh Pasek 2016; O'Sullivan et al. 2018).

Self-regulation skills are now considered a better predictor of longer-term wellbeing and academic achievement than more traditional measures of intelligence (McClelland et al. 2013). Self-regulation (including metacognitive knowledge, metacognitive regulation and motivational and emotional regulation) makes a significant contribution to young children's emerging ability to engage in self-directed learning (Whitebread 2012). Given the associations between self-regulation and academic achievement, it is important that all children have plenty opportunities, in the early years, to develop these skills. For some children with additional needs, delays in development can influence the emergence of self-regulation (Coelho et al. 2018). Given the significance of engagement, for learning, strategies which support children with additional needs to develop important self-regulation skills, are critical to improving educational outcomes (Coelho et al. 2018). Play can naturally foster emerging self-regulation skills, as children will be much more likely to regulate feelings, behaviour and thinking when the activity is of interest, intrinsically motivating and when they have an element of autonomy (Gray 2015; King and Howard 2016). Moreover, in the context of social play, peers provide an important scaffold for the development of these skills (Bodrova and Leong 2015). Overscheduling children's day with various interventions can sometimes reduce the opportunities children with additional needs have to engage in self-directed play (Mastrangelo 2009). Clearly, a truly inclusive curriculum should afford all children opportunities to practice directing their own activity and learning. In addition to child-initiated play, McClelland and Tominey (2015) provide numerous examples of playful games, which educators can use to encourage young children to regulate their own behaviour, thinking and feelings.

Playful learning has the added advantage of promoting social inclusion in a context, which is meaningful, for all children. Being present in mainstream educational settings, however, may be inadequate to promote the full inclusion of children with additional needs, in play (Saracho 2012). Research suggests that membership of the playgroup can sometimes be a challenge for children with additional needs who may be more likely, than their peers, to play alone or to engage in play with adults (Hestenes and Carroll 2000; Brown and Bergen 2002; Bray and Cooper 2007; Saracho 2012). The relationship between play and the social development of children with additional needs is complex. While play is considered a supportive and naturalistic context in which to develop social competence, social and communication differences can create a barrier to engaging in the social play experiences, which propel social competence (Hestenes and Carroll 2000). Sensitive adult scaffolding, which supports children developing the skills needed to initiate and sustain social play with peers should be a pedagogical priority in an inclusive curriculum (Okimoto, Bundy and Hanzlik 2000). Hestenes and Carroll (2000) underscore the importance of supporting peer understanding of individual children's unique needs and interests. This can increase acceptance and empathy and encourages children to differentiate their interactions when playing with the child with additional needs. Moreover, it can increase the success of play interactions, which in turn motivates children to continue to play together.

> ### The Potential of Play to Propel Learning and Development
>
> - Play is associated with a range of benefits including benefits for wellbeing, self-regulation and social competence.
> - Play promotes wellbeing as children experience autonomy and social interaction.
> - Play promotes self-regulation, which is important for engagement and learning achievement.
> - Play promotes social competence through providing a meaningful context in which children with additional needs can develop important social skills.

Curriculum, Play and Inclusion

Aistear: The Early Childhood Curriculum Framework (NCCA 2009) aims for each child to develop as a confident and competent learner through playful emergent inquiry-based learning and reflecting its sociocultural orientation, through interactions with others. Aistear articulates learning as involving a broad range of knowledge and understanding, skills, dispositions, attitudes and values (NCCA 2009). It is an integrated and holistic framework, which sees children learning many things at the same time and places equal value on all areas of learning and development. Given that Aistear is intended to be a flexible and guiding framework, the Aistear guidelines for good practice (NCCA 2009) and the Aistear Síolta Practice Guide (NCCA 2015) offer further guidance in relation to welcoming and valuing difference and ensuring that all children are fully included and supported to achieve their potential. The flexible and emergent orientation of Aistear lends itself to learning experiences, which are based on individual children's strengths and interests (NCCA 2009). Odom and colleagues (2011), identify this type of individualisation as a measure of the quality of inclusive early childhood education. While Aistear (NCCA 2009) clearly articulates a playful and inclusive curriculum, developing a playful pedagogical approach requires a deliberate and reflective focus that acknowledges the complexity of moving towards a model of playful learning, which is responsive to all children's learning needs and interests (Moyles 2010; Ring and O'Sullivan 2019).

> Keynote Signposts: Curriculum, Play and Inclusion
>
> - Aistear: The Early Childhood Curriculum Framework (National Council for Curriculum and Assessment (NCCA) 2009) sets out what children should learn and develop in the early years and provides guidance in relation to how this learning and development can be supported. It identifies play as a key context through which children learn and develop.
> - Aistear (NCCA 2009) promotes an inclusive emergent and inquiry-based curriculum where each child is valued and welcomed and supported to reach their potential.
> - Developing a playful pedagogical approach requires a deliberate and reflective focus that acknowledges the complexity of moving towards a model of playful learning, which is responsive to all children's learning needs and interests (Ring and O'Sullivan 2019).

Effective Pedagogy for Inclusive Playful Learning

Wood (2009), defines a pedagogy of play as making

> provision for play and playful approaches to learning and teaching, how they design play/learning environments, and all the pedagogical decisions, techniques and strategies they use to support or enhance learning and teaching through play. (Wood 2009: 27)

Siraj-Blatchford and Sylva (2004) further delineate pedagogical framing (aspects of pedagogy which include planning, resources and establishment of routines), from pedagogical interactions (specific adult behaviours during learning experiences). While the research supports the view that play is an effective medium through which children can be supported to work towards a range of curriculum learning goals (Michnik Golinkoff and Hirsh-Pasek 2016; Weisberg et al. 2016), there is a danger that the global education reform movement (GERM) coupled with the 'play as education' rhetoric may, inadvertently, reduce opportunities for play in the curriculum (Saracho 2012; Wood and Chesworth 2017; Sahlberg and Doyle 2019). Consequently, it is imperative to find a mechanism for harnessing the potential of play without eroding the very qualities, which optimise learning. Zosh and colleagues (2018), argue for redefining play as a spectrum, which incorporates free-play, guided-play and playful structured activities. Such an approach alleviates concerns that children's learning may not be maximised in free-play and creates important connections across all learning experiences. Playfulness, as such, becomes

> characteristic of the interaction between adult and the child and not just characteristic of child-initiated versus adult-initiated activities, or of play-time versus task-time. (Walsh et al. 2011:107)

Achieving this intricate balance of child- and adult-initiated playful learning can be particularly difficult for children with additional needs whose educational experience can be more tightly structured and teacher controlled (Mastrangelo 2009).

Pedagogical Framing for Inclusive Playful Learning

Generally speaking, children need in the region of one hour to plan, develop and sustain complex play (Miller and Almon 2009). An individualised approach should be adopted for children with additional needs and through careful assessment, educators can determine if time allocation is appropriate. As with all children, we would hope that children with additional needs would become more able for extended engagement in free-play, with time and experience in the educational setting.

The Reggio Emilia curriculum emphasises the early learning environment as a third teacher, in light of its potential to promote positive interactions and learning (Gandini 2012). This is discussed further by the authors in Chapter 8. The recently launched Universal Design (UD) Guidelines for Early Learning and Care Settings, provide guidance on how early learning environments can be designed so that they can be accessed, understood and used to their potential by all people, irrespective of ability (Grey et al. 2019). In terms of the indoor play environment, centres (i.e. pretend play area) with their own specific play materials can offer children with additional needs an element of structure and predictability (Ring et al. 2019). Clearly identified boundaries and pathways between these centres can also promote independent play. Structured centres should be complemented with more open-ended areas, which do not suggest any one way of playing as these areas can increase social interaction and creativity (Broadhead 2010). Moreover, large open spaces increase opportunities for children to play together in larger groups and may be particularly important in allowing space for children with additional physical needs to come together with others (Ring et al. 2019). Extra supports such as visual cues for children with additional hearing or language needs or tactile cues for children with visual needs can support children independently navigating their play environment.

Opportunities to play in the natural and dynamic outdoor environment make an important contribution to the learning and development of all children (Tovey 2007). Similar consideration should be given to supporting children to independently navigate the outdoor environment through reflecting carefully on the layout and ensuring a balance of designated and more open-ended play spaces (Ring et al. 2019). The outdoor environment has many affordances – it allows more space which can increase children's confidence to engage in certain types of play (Bray and Cooper 2007). It also has significant advantages in terms of the sensory stimulation more natural spaces can afford (Brewer 2016). For children with additional needs, in particular, educators can find it challenging to balance children's play needs with their health and safety needs when playing outside (Ring et al. 2019). As Tovey (2007), suggests we should aim to make the outdoor environment, safe enough rather than as safe as possible.

Toys and play materials also have a significant influence on the quality of play as 90 per cent of play involves toys or play materials (Trawick-Smith, Russell and Swaminathan 2010). The interests of children should clearly inform the provision of toys and play materials as interest is critical to fostering motivation and engagement. In so far as possible, storage and displays should be easily accessible to all children. Children will benefit from opportunities to revisit favoured toys and play materials but also from the gradual and ongoing introduction of novel resources (Ring et al. 2019). Educators need to assess the affordance of toys and play materials as underestimation of children's play abilities can sometimes lead to the provision of less complex materials, for children with additional needs (Hughes 2010). Consideration should be given to the potential of toys and play materials to promote autonomy, social interaction and thinking and learning behaviours (Trawick-Smith et al. 2014). It is also important to balance specific toys and materials with more open-ended or loose parts materials (Trawick-Smith et al. 2014). While open-ended resources might have an edge for creativity and problem-solving, more structured toys and play materials can offer an important scaffold for children with additional needs. The provision of realistic props, for example, has been found to increase the quantity and quality of the pretence of younger learners and those with additional needs (Hestenes and Carroll 2000; Doctoroff 2001). The quantity of materials provided is also worthy of reflection as a room overly packed with resources may prove distracting and overly stimulating, potentially creating a barrier to engagement in sustained complex play (Howard and McInnes 2013). Overall, the toys and play materials available in the educational setting should reflect the diverse play needs and interests of its community of learners. In some circumstances this may require such resources to be adapted to meet the needs of children with specific physical or sensory needs (Doctoroff 2001).

Pedagogical Interactions for Inclusive Playful Learning

During play, educators may need to calibrate their interactions to meet the needs of individual children. For example, a child with additional needs may require more guidance than might usually be given to plan, engage and sustain play, particularly social play with peers. Educators can support play through engaging children in play planning and through encouraging them becoming more intentional and engaged in their play (Bodrova and Leong 2007). Critically, educators need to provide the emotional warmth and security which is pre-requisite to engaging in playing and learning (Whitebread and Cotman 2011). This can be achieved through showing a genuine interest in children's play ideas, supporting autonomy, engaging playfully and providing just the right level of guidance (Whitebread and Coltman 2011). During play, simple strategies such as modelling (i.e. how a particular role is enacted in pretend play), suggesting (i.e. the possibilities for constructing with bricks), open-ended questioning (i.e. what is happening when we mix the sand with the water?) describing (i.e. that the play-dough is soft and sticky) and reflecting (i.e. that the child enjoyed running in the grass), can be highly effective in guiding children's play in a manner which does not erode its child-initiated qualities. Moreover, this type of adult scaffolding should have the net effect of enhancing independent play with peers as young children with additional needs generalise the play skills being developed in the context of adult guided-play.

Promoting social interactions between peers is a key aim of inclusive programming. There are many strategies which can be used to support children with additional needs engaging, meaningfully, with peers. More structured approaches such as Wolfberg's (2003) Integrated Play Groups® (IPG) have been shown to increase the social play of autistic children and can be used alongside naturally occurring play. Children with certain additional needs may engage in play, at a level, developmentally below their peers (Odom and Diamond 1998; Bray and Cooper 2007). Consequently, educators need to consider if opportunities to play in mixed-aged groups might have an advantage in terms of scaffolding play skills (Odom and Diamond 1998; Gray 2013). Peer buddy systems can also be effective in promoting social play in inclusive settings (Odom and Diamond 1998). Educators directing who plays with whom can be problematic, however, as when educators act as social engineers it can alter the autonomy inherent in play (Trawick-Smith 2006; King and Howard 2016). Assessment and evaluation of local needs, in each educational setting, will allow educators to carefully reflect on what approach works bests for individual learners.

Educators can also support the play of children with additional needs, away from the play itself. Opportunities to plan for, and review, play are important for all children to the extent that they provide opportunities for children to reflect upon and articulate their thinking (Schweinhart and Weikart 1997; Bodrova and Leong 2007; Whitebread and Coltman 2011). Creative use of verbal and visual cues and props can engage children with diverse needs, in the review process. Providing children with direct experiences of topics, which are of particular interest to them, can also support engagement in play (Smilansky 1990; Karpov 2005). An interest in cars, for example, could be extended through a visit to the Petrol Station, through fiction and-non-fiction books about cars, accessing video clips or engaging in extended projects. Such an approach builds children's knowledge and understanding which can then be used and elaborated upon, in play. Ultimately, careful observation and assessment ensure that educators have a good understanding of individual children's play abilities and interests. Only then, can interactions be calibrated to respond to, and maximise upon, each learner's unique needs and interests, which remains a key principle of pedagogy and curriculum at ELC and primary level in Ireland (NCCA 1999; 2009; 2020).

> ### Keynote Signposts: Effective Pedagogy for Inclusive Playful Learning
>
> - Inclusive play can be promoted through pedagogical framing and pedagogical interactions (Siraj-Blatchford and Sylva 2004).
> - Pedagogical framing involves adults scheduling play, organising the indoor and outdoor learning environment and providing toys and play materials, which nurture inclusive play.
> - Pedagogical interactions both within and outside of the play, when attuned to individual children's play needs and interests, support engagement and learning.

Conclusion: Building and Sustaining High-Quality Inclusive Play

The research evidence clearly articulates that the learning and development of children, with additional needs, are optimised within an inclusive educational environment (Odom and Diamond 1998; Kemp et al. 2012). While opportunities for inclusive play are identified as a key feature of high-quality inclusive early years programmes, providing the type of inclusive play, which allows all children to flourish requires early childhood teachers to adopt a deliberate and reflective focus that acknowledges the complexity of moving towards an effective and responsive model of playful learning (Ring and O'Sullivan 2019). Going forward, the possibilities for all children inherent in building and sustaining high-quality inclusive play are limitless and it therefore remains our collective responsibility to continue to develop evidence-based practices which uphold the rights of all children to learn and develop through play.

Bibliography

Baines, E., and Blatchford, P. (2011). 'Children's Games and Playground Activities in School and Their Role in Development'. In A. D. Pellegrini (ed), *The Oxford Handbook of the Development of Play*, pp. 260–283. Oxford: Oxford University Press.

Barnett, L. A., and Owens, M. H. (2015). 'Does Play Have to Be Playful?'. In J. E. Johnson, S. G. Eberle, T. S. Henricks, and D. Kuschner (eds), *The Handbook of the Study of Play*, pp. 453–460. Lanham: Rowan & Littlefield.

Blaustein, M. (2005). 'See, Hear, Touch: The Basics of Learning Readiness', *Beyond the Journal: Young Children on the Web*. Washington, DC: National Association for the Education of Young Children, <http://citeseerx.ist.psu.edu/viewdoc/download;jsessionid=4B5AA77762FEAFFA9C52616D034ABC5E?doi=10.1.1.588.4838&rep=rep1&type=pdf>, accessed 09 September 2020.

Bodrova, E., and Leong, D. J. (2007). *Tools of the Mind: The Vygotskian Approach to Early Childhood Education*. Upper Saddle River, NJ: Pearson Merrill Prentice Hall.

Bodrova, E., and Leong, D. J. (2015). 'Vygotskian and Post-Vygotskian Views on Children's Play', *American Journal of Play*, 7(3), 371–388.

Bray, P., and Cooper, R. (2007). 'The Play of Children with Special Needs in Mainstream and Special Education Settings', *Australian Journal of Early Childhood Education*, 32(2), 36–42.

Brewer, K. (2016). 'Nature Is the Best Way to Nurture Pupils with Special Educational Needs', *The Guardian*, 1 May, <https://www.theguardian.com/teacher-network/2016/may/01/nature-nurture-pupils-special-educational-needs-outdoor-education>, accessed 8 December 2019.

Broadhead, P. (2010). 'Cooperative Play and Learning from Nursery to Year One'. In P. Broadhead, J. Howard, and E. Wood (eds), *Play and Learning in the Early Years*, pp. 43–60. London: Sage.

Brown, M., and Bergen, D. (2002). 'Play and Social Interaction of Children with Disabilities at Learning/Activity Centers in an Inclusive Preschool', *Journal of Research in Early Childhood Education*, 17(1), 26–37.

Buchanan, M., and Giovacco Johnson, T. (2009). 'A Second Look at the Play of Children with Disabilities', *American Journal of Play*, 2(1), 41–59.

Carlson, F. (2011). 'Rough Play: One of the Most Challenging Behaviours', *Young Children*, July 2011, 18–25.

Coelho, V., Cadima, J., Pinto A. I., and Guimaraes, C. (2018). 'Self-Regulation, Engagement, and Developmental Functioning in Preschool-Aged Children', *Journal of Early Intervention*, 41(2), 1–20.

Deci, E. L., and Ryan, R. M. (2008). 'Self-Determination Theory: A Macrotheory of Human Motivation, Development and Health', *Canadian Psychology*, 49(3), 182–185.

Dewey, S., Lord, C., and Magill, J. (1988). 'Qualitative Assessment of the Effect of Play Materials in Dyadic Peer Interactions of Children with Autism', *Canadian Journal of Psychology*, 42(2), 242–260.

Doctoroff, S. (2001). 'Adapting the Physical Environment to Meet the Needs of All Young Children for Play', *Early Childhood Education Journal*, 29(2), 105–109.

Douglas, S., and Stirling, L. (2012). 'Metacommunication, Social Pretend Play and Children with Autism', *Australasian Journal of Early Childhood*, 37(4), 34–43.

Eisele, G., and Howard, J. (2012). 'Exploring the Presence of Characteristics Associated with Play within the Ritual Repetitive Behaviour of Autistic Children', *International Journal of Play*, 1(2), 139–150.

Elias, C. L., and Berk, L. E. (2002). 'Self-Regulation in Young Children: Is There a Role for Sociodramatic Play?', *Early Childhood Research Quarterly*, 17(2), 216–238.

El-Ghoroury, N. H., and Romanczyk, R. (1999). 'Play Interactions of Family Members towards Children with Autism', *Journal of Autism and Developmental Disorders*, 29(3), 249–258.

Gandini, L. (2012). 'Connecting through Caring and Learning Spaces'. In C. Edwards, L. Gandini, and G. Foreman (eds), *The Hundred Languages of Children* (3rd ed.), pp. 317–341. Santa Barbara, CA: PRAEGER.

Gascoyne, S. (2019). 'Coming to Our Senses', *Teach Nursery*, 40–43, <https://www.teachearlyyears.com/images/uploads/article/supporting-sensory-play.pdf>, accessed 09 September 2020.

Goldschmied, E., and Jackson, S. (1994). *People under Three: Young Children in Day-Care*. Abingdon: Routledge.

Gray, P. (2013). *Free to Learn: Why Unleashing the Instinct to Play Will Make Our Children Happier, More Self-Reliant and Better Students for Life*. New York, NY: Basic Books.

Gray, P. (2015). 'Studying Play without Calling It that: Humanistic and Positive Psychology'. In J. Johnson, S. Eberle, T. Henricks, and D. Kuschner (eds), *The Handbook of the Study of Play*, pp. 121–138. New York, NY: Rowman & Littlefield.

Grey, T. Corbett, M., Sheerin, J., Heeney, T., Ring, E., and O'Sullivan, L. (2019). *Universal Design Guidelines for Early Learning and Care Settings*. Dublin: Department of Children and Youth Affairs in collaboration with the Centre for Universal Design and the National Disability Authority, <https://aim.gov.ie/wp-content/uploads/2019/06/universal-design-guidelines-for-elc-settings-introduction-1.pdf>, accessed 30 December 2019.

Hestenes, L. E., and Caroll, D. E. (2000). 'The Play Interactions of Young Children with and without Disabilities: Individual and Environmental Influences', *Early Childhood Research Quarterly*, 15(2), 229–246.

Howard, J., and McInnes, K. (2013). *The Essence of Play: A Practice Companion for Professionals Working with Children and Young People*. London: Routledge.

Hughes, F. P. (2010). *Children, Play and Development* (4th ed.). Newbury Park, CA: Sage.

Ireland. (2004). *Education for Persons with Special Educational Needs Act, 2004*. Dublin: The Government Publications Office.

Jarrold, C., and Conn, C. (2011). 'The Development of Play in Children with Autism'. In A. D. Pellegrini (ed), *The Oxford Handbook of the Development of Play*, pp. 308–321. Oxford: Oxford University Press.

Johnson, J., Christie, J., and Wardle, F. (2005). *Play Development and Early Education*. Boston, MA: Pearson Merrill Prentice Hall.

Jolly, R. P. (2010). *Children and Pictures: Drawing and Understanding*. Sussex: Wiley Blackwell.

Karpov, Y. V. (2005). *The Neo-Vygotskian Approach to Child Development*. Cambridge: Cambridge University Press.

Kasari, C., Chang, Y., and Patterson, S. (2013). 'Pretending to Play or Playing to Pretend: The Case of Autism', *American Journal of Play*, 2(4), 124–135.

Kemp, C., Kishida, Y., Carter, M., and Sweller, N. (2013). 'The Effect of Activity Type on the Engagement of Children with Disabilities in Inclusive Childcare Settings', *Early Childhood Research Quarterly*, 28, 134–143.

King, P., and Howard, J. (2016). 'Free Choice or Adaptable Choice: Self-Determination Theory and Play'. *The American Journal of Play*, 9(1), 56–70.

Lewis, V. (2003). *Development and Disability* (2nd ed.). Oxford: Blackwell Publishing.

Liu, C., Solis, S. L., Jensen, H., Hopkins, E., Neale, D., Zosh, J., Hirsh-Pasek, K., and Whitebread, D. (2017). *Neuroscience and Learning through Play: A Review of the Evidence*. Billund, Denmark: The Lego Foundation.

Mastrangelo, S. (2009). 'Harnessing the Power of Play: Opportunities for Children with Autistic Spectrum Disorders', *Teaching Exceptional Children*, 42(1), 34–44.

Maude, P. (2015). "How Do I Do This Better?' From Movement into Physical Literacy'. In D. Whitebread and P. Coltman (eds), *Teaching and Learning in the Early Years* (4th ed.), pp. 209–228. Abingdon: Routledge.

McClelland, M. M., Acock, A. C., Piccinin, A., Rhea, S. A., and Stallings, M. C. (2013). 'Relations between Preschool Attention Span-Persistence and Age 25 Educational Outcomes', *Early Childhood Research Quarterly*, 28(2), 314–324.

McClelland, M. M., and Tominey, S. L. (2015). *Stop, Think, Act: Integrating Self-Regulation in the Early Childhood Classroom*. New York, NY: Routledge.

Michnick Golinfoff, R., and Hirsh-Pasek, K. (2016). *Becoming Brilliant: What Science Tells Us about Raising Successful Children*. Washington, DC: American Psychological Association.

Miller, E., and Almon, J. (2009). *Crisis in the Kindergarten: Why Children Need to Play in School*. College Park, MD: Alliance for Childhood.

Mistry, J., Rogoff, B., and Herman, H. (2001). 'What is the Meaning of Meaningful Purpose in Children's Remembering? Istomina Revisited', *Mind, Culture, and Society*, 8(1), 28–41.

Monighan Nourot, P. (2015). 'Sociodramatic Play: Pretending Together'. In D. Fromberg and D. Bergen (eds), *Play from Birth to Twelve. Contexts,*

Perspectives and Meanings (3rd ed.), pp. 119–134. New York, NY: Routledge Taylor and Francis Group.

Moyles, J. (2010). 'Practitioner Reflection on Play and Playful Pedagogies'. In J. Moyles (ed.), *Thinking about Play: Developing a Reflective Approach*, pp. 13–29. Maidenhead: Open University Press.

National Council for Curriculum and Assessment. (1999). *Primary School Curriculum*. Dublin: The Stationery Office, <https://curriculumonline.ie/getmedia/93de2707-f25e-4bee-9035-92b00613492e/Introduction-to-primary-curriculum.pdf>, accessed 04 July 2020.

National Council for Curriculum and Assessment. (2009). *Aistear: The Early Childhood Curriculum Framework*. Dublin: National Council for Curriculum and Assessment, <https://www.ncca.ie/en/early-childhood/aistear>, accessed 29 October 2019.

National Council for Curriculum and Assessment. (2015). *Aistear/Síolta Practice Guide*. Dublin: National Council for Curriculum and Assessment, <www.ncca.ie/en/Practice-Guide>, accessed 04 July 2020.

National Council for Curriculum and Assessment. (2020). *Draft Primary Curriculum Framework. for Consultation*. Dublin: National Council for Curriculum and Assessment, <https://ncca.ie/media/4456/ncca-primary-curriculum-framework-2020.pdf>, accessed 06 September 2020.

Odom, S. L., Buysse, V., and Soukakou, E. (2011). 'Inclusion for Young Children with Disabilities: A Quarter of a Century of Research Perspectives', *Journal of Early Intervention*, 33, 344–356.

Odom, S. L., and Diamond, K. E. (1998). 'Inclusion of Young Children with Special Educational Needs in Early Childhood Education: The Research Base', *Early Childhood Research Quarterly*, 13(1), 3–25.

Okimoto, A. M., Bundy, A., and Hanzlik, J. (2000). 'Playfulness in Children with and without Disability: Measurement and Intervention', *American Journal of Occupational Therapy*, 54(1), 73–82.

Orr, R. (2000). *My Right to Play: A Child with Complex Needs*. Maidenhead: Open University Press.

O'Sullivan, L. (2018). 'A Right to Play: Our Responsibility to Include Play in the Curriculum for Children with Autism Spectrum Difference'. In E. Ring, P. Daly, and E. Wall (eds), *Autism from the Inside Out: Signposts for Parents, Early Childhood, Primary, Post-Primary and Special School Settings*, pp. 45–66. Oxford: Peter Lang.

O'Sullivan, L., and Ring, E. (2018). 'Play as Learning: Implications for Educators and Parents from Findings of a National Evaluation of School Readiness in Ireland', *International Journal of Play*, 7(3), 266–289.

O'Sullivan, L., Ring, E., and Horgan, K. (2018). 'The Power of Play to Promote Wellbeing and Connections with Others in Children with Autism Spectrum Differences', *Children's Research Digest*, 5(2), 59–65.

Pellegrini, A. D. (2009). *The Role of Play in Human Development*. New York, NY: Oxford University Press.

Piaget, J. (1962). *Play, Dreams and Imitation in Childhood* (Translated by C. Gattegno and F. M. Hodgson). New York, NY: W.W. Norton & Company Inc.

Ring, E., Grey, T., O'Sullivan, L., Corbett, M., Sheerin, J., and Heeney, T. (2019). *Universal Design Guidelines for Early Learning and Care Settings: Literature Review*. Dublin: Department of Children and Youth Affairs in collaboration with the Centre for Universal Design and the National Disability Authority, <https://aim.gov.ie/wp-content/uploads/2019/06/universal-design-guidelines-for-elc-settings-literature-review-2.pdf>, accessed 3 January 2020.

Ring, E., and O' Sullivan, L. (2019). 'Creating Spaces Where Diversity Is the Norm, an Innovative Competency-Based Blended Learning Teacher Education Program in Ireland', *Childhood Education*, 95(2), 29–39.

Sahlberg, P., and Doyle, M. (2019). *Let the Children Play: How More Play Will Save Our Schools and Help Children Thrive*. New York, NY: Oxford University Press.

Saracho, O. N. (2012). *An Integrated Play-Based Curriculum for Young Children*. New York, NY: Routledge.

Sarama, J., and Clemments, D. H. (2009). 'Building Blocks and Cognitive Building Blocks: Playing to Know the World Mathematically', *American Journal of Play*, 1, 313–337.

Sawyer, K. R. (1997). *Pretend Play as Improvisation: Conversations in the Preschool Classroom*. New Jersey: Lawrence Erlbaum Associates Publishers.

Schweinhart, L. J., and Weikart, D. P. (1997). *Lasting Differences: The HighScope Preschool Curriculum Comparison Study through Age 23. Monographs of the HighScope Educational Research Foundation, 12*. Ypsilanti, MI: HighScope Press.

Siraj-Blatchford, I., and Sylva, K. (2004). 'Researching Pedagogy in English Preschools', *British Educational Research Journal*, 30(5), 713–730.

Sit, C. H. P., McKenzie, T. L., Cerin, E., Chow, B. C., Huang, W. Y., and Yu, J. (2017). 'Physical Activity and Sedentary Time among Children with Disabilities at School', *Medicine and Science in Sports and Exercise*, 49(2), 292–297.

Smilansky, S. (1990). 'Sociodramatic Play: Its Relevance to Behavior and Achievement in School'. In E. Klugman and S. Smilansky (eds), *Children's Play and Learning. Perspectives and Policy Implications*, pp. 198–142. New York, NY: Teachers College Press.

Snell, R. (1997). 'Gross Motor Development in Infants with Motor Disabilities'. In D. Chen (ed), *Effective Practices in Early Intervention: Infants Whose Multiples Disabilities Include Both Vision and Hearing Loss*. Northridge, CA: California State University, <https://files.eric.ed.gov/fulltext/ED406795.pdf>, accessed 8 August 2019.

Tomchek, S. D., and Dunn, W. (2007). 'Sensory Processing in Children with and without Autism: A Comparative Study Using the Short Sensory Profile', *The American Journal of Occupational Therapy*, 61(2), 190–200.

Tovey, H. (2007). *Playing Outdoors: Spaces and Places, Risk and Challenge*. London: McGraw-Hill Education.

Trawick-Smith, J. (2006). 'Social Play in School'. In D. Fromberg and D. Bergen (eds), *Play from Birth to Twelve. Contexts, Perspectives and Meanings* (2nd ed.), pp. 173–180. New York, NY: Routledge Taylor & Francis Group.

Trawick-Smith, J. (2010). 'Drawing Back the Lens on Play: A Frame Analysis of Young Children's Play in Puerto Rico', *Early Education and Development*, 21(4), 1–32.

Trawick-Smith, J., Russell, H., and Swamnathan, S. (2010). 'Measuring the Effects of Toys on the Problem-Solving, Creative and Social Behaviours of Preschool children', *Early Childhood Development and Care*, 181(7), 909–927.

Trawick-Smith, J., Wolff, J., Koschel, M., and Vallarelli, J. (2014). 'Which Toys Promote High-quality Play? Reflections on the Five Year Anniversary of the TIMPANI Toy Study', *Young Children*, 69(2), 40–47.

Tremblay, A., Strain, P. S., Hendrickson, J. M., and Shores, R. E. (1981). 'Social Interactions of Normal Preschool Children: Using Normative Data for Subject and Target Behaviour Selection', *Behaviour Modification*, 5(2), 237–253.

Vygotsky, L. S. (1978). *Mind in Society. The Development of Higher Psychological Processes* (M. Cole, V. John-Steiner, S. Scribner, and E. Souberman, eds). Cambridge, MA: Harvard University Press.

Walsh, G., Sproule, L., McGuiness, C., and Trew, K. (2011). 'Playful Structure: A Novel Image of Early Years Pedagogy for Primary School Classrooms', *Early Years*, 31, 107–119.

Weisberg, D. S., Hirsh-Pasek, K., Michnick Golinkoff, R., Kittredge, A. K., and Klahr, D. (2016). 'Guided Play: Principles and Practices', *Current Directions in Psychological Science*, 25(3), 177–182.

Whitebread, D. (2012). *Developmental Psychology and Early Childhood Education*. London: Sage.

Whitebread, D. (2015). 'Young Children Learning and Early Years Teaching'. In D. Whitebread and P. Coltman (eds), *Teaching and Learning in the Early Years* (4th ed.), pp. 1–21. London: Routledge.

Whitebread, D., and Coltman, P. (2011) 'Young Children as Self-Regulating Learners'. In J. Moyles, J. Georgeson, and J. Payler (eds), *Beginning Teaching: Beginning Learning: In Early Years and Primary Education*, pp. 122–138. Maidenhead: Open University Press.

Whitebread, D., Neale, D., Jensen, H., Liu, C., Solis, S. L., Hopkins, E., Hirsh-Pasek, K., and Zosh, J. M. (2017). *The Role of Play in Children's Development: A Review of the Evidence*. Billund, Denmark: The LEGO Foundation.

Whitebread, D., and O'Sullivan, L. (2012). 'Preschool Children's Social Pretend Play: Supporting the Development of Metacommunication, Metacognition and Self-regulation', *International Journal of Play*, 1(2), 197–213.

Wolfberg, P. J. (2003). *Peer Play and the Autism Spectrum: The Art of Guiding Children's Socialization and Imagination*. Kansas, MO: Autism Asperger Publishing Co.

Wolfgang, C., Stannard, L., and Jones, I. (2003). 'Advanced Constructional Play with LEGOs among Preschoolers as a Predictor of Later School Achievement in Mathematics', *Early Child Development and Care*, 173, 467–475.

Wood, E. (2013). *Play, Learning and the Early Childhood Curriculum* (3rd ed.). London: Sage.

Wood, E., and Chesworth, L. (2017). 'Play and Pedagogy'. In J. Payler, J. Georgeson, and E. Wood (eds), *BERA/TACTYC Early Childhood Research Academic Review 2003-2017*, British Educational Research Association and Association for Professional Development in Early Years, <http://www.childrens-mathematics.net/BERA-TACTYC-Full-Report.pdf>, accessed 9 September 2020.

Zosh, J., Hirsh-Pasek, K., Hopkins, E. J., Jensen, H., Liu, C., Neale, D., Solis, S. L., and Whitebread, D. (2018). 'Accessing the Inaccessible: Redefining Play as a Spectrum', *Frontiers in Psychology*, 9, 1124, <https://www.frontiersin.org/articles/10.3389/fpsyg.2018.01124/full>, accessed 09 September 2020.

SARAH KELLEHER AND EDEL FENLON

Chapter 8 Making the Environment the Third Teacher

ABSTRACT
The competencies associated with leading inclusion in the early years identified by the Leadership for INClusion in the Early Years (LINC) Programme Consortium highlight the importance of child-centred stimulating environments that are warm and inviting, and representative of the culture, values, attitudes and ideas of all the stakeholders (LINC 2016–2020; Ring et al. 2019). Recognising the environment as a third teacher can contribute significantly to the creation of an inclusive early childhood environment where all children can flourish. Stemming from the philosophy of early childhood education developed in Reggio Emilia in Northern Italy, this chapter, explores research concerning the potential of the environment as a third teacher. Throughout the chapter the implications of this research for early childhood teachers in early learning and care (ELC), primary and special school settings are identified in order to support all children's wellbeing, learning and development from the outset (Edwards, Gandini and Foreman 2012).

Introduction

Based on the concept of the environment as a third teacher, this chapter will explore how different environments create different expectations for children and impact on their wellbeing, learning and development (Edwards, Gandini and Forman, 2012; Ring, 2018a). The three dimensions of the environment isolated by Pairman and Terreni (2001) – the physical, temporal and interactional environments – will be deconstructed and applied specifically to providing for children in early childhood environments. The negative impact of chaotic environments on young children's wellbeing will be considered and the importance of communicating with parents in relation to the role of the environment in their children's wellbeing will be highlighted. Reference will be made to the range of supports that can be provided in the environment to stimulate children's interest and support their engagement, such as visual schedules; clearly delineated areas; well-organised and accessible materials, in addition to the importance of creating attractive areas where the child can take movement breaks and have opportunities to self-regulate (Feeney 2018; Ring 2018a).

The Reggio Emilia Approach to Early Childhood Education

The Reggio Emilia approach to early childhood education is an approach to early childhood education, underpinned by a unique philosophy of education (Edwards et al. 2012). This unique approach originated in the city of Reggio Emilia in Northern Italy, and developed following the devastation of the area during the Second World War. A significant factor in its development, was the coming together of the community to create this pioneering approach grounded in parental collaboration and the education of young children in a democratic manner (Edwards et al. 2012). Loris Malaguzzi was the principal founder of the approach; his pioneering ideas for education were influenced by a variety of philosophies of education including those espoused by Friedrich Froebel (1782–1852); John Dewey (1859–1952); Maria Montessori (1870–1952); Lev Vygotsky (1896–1934); Jean Piaget (1896–1980) and Erik Erikson (1902–1994) (Edwards et al. 2012; Ring 2018a). The Reggio Emilia experience evolved over the last sixty years to encompass its own set of innovative pedagogical and philosophical assumptions, that foster 'children's intellectual development through a systematic focus on symbolic representation' (Edwards et al. 2012: 6). Children are encouraged to explore and experiment in their environments with peers and early childhood teachers. Communication, expression and reflection are core competencies; and learning processes are the focus rather than repetitive practising of specific skills (Edwards et al. 2012). Furthermore, Reggio Emilia is viewed as an inclusive community where Malguzzi recognised that children with additional needs stimulate early childhood teachers to broaden pedagogical practices for all children (Soncini 2012). Children with additional needs are typically referred to as children with 'special rights', recognising the variety of differences of all learners and the rights of all children to enriching early childhood experiences (Soncini 2012).

Internationally the Reggio Emilia approach is held in high regard and has been hugely influential in the pedagogy and practice of early childhood education internationally in recent decades (Gardner 2012). Dahlberg, Moss and Pence (1999) explored quality early childhood experiences and established that quality experiences are inextricably linked with specific historical and cultural dimensions. With this in mind, a Reggio Emilia approach cannot be transferred directly to another jurisdiction as it is culturally and historically linked to the city of Reggio Emilia (Edwards et al. 2012). However we can adopt and adapt the principles underpinning this approach in order to meet the unique needs and cultural contexts of our own early childhood settings. Edwards et al. (2012: 15) outline the key terms or areas of discourse most commonly referred to in respect of this approach: 'visibility, context, pedagogical documentation, projected curriculum, image of the child, education as relationship, revisiting, cognitive knots and participation'. These key terms are summarised in Table 8.1.

The Reggio Emilia approach is similar to the pedagogy and practice supported in the Irish national context, in that it promotes a childhood which is celebrated as a 'time of being' (National Council for Curriculum and Assessment (NCCA) 2009: 6) and endorses a child-centred approach that acknowledges the bioecological lens referred to in Chapter 1 previously (NCCA 1999; 2015; 2019; 2020; Centre for Early Childhood Development and Education (CECDE) 2007). The approach also aligns with the principles articulated in Chapter 2 and reflects Article 12 of the United Nations (UN) Convention on the Rights of the Child (UNCRC) in recognising that children have the right to have their opinions taken into account and their views respected in relation to decision-making that affects them (UN 1989).

Table 8.1. Key Terms Associated with the Pedagogy and Practice of a Reggio Emilia Approach to Early Childhood Education

• *Visibility*: Public visibility of early childhood settings, championing the significant time that is childhood and early years education on the education continuum. • *Context*: Recognition of Reggio Emilia as a culturally and geographically specific context. • *Pedagogical Documentation*: Is a means through which learning is made visible to children, families and the wider community. • *Projected Curriculum*: Curriculum centred on project-based learning, which involves children, teachers, parents and the wider community. • *Image of the Child*: Image of the child as competent, strong, powerful and rich in potential. • *Education as Relationship*: Education, which focuses on interactions as a central premise of learning, with a core focus on building and sustaining relationships. • *Revisiting*: Linked to pedagogical documentation, where children can revisit and recall previous learning experiences, the teacher notes events of the day and revisits or often recaps this information with the children to promote reflection and deeper understanding. • *Cognitive Knots*: Complex questions or problems that emerge during learning experiences, which provide the correct amount of challenge to motivate the child to problem-solve the issue or knot. • *Participation*: The participation of families and recognition of children as children as citizens, driven by relationships in the early childhood setting.

Environmental Diversity in the Irish Landscape

The Leadership for INClusion in the Early Years (LINC) Programme is a special purpose higher education award, located at level six on the national qualifications framework in Ireland (LINC 2016–2020; Quality and Qualifications Ireland (QQI) 2020; Ring et al. 2019). The LINC programme is designed to support early childhood teachers to provide inclusive learning experiences for all children, with a specific focus on children with additional needs. As authors of this chapter, our experience,

Making the Environment the Third Teacher

as LINC tutors, in completing mentoring visits to support early childhood teachers during their participation in the LINC programme has been of paramount importance to us and we have been fortunate to visit hundreds of early learning and care (ELC) settings in this context. As Pairman and Terreni (2001) note, this has provided us with a unique perspective, that of insider and visitor to numerous ELC settings in Ireland. Visitors to early childhood settings can develop a sense of the setting within moments of entering the space. Gandini (2012), for example, highlights the emphasis of Reggio Emilia approach on the creation of a welcoming space that is evident from the moment one enters a setting. The nature of ELC settings in the Irish context is widely varied, from purpose built to converted spaces, rented and owned, with no two centres being the same (Grey et al. 2019). Some may be in shared spaces where the space is an ELC setting in the morning and a scout troop's den or community meeting space by night. Similar variations and associated challenges exist in the environment in primary and special schools in Ireland (Ring 2018b). All of these factors will influence the aesthetics of the environment. Regardless of these factors, what remains constant across all spaces is the need for well-designed learning spaces to support all children across ELC, primary and special school settings.

> **Key Signposts: Environmental Diversity in the Irish Landscape**
>
> - Gandini (2012) highlights the emphasis of the Reggio Emilia approach on the creation of a welcoming space that is evident from the moment one enters a setting.
> - The nature of early childhood settings in the Irish context is widely varied across early learning and care (ELC), primary and special school settings (Ring 2018b; Grey et al. 2019)
> - What remains constant across all spaces is the need for well-designed learning spaces to support all children across ELC, primary and special school settings.

The Environment as a Third Teacher

Many early childhood teachers take the view that the larger the space the better it will be for creating enriched learning experiences for children; however, this is not necessarily true. Gandini (2012) suggests that it is more than just the square metres of a space that matter, it is how this space is utilised, its functions and its aesthetics. An early childhood space or classroom has a number of functions, one function of the space is the manner in which children and adults are facilitated in moving through the space. Providing clear travel spaces, designed to enable seamless movement through the environment for all users, and avoiding overly cluttered spaces, which inhibit the users, should be considered. Environments can be purposefully designed to promote children's independence, for example, including a child-level sink in the space to promote handwashing as opposed to handwashing only being available in a bathroom, located external to the classroom. Aesthetics can be defined as the appreciation of sensory experiences, which are pleasant for a child or adult (Dissanayake 1992). Examining the aesthetics of a classroom, it is important to consider the colour palette, for example, ensuring the walls and floors are a neutral colour and free from strong colours and murals (Department of Education and Skills (DES) 2012; Ring 2018b; NCCA 2019). Neutral tones are aesthetically pleasing and less distracting or overwhelming for a child, whereas a visually busy colour palette may impact on the child's ability to engage in learning as they may become overwhelmed or distracted by the colours and patterns.

In the context of the environment as a third teacher, Malaguzzi in interview with Gandini states that 'the environment becomes part of the individual' (Gandini 2012: 321). This can be both positive and negative and influences how the children use and interact with the environment. Síolta: The National Quality Framework for Early Childhood Education invites us to reflect on the experiences that our environments both indoors and outdoors provide for our children (CECDE 2006). Use of the Aistear Síolta Practice Guide Self-Evaluation tool and the Universal Design Guidelines for Early Learning and Care Settings are useful self-assessment tools to critically reflect on the opportunities and experiences the environment provides for the children attending the setting (NCCA 2015; Grey et al. 2019). While all themes from Aistear: The Early Childhood Curriculum Framework can be seen in action in the environment, Exploring and Thinking in particular in the context of the third teacher is ever present as all children develop cognitively and physically through exploration of their environment. Gandini (2012) recommends environments that are populated with invitations to play and provocations for the child to explore and inquire freely, in both small and large groups, thus encouraging positive learning dispositions and a sense of awe and wonder in the learning environment (NCCA 2009). Westwood (2013) suggests that the environment we create can be the basis upon which an inclusive society is created. It is well established that children learn best in an environment that teaches; one that is warm and inviting and mirrors the culture, values, attitudes and ideas of all of the stakeholders (NCCA 2009; Gandini 2012; Westwood 2013). Furthermore, it is important to consider the images our environment portrays to children and adults (Murray and Urban 2012). Does the environment promote autonomy, curiosity and enquiry-based learning dispositions? Are children and families represented in a meaningful and non-tokenistic manner?

> ### Key Signposts: The Environment as a Third Teacher
>
> - It is more than just the square metres of a space that matter, it is how this space is utilised, its functions and its aesthetics (Gandini 2012).
> - It is useful to consider and reflect on the opportunities and experiences that our environments, both indoors and outdoors, provide for our children.
> - Early childhood environments that are populated with invitations to play and provocations for the child to explore and inquire freely, in both small and large groups, encourage positive learning dispositions and a sense of awe and wonder in the learning environment (NCCA 2009; 2015; Grey et al. 2019).
> - Consider that the environment we create can be the basis upon which an inclusive society is created (Westwood 2013).

The Physical Environment

The physical environment refers to the organisation, resources and aesthetics of the early childhood classroom, both indoor and outdoor (NCCA 2009). Quality play-based learning experiences are optimised when the physical environment meets the needs of all the children it serves through providing the opportunity to engage in play (NCCA 2015). The organisation and layout of the classroom should be carefully considered in a planned and structured approach to ensure all children's learning, wellbeing and development are supported (CECDE 2006). Organising the location of people and materials in the space is a key consideration and providing clearly defined areas of observed interest will provide support for a child who may experience difficultly in planning play (AsIAm 2018).

As previously outlined, in an Irish landscape early childhood settings vary considerably in size, structure and design; therefore, it is vital to ensure unique structural features are utilised. Windows with views or unlevel surfaces outdoors, for example, can be used effectively to create a unique space of interest and challenge (Pairman and Terrini 2001). Consideration can also be given to creating boundaries within spaces, ensuring areas are divided into small and separated areas such as an art and craft area, a construction area, or a relaxing book corner (NCCA 2009). These boundaries can include the use of partitions, changes in floor covering from vinyl to carpeted areas, flexible low-level units, which are multi-functional and can be used for sitting or an additional play surface (Pairman and Terrini 2001; CECDE 2006; NCCA 2009; Grey et al. 2019).

Storage and display of materials and resources should be at the child's level and be open and accessible to them. It is important to consider how children with specific needs such as visual or motor challenges can access materials. Labelling of materials and storage containers with textures, images and text can assist all children in locating and selecting play materials. A wide variety of open-ended materials and props should be accessible for all children. Additionally, consideration can be given to the identified sensory needs of the children in the class, through the creation of a sensory plan for children (AsIAm 2018). When the early childhood teacher is planning for play and resourcing the physical environment, s/he can ensure that activities and resources in the environment are not sensory triggers for children, which could lead to a child's non-participation. Children should be represented in their environment, ensuring displays reflect the identity of the children and families. Ensuring representations from different cultures, backgrounds and abilities can be used to promote and acknowledge similarities and differences.

> ### Key Signposts: The Physical Environment
>
> - Quality play-based learning experiences are optimised when the physical environment meets the needs of all children it serves through providing the opportunity to engage in play (NCCA 2015; 2019; Grey et al. 2019).
> - Unique structural features of the environment can be effectively utilised, to create a unique space of interest and challenge (Pairman and Terrini 2001).
> - When the early childhood teacher is planning for play and resourcing the physical environment, s/he can ensure that activities and resources in the environment are not sensory triggers for children, which could lead to a child's non-participation.

The Temporal Environment

The temporal environment refers to the routines, schedules and the transitions that children experience throughout the day in the early childhood or school setting (Ring 2018a) and is inexplicably linked to the physical environment. Children's engagement can be enhanced by helping them to anticipate what happens, which provides them with a sense of security and control over their environment, supports their emotional regulation; reduces anxiety and stress, empowers children to be active learners and to develop decision-making skills and independence (CECDE 2006; NCCA

2009; Ring 2018a). Routines can help children to learn how their world is organised and what they need to do in order to interact successfully in that world (Sussmen 2011). Educational settings can assist children's engagement through the provision of visual and/or object schedules, which can reduce children's anxiety and contribute to their understanding of the sequence and structure of the day (Ring et al. 2018). The importance of managing transitions throughout the day sensitively and purposefully is also highlighted in Síolta: The National Quality Framework for Early Childhood Education (CECDE 2006). Transitions in the early childhood setting can be supported in a number of ways, including the use of sand timers and/or transitional songs, alerting children to the next activity and giving them sufficient time to transition from their previous activity.

We can also empower children and develop their independence through the use of task analysis. This involves analysing the child's abilities in relation to the task we wish to teach, for example, hand washing, self-feeding, zipping up a coat, in terms of what they currently know and what they need to learn to complete the requisite task successfully. Task analysis also requires an analysis of the task, through breaking down the steps required into a sequence and supporting the child through each step of the sequence (Mac Naughton 2003).

Key Signposts: The Temporal Environment

- The temporal environment is inextricably linked to the physical environment and refers to the embedding of routines and predictability in the child's day.
- By helping children to anticipate what happens next, children achieve a sense of security, reducing stress and anxiety and empowering children to become more independent.
- Useful resources include visual and object schedules designed to support children in understanding the sequence and structure of events in the day.
- Task analysis can be used to promote children's independence and autonomy.

The Interactional Environment

The interactional environment refers to the quality of social interactions children experience in the early childhood setting. Ryan in Chapter 4 has highlighted the critical importance of interactions in propelling children's development. The NCCA observes that 'children have a fundamental need to be with other people. They learn and develop through loving and nurturing relationships with adults and other children, and the quality of these interactions impacts on their learning and development' (NCCA 2009: 9). Consistent, responsive, sensitive and reciprocal relationships are essential to children's wellbeing and overall development (CECDE 2006). Adults who are not responsive may adversely impact children's early childhood experiences and the role of the adult is therefore crucial and must be constant in all interactions from greeting the child when they arrive in the setting, to saying goodbye when they depart (French and Murphy 2005; Lobman 2006). Early childhood teachers should strive to be respectful listeners and keen observers, willing to adapt their practice to meet the child's needs; sensitive and responsive to children's level of understanding and interests and intentions; supporting children to express themselves, initiate activities and to become increasingly independent (CECDE 2006; NCCA 2009; Irvin, Boyd and Odom 2015)

Through observing and supporting children in fostering the friendships that children are making early childhood teachers can assist children in sustaining these relationships, thereby nurturing the child's self-esteem and self-worth (CECDE 2006). Research has shown that during these interactions, particularly in unstructured settings or activities, children exhibit increasingly complex play and the development of social networks (Guralnick et al. 2006). Early childhood teachers can support and foster these relationships by providing space, materials and time for children to play together, including opportunities for social play, particularly in the pretend play areas, planned pairing and small group activities generated by children's observed and articulated interests (O'Sullivan 2018; O'Sullivan and Ring 2018; O'Sullivan, Ring and Horgan 2018). They can encourage children to play co-operative games and to assist one another during activities, play and routines, and can model social behaviour when interacting with adults and children alike (French 2003; CECDE 2006; NCCA 2009). Circle time can also be used as an opportunity to support social interaction and should be an interactive, fun, collaborative and spontaneous experience, which takes account of children's interests and supports children's learning and development (Mac Naughton and Williams 2009).

Practical ways in which we can provide an environment to support social interaction include using a variety of pedagogical strategies during interactions with children such as the use of open-ended questions and allowing sufficient time for children to answer (Mac Naughton and Williams 2004); observing children and providing open-ended opportunities for children to engage in play, active exploration and first-hand experiences and recognising that learning occurs in a holistic, non-compartmentalised way (Ring et al. 2018).

> **Key Signposts: The Interactional Environment**
>
> - The interactionist environment refers to the quality of social interactions children experience in the early childhood setting.
> - Early childhood teachers can effectively model positive social interactions when interacting with adults and children alike.
> - Early childhood teachers can observe and foster children's friendships and social interactions and provide opportunities, space, materials and time for children to play together, including opportunities for social play and unstructured play opportunities.

Conclusion

The three dimensions of the environment isolated by Pairman and Terreni (2001): the physical, temporal and interactional environments were discussed in the context of capturing the potential of the early childhood environment as a third teacher. The chapter has confirmed that how the environment is utilised matters significantly for all children's early childhood experiences. Quality play-based learning experiences are optimised when the physical environment meets the needs of all the children it serves through providing children with the opportunity to engage in play (NCCA 2015; Ring and O'Sullivan 2021). This is achieved when the organisation, resources and aesthetics of the classroom both indoor and outdoor are purposefully planned and reflected upon by early childhood teachers (NCCA 2009; Ring 2018a). Within the physical environment, the temporal environment supports children in predicting and managing routines, schedules and the transitions that they experience throughout the day in ELC, primary and special school settings (Ring 2018a). Finally, the interactional environment highlights the importance of consistent, responsive, sensitive and reciprocal relationships to children's wellbeing, learning and development (CECDE 2006; NCCA 2009).

Bibliography

AsIAm. (2018). *Teach Me As I Am: Early Years Autism Training Programme: Sensory Environment Observation*. Dublin: AsIAm.

Centre for Early Childhood Development and Education. (2006). *Síolta: The National Quality Framework for Early Childhood Education*. Dublin: Centre for Early Childhood Development and Education, <http://siolta.ie/media/pdfs/final_handbook.pdf>, accessed 20 October 2019, accessed 29 October 2010.

Dahlberg, G., Moss, P., and Pence, A. (1999). *Beyond Quality in Early Childhood Education and Care*. London: Falmer Press.

Department of Education and Skills. (2012). *Planning and Design Guidelines: Primary and Post Primary School Specialist Accommodation for Pupils with Special Educational Needs*. Offaly: Department of Education and Skills, <https://www.education.ie/en/School-Design/Technical-Guidance-Documents/Current-Technical-Guidance/pbu_tgd_026.pdf>, accessed 20 January 2019.

Dissanayake, E. (1992). *Homo Aesthetics: Where Art Comes from and Why*. New York, NY: The Free Press.

Edwards, C., Gandini, L., and Forman, G. (eds). (2012). *The Hundred Languages of Children* (3rd ed.). Santa Barbara, CA: Praeger.

Feeney, S. (2018). 'Addressing Children's Sensory Differences: Strategies for Practice'. In E. Ring, P. Daly, and E. Wall (eds), *Autism from the Inside Out: Signposts for Parents, Early Childhood, Primary, Post-Primary and Special School Settings*, pp. 67–96. Oxford: Peter Lang.

French, G. (2003). *Supporting Quality: Guidelines for Best Practice in Early Childhood Services* (2nd ed.). Dublin: Barnardos National Children's Resource Centre.

French, G., and Murphy, P. (2005). *Once in a Lifetime: Early Childhood Care and Education for Children from Birth to Three*. Dublin: Barnardos' National Children's Resource Centre.

Gandini, L. (2012). 'Connecting Through Caring and Learning Spaces'. In C. Edwards, L. Gandini, and G. Foreman (eds), *The Hundred Languages of Children* (3rd ed.), pp. 317–341. Santa Barbara, CA: Praeger.

Gardner, H. (2012). 'Foreword'. In C. Edwards, L. Gandini, and G. Forman (eds), *The Hundred Languages of Children: The Reggio Emilia Experience in Transformation* (3rd ed.), pp. xiii–xvi. Oxford: PRAEGER.

Grey, T., Corbett, M., Sheerin, J., Heeney, T., Ring, E., and O'Sullivan, L. (2019). *Universal Design Guidelines for Early Learning and Care Settings*. Dublin: Department of Children and Youth Affairs in collaboration with the Centre for Universal Design (CEUD), National Disability Authority (NDA), <https://aim.gov.ie/wp-content/uploads/2019/06/universal-design-guidelines-for-elc-settings-introduction-1.pdf>, accessed 24 January 2019.

Guralnick, M., Hammond, M., Connor, R., and Neville, B. (2006). 'Stability, Change, and Correlates of the Peer Relationship of Young Children with Mild Developmental Delays', *Child Development*, 77(2), 312–324.

Irvin, D. W., Boyd, B. A., and Odom, S. L. (2015). 'Adult Talk in the Inclusive Classroom and the Socially Competent Behaviour or Preschoolers with Autism Spectrum Disorder', *Focus on Autism and Other Developmental Disabilities*, 30(3), 131–142.

Leadership for INClusion in the Early Years Consortium. (2016–2020). *Competencies Associated with Providing for Inclusion in the Early Years*. Mary Immaculate College, Limerick: Leadership for INClusion in the Early Years Consortium.

Lobman, C. (2006). 'Improvisation: An Analytic Tool for Examining Teacher-Child Interactions in the Early Childhood Classroom', *Early Childhood Research Quarterly*, 21, 455–470.

Mac Naughton, G., and Williams, G. (2009). *Teaching Young Children: Choices in Theory and Practice* (2nd ed.). Mallory, NSW: Pearson Education Australia.

Mac Naughton, G. (2003). *Shaping Early Childhood: Learners, Curriculum and Contests*. Maidenhead: Open University Press.

Murray, C., and Urban, M. (2012). *Diversity and Equality in Early Childhood: An Irish Perspective*. Dublin: Gill and *Macmillan*.

National Council for Curriculum and Assessment. (1999). *Primary School Curriculum*. Dublin: National Council for Curriculum and Assessment.

National Council for Curriculum and Assessment. (2009). *Aistear: The Early Childhood Curriculum Framework*. Dublin: National Council for Curriculum and Assessment, <https://www.ncca.ie/en/early-childhood/aistear>, accessed 29 October 2019.

National Council for Curriculum and Assessment. (2015). *Aistear/Síolta Practice Guide*. Dublin: National Council for Curriculum and Assessment, <www.ncca.ie/en/Practice-Guide>, accessed 29 October 2019.

National Council for Curriculum and Assessment. (2019). *Primary Language Curriculum*. Dublin: National Council for Curriculum and Assessment, <https://www.curriculumonline.ie/getmedia/2a6e5f79-6f29-4d68-b850-379510805656/PLC-Document_English.pdf>, accessed 12 January 2020.

National Council for Curriculum and Assessment. (2020). *Draft Primary Curriculum Framework. For Consultation*. Dublin: National Council for Curriculum and Assessment, <https://ncca.ie/media/4456/ncca-primary-curriculum-framework-2020.pdf>, accessed 06 September 2020.

O'Sullivan, L. (2018). 'A Right to Play: Our Responsibility to Include Play in the Curriculum for Children with Autism Spectrum Difference'. In E. Ring, P. Daly, and E. Wall (eds), *Autism from the Inside Out: Signposts for Parents, Early Childhood, Primary, Post-Primary and Special School Settings*, pp. 45–66. Oxford: Peter Lang.

O'Sullivan, L., and Ring, E. (2018). 'Play as Learning: Implications for Educators and Parents from Findings of a National Evaluation of School Readiness in Ireland', *International Journal of Play*, 7(3), 266–289.

O'Sullivan, L., Ring, E., and Horgan, K. (2018). 'The Power of Play to Promote Wellbeing and Connections with Others in Children with Autism Spectrum Differences', *Children's Research Digest*, 5(2), 59–65.

Pairman, A., and Terreni, L. (2001). *If the Environment Is the Third Teacher What Language Does She Speak*. Wellington: Ministry of Education.

Quality and Qualifications Ireland. (2020). *National Framework of Qualifications*. Quality and Qualifications Ireland: Dublin, <https://www.qqi.ie/Articles/Pages/National-Framework-of-Qualifications-(NFQ).aspx>, accessed 12 September 2020.

Ring, E. (2018a). 'Harnessing the Reggio Emilia Concept of the Environment as the "Third Teacher" for Children with Autism Spectrum Difference'. In E. Ring, P. Daly, and E. Wall (eds), *Autism from the Inside Out: Signposts for Parents,*

Early Childhood, Primary, Post-Primary and Special School Settings, pp. 181–198. Oxford: Peter Lang.

Ring, E. (2018b) 'The Case of Inclusion: Why Hard Cased Make Good Law: Exploring Research-Informed Practical Strategies for Inclusion', *Irish National Teachers' Organisation Consultative Conference on Education: The Teaching Profession – 150 Years on*, Athlone, 16–17 November, Athlone: Hodson Bay Hotel, <https://www.into.ie/app/uploads/2019/07/EdConf2018_EmerRyng.pdf>, accessed 12 September 2020.

Ring, E., Kelleher, S., Breen, F., Heeney, T., McLoughlin, M., Kearns, A., Stafford, P., Skehill, S., Campion, K., Comerford, D., and O'Sullivan, L. (2019). *Interim Evaluation of the Leadership for Inclusion in the Early Years (LINC) Programme*. Limerick: Mary Immaculate College, <https://documentcloud.adobe.com/link/track?uri=urn:aaid:scds:US:d8c95d7d-2d75-40a8-9f65-b6582908c08d>, accessed 6 January 2019.

Ring, E., and O'Sullivan, L. (2021). 'Exploring the Possibilities of the Environment and Universal Design in Realising Aspects of Structural and Process Quality in Early Childhood Education and Creating Spaces where Diversity Is the Norm'. In O. Saracho (ed.), *Contemporary Perspectives in Early Childhood Education*. Charlotte, NC: Information Age Publishing, [In press].

Ring, E., O'Sullivan, L., Ryan, M., and Burke, P. (2018). *A Melange or a Mosaic of Theories? How Theoretical Perspectives on Children's Learning and Development Can Inform a Responsive Pedagogy in a Redeveloped Primary School Curriculum*. Dublin: National Council for Curriculum and Assessment, <https://www.ncca.ie/media/3863/seminar_four_er_los_mr_pb_paper.pdf>, accessed 16 January 2020.

Soncini, I. (2012). 'The Inclusive Community'. In C. Edwards, L. Gandini, and G. Foreman (eds), *The Hundred Languages of Children* (3rd ed.), pp. 187–212. Santa Barbara, CA: Praeger.

Sussmen, F. (2011). *The Power of Using Everyday Routines to Promote Young Children's Language and Social Skills*. Toronto: The Hanen Centre®, <http://www.hanen.org/SiteAssets/Articles---Printer-Friendly/Public-Articles/The-Power-of-Using-Everyday-Routines-.aspx>, accessed 12 September 2020.

United Nations. (1989). *Convention on the Rights of the Child*. New York, NY: United Nations, <http://www.ohchr.org/EN/ProfessionalInterest/Pages/CRC.aspx>, accessed 29 October 2019, accessed 12 January 2020.

Westwood, P. (2013). *Inclusive and Adaptive Teaching: Meeting the Challenge of Diversity in the Classroom*. Oxon: Routledge.

Leadership for Including all Children

SHARON SKEHILL

Chapter 9 Leadership in the Early Learning and Care Setting

ABSTRACT
In recognition of the essential importance of early intervention in supporting all learners to reach their full potential, recent policy attention in Ireland has focussed on supporting access to and inclusion in early learning and care (ELC) settings. To support this development, it was decided that nominated INclusion COordinators (INCOs) would lead this change within their settings. In order to meet the professional development requirements of these INCOs, a Leadership for INClusion in the Early Years (LINC) Programme was developed and offered to early childhood teachers across the country (Ring et al. 2019). This chapter explores the key features of effective leadership for inclusion which underpin the LINC programme. It also examines the barriers for INCOs within the Irish context and outlines the ways in which the LINC programme supports INCOs in navigating these challenges. The chapter explores what it means to be an INCO in practice; the skills required, the process of facilitating change and the core responsibilities of the role. Practical guidance is offered for early childhood teachers and INCOs and key signposts for practice are identified in terms of communicating with colleagues; facilitating diversity, equality and inclusion; sharing information with parents and professional colleagues and harnessing the voice of the child.

Introduction: Leadership for Inclusion Policy and Provision in the Irish Policy Context

The Inclusion Charter (Department of Children and Youth Affairs (DCYA) 2016) outlines the requirement for early learning and care (ELC) settings in Ireland to 'provide opportunities for all children to thrive in early education through the promotion of positive identities and abilities, the celebration of diversity and difference and the provision of an inclusive, participative culture and environment' (DCYA 2016: 4). The Access and Inclusion Model (AIM) was introduced into the ELC sector in Ireland to support the implementation of the Diversity, Equality and Inclusion Charter and Guidelines for Early Childhood Care and Education (Inter-Departmental Group (IDG) 2015; DCYA 2016) comprising seven different levels of support. As part of this model the role of the INclusion CO-ordinator (INCO) was established. Early learning and care settings can apply for additional capitation once a qualified INCO is designated in their setting. The role is designed to support the inclusion of all children with a specific focus on children with additional needs in the ELC setting. In order to support the professional development of potential INCOs, the Leadership for Inclusion in the Early Years (LINC) Programme was developed under Level 3 of AIM. This programme seeks to provide a high-quality continuing professional development (CPD) programme for early childhood teachers working in the sector who wish to pursue this leadership role. The modules included in this Special Purpose Award, located at Level 6 on the National Framework of Qualifications (NFQ) (Quality and Qualifications Ireland (QQI) 2020), are Child Development, Curriculum for Inclusion, Leadership for Inclusion, Collaborative Practice, and Inclusion in the Early Years' Setting: Concepts and Strategies. This blended learning programme is delivered through a combination of online and face-to-face sessions for each module. Students also receive a mentoring visit from their tutor over the course of the academic year to support them in incorporating their learning from the programme in their practice with children. On completion of the LINC programme, graduates are qualified to take on the leadership role of INCO, which involves supporting management in the provision of leadership and guidance for the inclusion and full participation of all children in the early childhood care and education (ECCE) programme (DCYA 2020).

Effective Leadership Practice

Siraj-Blatchford and Manni's (2007) study of leadership in the ELC sector identifies ten categories of effective leadership practice including; the ability to create a shared vision and ensure shared understanding and communication of that vision; the ability to encourage reflection while also supporting and assessing practice; the ability to build and support the learning community within the setting and creating a balance between leading and managing. Moyles (2001) and Osgood (2010) emphasise the need for confidence to take on a leadership role, in order to support professional learning and to develop and sustain the complexities of team relationships and interactions in the ELC setting (Sullivan 2010; Colmer 2017). Traditionally, the concept of leadership within the ELC setting resided with the manager (Rodd 2004; Moloney and Pettersen 2017; Moloney and McCarthy 2018), and the paradigms of leadership are largely associated with the concepts of power and authority (McDowall Clark 2012; Murray 2013).

Fitzgerald (2018) discusses the transformational approaches to leadership in promoting inclusion in educational settings, and emphasises the importance of having leaders working close to the site of learning, thereby recommending a process of distributed leadership in the education setting. Distributed leadership involves recognising the skills and qualifications of the team, and determining how teachers can best work together to effectively implement a quality and inclusive programme. This necessitates an understanding of the difference between management and leadership in the ELC setting, and simultaneously how they are both interwoven in practice. Rodd (2004) argues that an effective leader needs to be an effective manager, yet 'management skills do not equate with leadership skills' (p. 6). Adherence to legislation and best practice guidelines requires good management and organisational skills, together with the leadership skills to motivate the team in taking responsibility for their role in supporting quality and inclusive practice in a safe and stimulating environment. Leithwood and Sea-Shore Louis (2011) outline the key practices associated with leadership for learning in educational settings, which include the process of motivating the team, as well as providing support to develop competence by modelling quality practice and supporting professional learning.

> **Key Signposts: Effective Leadership Practice**
>
> - According to Siraj-Blatchford and Manni (2007) effective leadership practice includes; the ability to create a shared vision and ensure shared understanding and communication of that vision; the ability to encourage reflection while also supporting and assessing practice; the ability to build and support the learning community within the setting and creating a balance between leading and managing.
> - Traditionally, leadership in early learning and care (ELC) has been associated with management, authority and power.
> - In order to support inclusion, leaders should be close to the site of learning.
> - A model of distributed leadership, which recognises the skills and expertise of all staff is recommended to support inclusion (Fitzgerald 2018).
> - Effective leaders should model quality practice and support the professional learning of staff (Leithwood and Sea-Shore Louis 2011).

Early Childhood Teacher Education and Qualifications

Urban and Rubiano (2014) highlight the mismatch in the ELC sector in Ireland, whereby there are high expectations for the quality of teaching but minimal qualifications required for staff to navigate the curriculum and quality frameworks: Aistear: The Early Childhood Curriculum Framework (National Council for Curriculum and Assessment (NCCA) 2009) and Siolta: The National Quality Framework for Early Childhood Education (Centre for Early Childhood Development and Education (CECDE) 2006). Despite the ongoing call for a graduate-led workforce in the ELC sector (DES 2016; Government of Ireland (GoI) 2018), the Early Years Sector Profile Report 2017/2018 (Pobal 2018) notes that only 14.2 per cent of the staff team working with children in ELC settings hold a Level 8 degree. A further 6.4 per cent hold a Level 7 qualification on the National Framework of Qualifications (NFQ) and 43.1 per cent hold a Level 6, which is the minimal requirement to lead a room with the ECCE sessional group (Pobal 2018). Ring and colleagues (2019) discuss the myriad of qualifications recorded in the ELC sector in Ireland. They highlight the gaps that exist in relation to education and pay, as well as the need for a stronger focus on the inclusion of children with additional needs (Ring et al. 2019). The complexity of qualifications and experiences within this context over the past number of years has given cause for concern regarding the early childhood teacher's capabilities and skills to implement an effective early years curriculum and to adhere to best practice standards within the sector (Urban et al. 2011; Urban, Robson and Scacchi 2017; Ring et al. 2019). This context calls for effective leadership within settings to recognise the various skills and qualifications of the team in order to develop a high-quality and inclusive practice.

Oberhuemer (2015) outlines the education path for early childhood teachers in other countries, such as Sweden, Norway and Italy, whereby early childhood teachers are educated alongside their peers who are preparing for the primary school sector, with specific qualifications required for roles within the ELC setting. This potentially helps to create a stronger sense of identity for early childhood teachers within the teaching profession. Peeter, Sharmahd and Budginaité (2017) support Urban's (2008) argument, reiterated in articles with colleagues in 2011 and 2017, in relation to the need to establish a competent system to create a solid foundation for quality in the ELC sector, however, they also note that this competent system must be one that is based on access to a robust professional education continuum for those working in the sector (Peeters et al. 2017). Access to and engagement with a robust professional education continuum present the possibility of early childhood teachers having a more in-depth knowledge of child development, a better understanding of how to support children's holistic development and a deeper empathy for children (GoI 2018; Trodd and Dickerson 2018). Beavers, Orange and Kirkwood (2017) argue that a degree qualification alone is not sufficient to constitute quality, suggesting rather that there is a requirement for a blend of knowledge, skills and reflection on practice, with supports in place to guide reflective thinking. The emphasis on blending knowledge skill and reflection in the LINC programme enhances the potential to bridge this gap between qualifications and experience; policy and practice (Ring et al. 2019; Skehill 2019).

The importance of mentoring and pedagogical coaching for early childhood teachers has been identified as a key element in supporting reflective practice and developing confidence and competence Oberhuemer 2015; Beavers et al. 2017; Peeters et al. 2017; Urban et al. 2017; Ring et al. 2018). Osgood (2010) considers this mentoring process, the practical experience working with children, in addition to the process of reflective practice, as most valuable to practitioners in increasing their skills, and their confidence in their ability to apply theory to practice in their work with children. The INCO, through sharing the learning and supporting the staff team in cultivating inclusive practice, has the potential to provide such guidance during support and supervision sessions, as well as team meetings, which are advocated in the LINC programme together with quality guidance (CECDE 2006; DES 2016; Ring et al. 2019).

Waters and Payler (2015) reported on international projects to increase quality within the ELC sector, and similar to the Irish ELC sector, the gradual upskilling of an experienced and vocationally trained workforce to obtaining graduate qualifications on a part-time basis, has created a blur between initial teacher education (ITE) and CPD. The struggle to provide a consistent level of qualification for the knowledge, practice and values (Urban et al. 2017) required to work within the ELC setting, and to support and implement the policy developments of the sector is an ongoing challenge. Murray (2013) discusses the role of the early years' practitioner (EYP) in the English system who is viewed as an agent of change, responsible for implementing policy developments and raising standards of practice and professionalism through their transformational leadership (Department for Education and Skills (DfES) 2006). Similarly, in the Irish context, the high quality of practice and provision delineated in policy aspirations demands broad skills, shared reflection and responsibility from the ELC sector (Fortunati, Pagni and Pucci cited in Ring et al. 2019).

Key Signposts: ELC Teacher Education and Qualifications

- Researchers have highlighted a mismatch between high expectations for quality and minimal qualification requirements for the early learning and care (ELC) sector in Ireland (Urban and Rubiano 2014).
- There is significant variation in the qualifications of staff working within the ELC sector in Ireland; 14.2 per cent of the staff team working with children hold a Level 8 degree; 6.4 per cent hold a Level 7 qualification and 43.1 per cent with hold a Level 6 (Pobal 2018).
- In Sweden, Norway and Italy, ELC teachers and primary teachers prepare for their future teaching roles alongside each other thus potentially contributing to enhancing the sense of teacher identity amongst early childhood teachers (Oberhuemer 2015).
- Access to and engagement with a robust professional education continuum present the possibility of early childhood teachers having a more in-depth knowledge of child development, a better understanding of how to support children's holistic development and a deeper empathy for children (GoI 2018; Trodd and Dickerson 2018). Degree qualifications alone are not sufficient to ensure quality; early childhood teacher education should include a blend of knowledge, skills and reflection on practice (Beavers, Orange and Kirkwood 2017).
- Mentoring and pedagogical coaching has been identified as a key element in supporting reflective practice and developing ELC teachers' confidence and competence (Peeters, Sharmahd and Budginaité 2017; Oberhuemer 2015; Beavers et al. 2017; Urban et al. 2017; Ring et al. 2018).

Developing Leadership Skills

Heikka and Hujala (2013) found that leadership responsibilities in their Finnish study focused on quality improvement, pedagogical leadership as well as ensuring management of daily routines and human resource issues, they noted however, that these increasing managerial duties were having an impact on the time allocated for quality improvement. Hoas Moen and Granrusten (2013) identified a similar issue in the Norwegian sector whereby pedagogical leaders reported that they were spending less time with the children owing to other commitments relating to supporting staff members.

Leadership is based on relationships and interactions within a group, and there are many factors that might impact the dynamics and the effectiveness of the team. The LINC programme places an emphasis on distributive leadership within the ELC setting (Ring et al. 2019). Lárusdóttir and O'Connor (2017) identify a consistent move towards strategies for distributive leadership within school and teaching environments, but also question the delegation process and whether, in reality, these decisions are based on hierarchical control. Allred and Hancock (2015) identify pressures to create a 'professional culture' within the ELC setting, and question how shared power with colleagues and families can be established in a family-centred setting. Moloney and McCarthy (2018: 66) assert that distributed leadership in the ELC setting can create opportunities to utilise the skills and expertise of the whole team but express concern that the single role of INCO 'may be spread too thinly across too many areas'. An alternative perspective might consider the role of the INCO as part of the solution to support shared knowledge and peer learning in ELC settings as advocated by Irish policy reports (DES 2016; GoI 2018).

Fortunati and colleagues, cited in Ring et al. (2019) reported on the findings of the evaluation of LINC students' perceptions of their preparation to lead inclusive culture, practice and pedagogy within their settings. Although over 95 per cent of students in the academic year 2017/2018 felt they had acquired such leadership skills through engagement with the LINC programme, engagement with the responsibilities of the role of INCO may be dependent on a number of factors within the ELC setting. In this context therefore it is useful to consider management structures in place; the number of staff and children within the service; the willingness of the staff team; non-contact time allocated for leadership responsibilities as well as the time and funding available (Skehill 2019).

The first step for the INCO is to determine the specifics of his/her role with the manager and/or the Board of Management of the ELC setting.

While the DCYA (2020) has devised a comprehensive list of the INCO's responsibilities, these are subject to adaptation and adjustment in order to facilitate the pre-existing role of the INCO as a manager or an early childhood teacher. The responsibilities may also depend on the type of service provided, the number of children requiring AIM support within the setting under Level 7, and the existing competencies of the staff team in implementing an inclusive culture and pedagogy. It is advisable then that the new INCO requests a meeting with management to discuss what the role will look like in his/her setting and what time needs to be allocated to effectively carry out additional duties. The module on leadership for inclusion in the LINC programme provides guidance on effective communication and strategies to engage with colleagues and management in order to have the role recognised and valued for the significant benefits it can provide for children and their families. It is advisable that the INCO and the management team negotiate the terms and conditions of the additional responsibilities alongside their pre-existing role within the ELC setting prior to signing the contract with Pobal, a government body to support communities and local agencies towards achieving social inclusion and development, in order to secure the additional capitation associated with the INCO position.

> **Key Signposts: Developing Leadership Skills through the LINC Programme**
>
> - International research has highlighted that many pedagogical leaders report they are spending less time with the children owing to increasing managerial duties and commitments relating to supporting staff members (Heikka and Hujala 2013; Hoas Moen and Granrusten 2013).
> - The LINC Programme places an emphasis on distributive leadership within the early learning and care (ELC) setting (Ring et al. 2019)
> - INclusion COordinators (INCOs) will need to consider many factors in engaging with their roles and responsibilities; the management

> structures in place; the number of staff and children in the service; the willingness of the staff team; non-contact time allocated for leadership responsibilities as well as the time and funding available (Skehill 2019).
> - The LINC programme provides guidance on effective communication and strategies to engage with colleagues and management.
> - The first step for the INCO is to determine the specifics of his/her role in consultation with the manager and/or or the Board of Management of the ELC setting.

Leading Inclusive Practice and Pedagogy

Leading inclusive practice means guiding and mentoring the staff team so that the knowledge and learning of the INCO is incorporated into practice and embedded into the culture of the setting (Ring et al. 2019). The role of the INCO includes that of cascading learning throughout the staff in the setting to support the development of a shared understanding and an inclusive culture (Ring et al. 2019; DCYA 2020) Leading the staff team also includes the need to support colleagues in the implementation of inclusive practices in relation to planning, documenting and evaluating the curriculum in addition to sharing learning and good practice regarding observations and engagement with the Aistear Siolta Practice Guide (NCCA 2015). The INCO is also expected to model good practice and strategies for collaborating with other early childhood teachers in order to promote effective communication with children.

Northouse (2013) emphasises the leadership qualities of intelligence, wisdom and confidence that are required to effectively engage and motivate the staff team, together with being diligent in one's role in carrying out responsibilities as required. In order for the INCO to effectively support learning within the team, it is important that s/he can commit to keeping up-to-date with developments in the sector and be open to ongoing evaluation of practice. Graham (2017) outlines the importance of fostering positive teamwork to facilitate quality inclusive practice and to share the vision and goals for the service reiterating Siolta: The National Quality Framework for Early Childhood Education quality standard on professional practice (CECDE 2006). The leadership role of the 'registered provider' in the ELC setting is defined in the pre-school regulations in relation to one's responsibility in ensuring the quality and safety of care provided to those using the service (Tusla 2018) and is supported with guidance from the DES (2016) regarding leadership for management with the ECCE age group.

Moloney and Pettersen (2017: 153) discussed the importance of communication amongst the staff team, highlighting the need to share 'what is being done, why it is being done and how it is going to happen'. Effective communication creates a respectful environment where changes can happen within a willing and enthusiastic team. The what, why and how are very important within the ELC setting, as implementing changes and developing practices require a process and a plan. There needs to be an understanding of the daily routines and tasks involved when working with small children, which Fitzgerald (2018) sees as an essential element of leading inclusive practice. If the INCO has that working knowledge of the experience of the early childhood teacher, it is reasonable to assume that s/he will have an understanding of the realities of practice and how to implement changes.

The INCO might share the children's learning portfolios from the group with colleagues to illustrate how s/he identifies their interests, recognises their strengths, and devises learning goals based on this to support learning and development (Dunleavy-Lavin, Heaney and Skehill 2018). The INCO might also be charged with the responsibility of 'engaging with national and local developments related to inclusion in order to continue to lead the implementation of good practice in the setting (and) engaging with ongoing CPD to ensure adherence to good practice in relation to developments within the disability sector and in relation to the inclusion of children with additional needs' (DCYA 2020: 1, 2). There may be possible challenges in relation to this communication of information unless the INCO holds the role of registered provider or manager of the setting to whom all correspondence is generally sent from relevant external stakeholders. Fitzgerald (2018: 249) outlines the importance of designing 'collaborative systems' which facilitate the development of productive relationships within the education setting and considering how to address potential obstacles to progress. The reflective nature of the LINC programme encourages the INCO to think flexibly and to find solutions and strategies to share information effectively with all relevant stakeholders in the ELC setting.

Key Signposts: Leading Inclusive Practice and Pedagogy: What Does It Mean?

- Leading inclusive practice means guiding and mentoring the staff team so that the knowledge and learning of the INclusion COordinator (INCO) are incorporated into practice and embedded in the culture of the setting.
- Effective team-working skills and team motivation skills are essential for leading inclusive practice and pedagogy (Graham 2017).
- Effective communication creates a respectful environment where changes can happen within a willing and enthusiastic team.
- In considering the scope of any leadership duties within an early learning and care (ELC) setting there needs to be an understanding of the daily routines and tasks involved when working with small children (Fitzgerald 2018).

Managing Change as an INclusion CO-ordinator

For many early childhood teachers in ELC settings the inclusion of children with learning differences will be new and for some it may be quite daunting. Routine, process and procedure are important for the effective running of ELCs and often become deep rooted. Traditional policies, procedures, expectations and pedagogical approaches may need to be revised and adapted to support the setting in meeting the learning and care needs of diverse learners. The INCO will need to manage the changes

Leadership in the Early Learning and Care Setting

required carefully and sensitively provide for a culture in which the needs and best interests of the children and staff are met.

Lewin (1947) devised a three stage process to guide and manage change effectively, as illustrated in Figure 9.1. In the ELC setting, stage one of this process requires the skill of identifying what changes need to happen in order to develop or introduce new practices.

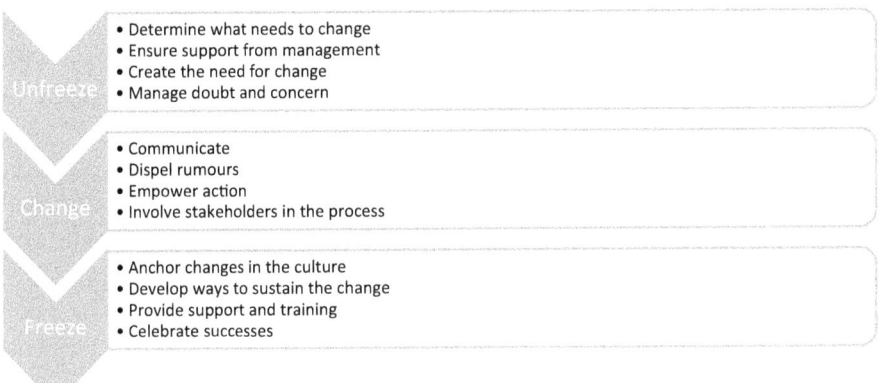

Figure 9.1. Lewin's Three-Step Process for Change (Adapted from Lewin 1947)

Lewin's process is very relevant for the role of the INCO and provides a framework for action to develop inclusive culture, practice and pedagogy. In the context of 'unfreezing' the INCO needs to prioritise tasks and determine what initial changes need to be implemented, or to identify what are the processes and practices that need to change, being mindful of ensuring that the child is at the centre of all such decisions and actions. Doubts and concerns will understandably be raised by colleagues, however the INCO will need to reassure colleagues by listening to their concerns and ensuring all voices, including those of the children, are heard in the process.

In order to facilitate the process of 'unfreezing', the INCO could consider providing time and opportunity for regular, meaningful and professional dialogue with colleagues. Support and supervision sessions provide both the leader and the team member with the opportunity to discuss issues or concerns that may be impacting quality practice and may uncover further issues that warrant a need for change (Lewin 1947). These meetings should focus on addressing and discussing these concerns, in a safe space whereby the team member is supported in reflecting on practice and guided in finding a solution. While working alongside each other enables this process of guiding and mentoring in practice for the leader and the early childhood teacher, there are so many distractions in the busy pre-school environment that it is very difficult to engage in meaningful conversations to address concerns, which can lead to frustration on all sides. Taking the time to listen and to have these conversations with colleagues indicates the value placed on their role, and a commitment to develop quality within the service.

It is beneficial to consider developing an action plan as a result of discussions at the support and supervision session. A plan can be devised on the basis of the issues addressed such as; completing a self-evaluation exercise based on the pre-school room (NCCA 2015); compiling a letter for parents as a reminder of collection times; organising a team building activity or organising an in-house CPD evening focused on observations. These actions are about finding practical solutions to any issues arising and for each party to commit to developing practice for the benefit of all stakeholders in the ELC setting. Making note of these commitments means that they are documented for discussion in the next support and supervision session, thereby creating a cycle of reflection and action within the team (Paige-Smyth and Craft 2011; Lindon and Trodd 2016). Quality within the ELC sector is inextricably linked with the adults working in the setting (GoI 2018) and therefore these support and supervision sessions are essentially about caring for the adults within the service leading to the development of a contentment and motivation in their role working with the children and their families.

Once the INCO has identified what needs to be 'unfrozen' (Lewin 1947), CPD topics can be prioritised and a plan implemented in accordance with the needs of the team and subsequently for the children and their families. Continuing professional development evenings and staff meetings can provide opportunities for discussion and dialogue, noting however that the importance of the INCO being in a position to mentor and guide the team in practice. This can involve working alongside colleagues, modelling strategies to support transitions (Egan 2018) and supporting conflict resolution when working in the room with the children (French 2012). INclusion COordinators should be mindful of clear communication and the potential for empowering colleagues, harnessing their interest, expertise and enthusiasm.

In considering ways to 'freeze' or maintain positive changes to the environment and to practice, support and supervision sessions also provide a valuable opportunity for the knowledge and expertise of the team to be acknowledged and celebrated. They provide a space for guidance, mentoring and support to develop a quality and inclusive practice. These sessions are opportunities where the INCO can recognise and acknowledge the work and achievements of the staff team on an individual basis. An inclusive culture advocates working from a strengths-based approach with the children, but also in recognising the strengths that a team member brings to the service.

Key Signposts: Managing Change as an INclusion CO-ordinator

- Lewin's (1947) three stage process to guide and manage change effectively (Unfreeze, Change, Freeze) provides a framework for INclusion COordinators (INCOs) to develop inclusive culture, practice and pedagogy.
- In considering change, INCOs should be mindful of ensuring that the child is at the centre of all decisions and actions.
- The INCO is in a pivotal position to facilitate professional dialogue.
- Support and supervision sessions between the INCO and the early learning and care (ELC) team member should be focused on addressing and discussing concerns in a safe space whereby the team member is supported in reflecting on practice and guided in finding a solution.
- Support and supervision sessions can be used as opportunities to celebrate the success and achievements of colleagues.

Information Sharing

The INCO is charged with the responsibility of sharing information on the AIM and inclusion more generally, to parents and staff (DCYA 2020). The INCO may also be required to assist with applications for AIM supports. This involves obtaining parental consent and completing a developmental checklist with the parents as a precursor to observations from the early years specialist. Early childhood teachers have identified this communication with parents as particularly challenging when raising concerns that they might have about a child's development (Skehill 2019).

The INCO needs to consider how to communicate and collaborate effectively with parents regarding their children's development. In Chapter 5, Barr and Hilliard have highlighted the critical importance of developing a seamless connection between the home and education setting for all children. O'Byrne (2018: 168) discusses the importance of 'cultivating and nurturing positive relationships between home and education' through effective communication and Chapter 5 of this publication details the importance of building relationships with parents. Síolta: The National Quality Framework for Early Childhood Education (CECDE 2006) sees this partnership with parents and families as central to quality practice in the early years and emphasises the need for ongoing opportunities for communication. Epstein's (2018) model for parental involvement and participation in education offers the INCO some strategies to develop relationships between the home and school environment. Involving parents in the ELC environment from the outset provides the basis for that mutual respect, whereby the teacher recognises the primary role of the parent in caring for the child and the essential knowledge that comes from the home environment, and in turn, the parents respect the role of the early childhood teacher in teaching and supporting the child's development. From the very outset, this relationship needs to be nurtured, and the INCO might consider sharing information at a parents' evening prior to enrolment to inform families about the inclusive culture and practice at the setting. A presentation of the benefits of the play-based approach, which have been discussed by O'Sullivan in Chapter 7, including visual representations of the inclusive pedagogy in practice and the theory that informs that practice can provide the foundation for a professional relationship. Documenting the children's development in learning portfolios that are sent home periodically ensures that parents are kept informed and are invited to contribute to this learning journal, placing value on parental involvement. If the INCO has established him/herself as one who is knowledgeable in early years education and in inclusive practice, it can be easier to communicate concerns with parents about a child's development, as the parent will recognise that this is coming from a place of respect and evidence-based knowledge and expertise. This partnership with parents will guide the application process and enable more effective collaboration with other professionals around the child.

The INCO may also be required to liaise with the early years specialist to develop strategies and an individual plan to support the child's participation in accordance with their individual needs, providing advice based on observations and knowledge of the child regarding any additional supports that might be required with reference to the different levels of support (see Chapter 10 for guidance on leading planning). This collaborative process and sharing of key information is key to supporting an effective and smooth transition to primary school. There is an ongoing process of identifying goals, working as a team to achieve such goals, and follow-up meetings with other professionals to discuss progress and plans. Throughout this process, the value of support and supervision sessions, team meetings and reflective practice are recognised as key to guiding this process to support inclusion and develop relationships (Moloney and McCarthy 2018).

Key Signposts: Information Sharing

- The INclusion COordinator (INCO) has the responsibility of sharing information on the AIM and inclusion more generally with parents and staff.
- Early childhood teachers have identified communication with parents regarding child development concerns, as particularly challenging (Skehill 2019).
- It is essential to cultivate and nurture positive relationships between home and education through effective communication (O'Byrne 2018).

- Documenting the children's development in learning portfolios that are sent home periodically ensures that parents are kept informed and are invited to contribute to this learning journal, placing value on their involvement.
- The INCO may be required to liaise with the early years specialist to develop strategies and an individual plan to support the child's participation in accordance with their individual needs.

Supporting Diversity, Equality and Inclusion

The INCO is responsible for promoting the guidance and best practice advocated in the Diversity, Equality and Inclusion Charter and Guidelines for Early Childhood Care and Education (DCYA 2016) within the setting, and sharing this information with colleagues and parents, as well as supporting the implementation of such guidance. The childcare committees nationwide have provided a series of CPD workshops focused on the Diversity, Equality and Inclusion Charter and Guidelines for Early Childhood Care and Education; and while it is not mandatory that the INCO attend this programme, it is advocated that at least one member of staff from the ELC setting complete this CPD. Collaborating with colleagues is a key element of distributed leadership in order to devise strategies to develop a more inclusive practice. The following section offers INCOs some strategies for supporting diversity, equality and inclusion in ELC settings.

Key Signposts: Strategies for Supporting Diversity, Equality and Inclusion in Your Setting

- *Inclusion Poster*: Sit with the early learning and care (ELC) team and consider the question asked in the Diversity, Equality and Inclusion Charter and Guidelines for Early Childhood Care and Education: What does inclusion in an early childhood service look like? (Department of Children and Youth Affairs (DCYA) 2016: 6) Consider creating a personalised poster for your setting by involving the early childhood teachers in writing their own individual images of inclusion (e.g. 'Inclusion is being part of their peer group, not being apart. / Inclusion is the child being actively involved in the curriculum') and finding photo examples from their key groups that illustrate what inclusion looks like in the setting. Share your completed project with parents and other stakeholders by creating a display in the hallway, or take photos of the display to share on your parents' group chats (ensuring adherence to General Data Protection Regulation (GDPR)).
- *Lead Reflective Dialogues*: Section 1 of the Guidelines (DCYA 2016: 17–19) encourages early childhood teachers to develop reflective practice skills in discussing the concepts of diversity, equality and inclusion. The statements here might be the focus of team meetings, whereby a safe space can be created where team members can discuss their views and their experiences, and learn from each other. Some examples of these statements include:

Discrimination hurts and influences how children and adults relate in the world.
Can I identify and empathise with adults and children affected by stereotyping, prejudice, discrimination and racism, sexism, homophobia, and understand the impact of these?

- *Consider Guideline Documents During Team Meetings:* Consider the Diversity, Equality and Inclusion Charter and Guidelines for Early Childhood Care and Education as an active document in your setting and keep it alive and active by using it as the basis of discussion

at team meetings on an ongoing basis. There are ideas for practice to support the design of the physical environment; and strategies to support families including guidance in relation to children with additional needs, diverse cultural background and heritage, gender, and Traveller/Roma communities. Certain aspects of the document will be more relevant at different times and with different groups of children, so it is important to share the information and use it effectively to guide your practice.
- *Lead an Inclusive Culture*: As INCO, sharing your knowledge of the Diversity, Equality and Inclusion Charter and Guidelines for Early Childhood Care and Education is very important in relation to inclusive practice, but it is equally as important to establish yourself as knowledgeable and informed of best practice in order to lead the development of an inclusive culture.

The Ultimate Responsibility

The final responsibility of the INCO is that of 'advocating on behalf of children and engaging in regular consultation with children to allow their ideas, feelings and thoughts to contribute to service provision and delivery' (DCYA 2020: 2). This may be the most important responsibility of all. The practice of making children's voices visible is discussed in greater detail in Chapter 2 of this publication by Ring, Harte and Harmon. The real indicator of excellence for an INCO is in how s/he views the children in her/his care, and if s/he can recognise the confident and competent learner (NCCA 2009) in every child, regardless of their age or stage of development. The INCO needs to see the strengths in every child, and see what they can do, rather than what they cannot. In modelling the respect that all children deserve, the INCO can ensure that children are actively listened to, are valued and are given a voice. Aistear: The Early Childhood Curriculum Framework (NCCA 2009) embraces Sorin's concept of the 'agentic child' (2005: 19), which challenges the notion of the innocent and powerless child, instead seeing children as partners in the educational environment. If the early childhood teacher can truly appreciate the confident and competent child (NCCA 2009), seeing what the child can do in a strengths-based approach, this sets the foundation for all other elements of practice in the ELC environment (NCCA 2015; DCYA 2016; Ring et al. 2018). Moloney and McCarthy (2018) concur with this point and identify meaningful inclusion as a combination of two primary factors – the empathic attitude of the adult working with the children in the ELC setting, and the leadership capacity within the service to model and support inclusion. Consideration of how one develops this empathy is at the heart of discussions relating to inclusion of children with additional needs in mainstream educational settings (NCCA 2015; Ring et al. 2016; Tynan 2018;).

Conclusion

This chapter examined the importance of leadership in the context of creating inclusive ELC settings. Policy changes in the Irish context were noted and the role of the INCO identified. The professional development initiative to support potential INCOs, the LINC programme, was discussed throughout the chapter in the context of the theory and research which underpin it (Ring et al. 2019). Particular challenges for the ELC settings were noted in terms of potential struggles between the role of manager and additional leadership roles. Models of leadership were explored and distributed leadership was identified as a valuable model for the ELC environment. This challenge of managing change in the ELC setting as an INCO was considered using Lewin's (1947) model for change, which provides a useful framework for thinking more systematically and strategically about change as an INCO. Consideration was given to the INCO's role in sharing important and sensitive information with parents and other professionals with guidance and suggestions offered. Ideas for supporting diversity, equality and inclusion were presented and the chapter concluded by outlining the most important role of the INCO: listening to, valuing and highlighting the voice of the child.

Bibliography

Allred, K. W., and Hancock, C. L. (2015). 'Reconciling Leadership and Partnership: Strategies to Empower Professionals and Families', *YC Young Children*, 70(2), 40–47.

Beavers, E., Orange, A., and Kirkwood, D. (2017). 'Fostering Critical and Reflective Thinking in an Authentic Learning Situation', *Journal of Early Childhood Teacher Education*, 38(1), 3–18.

Centre for Early Childhood Development and Education. (2006). *Síolta: The National Quality Framework for Early Childhood Education*. Dublin: Centre for Early Childhood Development and Education, <http://siolta.ie/media/pdfs/final_handbook.pdf>, accessed 20 October 2019, accessed 29 October 2019.

Colmer, K. (2017). 'Collaborative Professional Learning: Contributing to the Growth of Leadership, Professional Identity and Professionalism', *European Early Childhood Education Research Journal*, 25(3), 436–449.

Department of Children and Youth Affairs. (2016). *Diversity, Equality and Inclusion Charter and Guidelines for Early Childhood Care and Education*. Dublin: Department of Children and Youth Affairs, <https://assets.gov.ie/38186/c9e90d89d94b41d3bf00201c98b2ef6a.pdf>, accessed 14 October 2019.

Department of Children and Youth Affairs. (2019). *Early Childhood Care and Education (ECCE) or Free Preschool*. Dublin: Department of Children and Youth Affairs, <https://www.gov.ie/en/publication/d7a5e6-early-childhood-care-and-education-ecce-or-free-preschool/?referrer=/cat/en/childcare/211.htm/>, accessed 21 January 2020.

Department of Children and Youth Affairs. (2020). *Access and Inclusion Model: What Is the Role of the Inclusion Co-Ordinator?* Dublin: Department of Children and Youth Affairs, <https://aim.gov.ie/wp-content/uploads/2017/09/role-of-the-inclusion-co-ordinator.pdf>, accessed 12 September 2020.

Department for Education and Skills. (2006). *Children's Workforce Strategy: The Government's Response to the Consultation*. London: Department for Education and Skills.

Department of Education and Skills. (2016). *Survey of Early Years Practitioners: Consultation for the Review of Education and Training Programmes in Early Years*. Dublin: Department of Education and Skills, <https://www.education.ie/en/The-Education-System/Early-Childhood/Early-Years-Practitioner-Survey-Findings-2016.pdf>, accessed 08 January 2020.

Dunleavy-Lavin, M. M., Heaney, S., and Skehill, S. (2018). 'Individualised Planning: Bureaucratic Requirement or Critical for Effective Practice'. In E. Ring, P. Daly, and E. Wall (eds), *Autism from the Inside Out: A Handbook for Parents, Early Childhood, Primary, Post-Primary and Special School Settings*, pp. 121–138. Oxford: Peter Lang.

Egan, M. (2018). 'Effective Teaching Strategies to Promote Successful Learning'. In E. Ring, P. Daly, and E. Wall (eds), *Autism from the Inside Out: A Handbook for Parents, Early Childhood, Primary, Post-Primary and Special School Settings*, pp. 19–44. Oxford: Peter Lang.

Epstein, J. L. (2018). *School, Family and Community Partnerships: Preparing Educators and Improving Schools*. New York, NY: Routledge.

Fitzgerald, J. (2018). 'Leading Learning for Children with Autism Spectrum Difference'. in E. Ring, P. Daly, and E. Wall (eds), *Autism from the Inside Out: A Handbook for Parents, Early Childhood, Primary, Post-Primary and Special School Settings*, pp. 243–264. Oxford: Peter Lang.

French, G. (2012). 'The Highscope Approach to Early Learning'. In M. Mhic Mahuna and M. Taylor (eds), *Early Childhood Educations and Care: An Introduction for Students in Ireland'*, pp. 127–134. Dublin: Gill and MacMillan.

Government of Ireland. (2018). *First Five: A Whole-of-Government Strategy for Babies, Young Children and Their Families 2019–2028*. Dublin: The Government Publications Office, <https://assets.gov.ie/31184/62acc54f4bdf4405b74e53a4afb8e71b.pdf>, accessed 04 July 2020.

Graham, I. (2017). *Realising Potential: Equality, Diversity and Inclusive Practice in Early Years*. Dublin: Barnardos.

Heikka, J., and Hujala, E. (2013). 'Early Childhood Leadership through the Lens of Distributed Leadership', *European Early Childhood Education Research Journal*, 21(4), 568–580.

Hoås Moen, K., and Granrusten, P. T. (2013). 'Distribution of Leadership Functions in Early Childhood Centers in Norway Following Organisational Changes'. In E. Hujala, M. Waniganayake, and J. Rodd (eds), *Researching Leadership in Early Childhood Education*, pp. 79–96. Tampere: Tampere University Press.

Inter-Departmental Group. (2015). *Supporting Access to the Early Childhood Care and Education Programme for Children with a Disability*. Dublin: Inter-Departmental Group, <http://nda.ie/nda-files/Supporting-Access-to-the-Early-Childhood-Care-and-Education-for-Children-with-a-Disability.pdf>, accessed 21 January 2020.

Lárusdóttir, S. H., and O'Connor, E. (2017). 'Distributed Leadership and Middle Leadership Practice in Schools: A Disconnect?', *Irish Educational Studies*, 36(4), 423–438.

Leithwood, K., and Seashore-Louis, K. (2011). *Linking Leadership to Student Learning: Empirical Insights*. San Francisco, CA: Jossey Bass.

Lewin, K. (1947). 'Frontiers in Group Dynamics: Concept, Method and Reality in Social Science; Social Equilibria and Social Change', *Human Relations*, 1(1), 5–41.

Lindon, J., and Trodd, L. (2016). *Reflective Practice and Early Years Professionalism* (3rd ed.). London: Hodder Education.

McDowall Clark, R. (2012). 'I've Never Thought of Myself as a Leader But …: The Early Years Professional and Catalytic Leadership', *European Early Childhood Education Research Journal*, 20(3), 391–401.

Moloney, M., and McCarthy, E. (2018). *Intentional Leadership for Effective Inclusion in Early Childhood Education and Care: Exploring Core Themes and Strategies*. London: Routledge.

Moloney, M., and Pettersen, J. (2017). *Early Childhood Education Management: Insights into Business Practice and Leadership*. New York, NY: Routledge.

Moyles, J. (2001). 'Passion, Paradox and Professionalism in Early Years Education', *Early Years: An International Journal of Research and Development*, 21(2), 81–95.

Murray, J. (2013). 'Becoming an Early Years Professional: Developing a New Professional Identity', *European Early Childhood Education Research Journal*, 21(4), 527–540.

National Council for Curriculum and Assessment. (2009). *Aistear: The Early Childhood Curriculum Framework*. Dublin: National Council for Curriculum and Assessment, <https://www.ncca.ie/en/early-childhood/aistear>, accessed 09 January 2020.

National Council for Curriculum and Assessment. (2015). *Aistear Siolta Practice Guide*. Dublin: National Council for Curriculum and Assessment, <https://www.ncca.ie/en/early-childhood/aistear-siolta-practice-guide>, accessed 09 January 2020.

Northouse, P. G. (2013). *Leadership: Theory and Practice*. Los Angeles, CA: Sage.

Oberhuemer, P. (2015). 'Seeking New Cultures of Cooperation: A Cross-National Analysis of Workplace-Based Learning and Mentoring Practices in Early Years' Professional Education/Training', *Early Years*, 35(2), 115–123.

O'Byrne, A. (2018). 'Including Parents Right from the Start'. In E. Ring, P. Daly, and E. Wall (eds), *Autism from the Inside Out: A Handbook for Parents, Early Childhood, Primary, Post-Primary and Special School Settings*, pp. 163–180. Oxford: Peter Lang.

Osgood, J. (2010). 'Reconstructing Professionalism in ECEC', *Early Years*, 30(2), 119–133.

Paige-Smyth, A., and Craft, A. (2011). *Developing Reflective Practice in the Early Years*. London: Open University.

Peeters J., Sharmahd, N., and Budginaité, L. (2017). 'Early Childhood Education and Care (ECEC) Assistants in Europe: Pathways towards Continuous Professional Development (CPD) and Qualification', *European Journal Education*, 53(1), 45–57.

Pobal. (2018). *Early Years' Sector Profile 2016/2017*. Dublin: Pobal, <https://www.pobal.ie/app/uploads/2018/06/Early-Years-Sector-Profile-Report-2016-2017.pdf>, accessed 15 October 2019.

Quality and Qualifications Ireland. (2020). *National Framework of Qualifications*. Quality and Qualifications Ireland: Dublin,<https://www.qqi.ie/Articles/Pages/National-Framework-of-Qualifications-(NFQ).aspx>, accessed 12 September 2020.

Ring, E., Mhic Mhathuna, M., M., Hayes, N., Breatnach, D., Stafford, P., Carswell, D., Keegan, S., Kelleher, C., McCafferty, D., O'Keeffe, A., Leavy, A., Madden, R., and Ozonyia, M. (2016). *An Examination of Concepts of School-Readiness Among Parents and Educators in Ireland*. Dublin: Department of Children and Youth Affairs. <https://dspace.mic.ul.ie/handle/10395/2344>, accessed 12 September 2020.

Ring, E., Kelleher, S., Breen, F., Heeney, T., McLoughlin, M., Kearns, A., Stafford, P., Skehill, S., Campion, K., Comerford, D., and O'Sullivan, L. (2019). *Interim Evaluation of the Leadership for Inclusion in the Early Years (LINC) Programme*. Limerick: Mary Immaculate College, <https://documentcloud.adobe.com/link/track?uri=urn:aaid:scds:US:d8c95d7d-2d75-40a8-9f65-b6582908c08d>, accessed 6 January 2019.

Rodd, J. (2004). *Leadership in Early Childhood*. Berkshire: Open University Press.

Siraj-Blatchford, I., and Manni, L. (2007). *Effective Leadership in the Early Years Sector (The ELEYS Study)*. London: Institute of Education, University of London.

Skehill, S. (2019). ' Chapter Nine: Emerging Findings from a PhD study Focused on Evaluating the Impact of the Leadership for Inclusion in the Early Years Programme'. In E. Ring, S. Kelleher, F. Breen, T. Heeney, M. McLoughlin, A. Kearns, P. Stafford, S. Skehill, K. Campion, D. Comerfordand, and L. O'Sullivan, *Interim Evaluation of the Leadership for Inclusion in the Early Years (LINC) Programme*, pp. 94–115. Limerick: Mary Immaculate College, <https://documentcloud.adobe.com/link/track?uri=urn:aaid:scds:US:d8c95d7d-2d75-40a8-9f65-b6582908c08d>, accessed 6 January 2019.

Sorin, R. (2005). 'Changing Images of Childhood: Reconceptualising Early Childhood Practice', *International Journal of Transitions in Childhood*, 1, 12–21.

Sullivan, D. R. (2010). *Learning to Lead: Effective Leadership Skills for Teachers of Young Children* (2nd ed.). St. Paul, MN: Redleaf.

Trodd, L., and Dickerson, C. (2018). '"I Enjoy Learning": Developing Early Years Practitioners' Identities as Professionals and as Professional Learners', *Professional Development in Education*, 45(3), 356–371.

Tusla. (2018). *Quality and Regulatory Framework*. Dublin: Early Years' Inspectorate, Tusla, <https://www.tusla.ie/services/preschool-services/early-years-quality-and-regulatory-framework/>, accessed on 09 January 2020.

Tynan, F. (2018) 'Self-Evaluation: The Way Forward'. In E. Ring, P. Daly, and E. Wall (eds), *Autism from the Inside Out: A Handbook for Parents, Early Childhood, Primary, Post-Primary and Special School Settings*, pp. 265–294. Oxford: Peter Lang.

Urban, M. (2008). 'Dealing with Uncertainty: Challenges and Possibilities for the Early Childhood Profession', *European Early Childhood Education Research Journal*, 16(2), 135–152.

Urban, M., Robson, S., and Scacchi, V. (2017). *Review of the Occupational Role Profiles in Ireland in Early Childhood Education and Care*. Dublin: Department of Education and Skills, <https://www.education.ie/en/Publications/Education-Reports/Final-Review-of-Occupational-Role-Profiles-in-Early-Childhood-Education-and-Care.pdf>, accessed 09 January 2020.

Urban, M., and Rubiano, C. (2014). *Privatisation in Early Childhood Education (PECE). An Explorative Study on Impacts and Implications*. London: Education International, <http://download.ei-ie.org/Docs/WebDepot/EI2015_Privation ECE_EN_final.pdf>, accessed on 09 January 2020.

Urban, M., Vandenbroeck, M., Van Laere, K., Lazzari, A., and Peeters, J. (2011). *Competence Requirements in Early Childhood Education and Care. Final Report*. Brussels: European Commission, Directorate General for Education and Culture.

Waters, J., and Payler, J. (2015). 'The Professional Development of Early Years' Educators – Achieving Systematic, Sustainable and Transformative Change', *Professional Development in Education*, 41(2), 161–168.

ANN DONNELLAN, MARGARET JOYCE AND RACHAEL RYAN

Chapter 10   Leading and Implementing Whole-Setting and Individual Planning

ABSTRACT

In an ideal world, the inclusion of children with additional needs in early learning and care (ELC), primary and special school settings should be instinctive and be embedded in the whole-setting and individual planning that is in place for all children. However, at this point on the journey to achieving full inclusion, the evidence indicates that deliberate and focused planning is required. Planning remains a fundamental element in determining whether all children are supported in achieving their full potential, and is dependent on a whole-setting approach supported by elements of individual planning. Whole-setting approaches to inclusion work best when all professionals employed by the setting believe in all children having an opportunity to grow and develop in a space that reflects their strengths, needs and interests. This is achieved at the beginning through conscious efforts on the part of the manager in creating a culture of acceptance and inclusion. Comprehensive planning supports the manager to lead the team in inclusive practices and pedagogical approaches. This chapter identifies some planning frameworks, which reflect on whole-setting planning in ELC settings, primary and special school settings. It also considers the role of collaboration in supporting whole-setting and individual planning, with particular reference to the Access and Inclusion Model (AIM) and the role of the INclusion COordinator (INCO). The final section of the chapter deliberates on the importance of including the child's voice in the planning process. Strategies are identified for the reader to support the practice of consultation with children. This chapter allows for personal reflection supported by techniques to guide the reader in leading and implementing whole-setting and individual planning for children in the early years across ELC, primary and special school settings.

Introduction

According to the Centre for Early Childhood Development and Education (CECDE 2006a: 2), 'planning and evaluation are essential building blocks in the process of aiming for best practice', as they are integral to the realisation of achieving quality early childhood provision. Furthermore, both processes inform practice, determine review and facilitate change. While acknowledging the critical role of the teacher, the key principles presented by the European Agency for Special Needs and Inclusive Education (EASNIE 2011: 11) start from the learner's perspective, 'putting children at the heart of planning for their presence (access and attendance), participation (in quality learning experiences) and achievement (of outcomes through engagement in the learning process)'. The EASNIE (2017a; 2017b; 2017c; 2017d) consistently emphasis the centrality of placing an intentional focus on planning for the success of all learners in order to provide personalised opportunities for progress. Furthermore, planning should also include listening to the learner's voice and, through this, increase participation and engagement.

The New Zealand Ministry of Education (1996: 28) Early Childhood Curriculum, Te Wharike, advocates that planning and reviewing should be a 'continuous process, involving careful observation, identification of needs and capabilities, provision of resources, assessment and evaluation'. According to CECDE (2006b), guidelines for effective planning include establishing current conditions, being goal orientated by setting out objectives and associated goals logically, and adapting service plans to meet these goals. Furthermore, Kelly (2000) suggests that sequencing events is important, by outlining the steps required to meet the goal and the appropriate order in which those steps take place. 'Enriching and informing good practice within the setting requires a cycle of observation, planning, action and evaluation to be undertaken on a regular basis' (CECDE 2006b: 1) and key to this is the understanding that none of these four processes should stand alone, but should be both inter-dependent and inter-connected. Observations, for example, are not an end in themselves but are a tool for gathering information about a child. They can beneficially be analysed to inform planning (e.g. differentiate activities to meet the individual learning needs of different children) and used as the basis for formal and informal feedback to parents and, or to address concerns about any aspects of the child's learning and development (CECDE 2006b: 8). Additionally, in the primary and special school contexts, the National Council for Special Education's (NCSE's) improved model of support for inclusion highlights the critical importance of whole-setting and individual planning across the broad range of supports envisaged (NCSE 2017; 2018; Lynch et al. 2020). The Department of Education and Skills' (DES) inspectorate consistently highlights the critical role whole-setting and individual planning have in improving outcomes for all children (DES 2016a; 2016b; 2018).

 Key Signposts: Introduction

- Planning and evaluation are essential to good practice.
- Putting children at the heart of planning and valuing their voices, presence, and participation supports all children in achieving their potential.
- Good practice requires a cycle of observation, planning, action and evaluation to be undertaken on a regular basis.

Planning Frameworks

Effective planning for inclusion is a proactive rather than a reactive process, and involves examining and reviewing carefully, the existing provision so that structures for successful inclusion and systematic improvements to current provision can be made (NCSE 2010). Education systems need to move from compensatory approaches, towards more proactive intervention approaches that help to increase a school's capacity to provide high-quality support for all learners (EASNIE 2017a). Development planning at whole-school and early learning and care (ELC) setting level is an 'ongoing process that enables schools and ELC settings to enhance quality and manage change' (NCSE 2011: 24). Furthermore, it considers the aims and values of the school community, sets out a vision for future development and charts a course of action towards realising that vision. Development planning includes policies, practices and procedures in all areas of school life (NCSE 2010). It therefore 'provides a foundation of inclusive principles against which progress towards inclusion can be measured' (NCSE 2011: 24). Strategic planning facilitates the inclusion of all children through the equitable and effective deployment of resources, funding and staffing.

Within the context of supporting children with additional needs in ELC settings, the Inter-Departmental Working Group (IDG) (2015) developed a model of intervention to support the meaningful inclusion of children with additional needs accessing the Early Childhood Care and Education (ECCE) programme, termed the Access and Inclusion Model (AIM). The AIM model provides a suite of supports ranging from universal to targeted with reference to a seven step model of intervention. An Individual Access and Inclusion Plan and associated guidelines were developed to support the implementation of AIM (AIM 2017) and to promote the effective inclusion of children with additional needs in ELC settings. The Individual Access and Inclusion Plan is intended to support children's participation in the early years setting through identifying 'access and participation goals' and providing the supports needed to achieve these goals (AIM 2017). Designed as a live document that will remain in the ECCE setting, the plan enables the service to continually plan for the child's needs (AIM 2017). The plan recognises the importance of the relationship between the parent, the ELC staff and other professionals working collaboratively in planning for the needs of the child. Requiring collaboration and frequent review, the plan documents the child's strengths and interests and identifies the child's needs through 'goal themes' which are located under access, participation and supports. These 'goal themes' can then be 'linked to the Pillars of Practice in the Aistear Síolta Practice Guide' (AIM 2017: 4). The Aistear Síolta Practice Guide (NCCA 2015) supports early childhood teachers to lead the compilation of individual learning journals for all children, using their strengths and their interests in devising learning goals to support children's development. The role of the INclusion COordinator (INCO), the graduate of the Leadership for INClusion in the Early Years (LINC) Programme is to support the key worker and the staff team in 'devising strategies and plans to ensure the participation and inclusion of all children in the pre-school programme' (Ring et al. 2019a: 128). At all stages of the child's ECCE programme, goals should be planned and set in a sensitive, responsive and collaborative manner to support the child's transition to primary school (AIM 2017).

The NCSE guidelines advocate for the effective transition of children with additional needs from pre-school to primary school education and strongly advise that transition is planned for, and is included in the Individual Education Plan (IEP) process (NCSE 2006). The IEP process at primary and special school level mirrors the Individual Access and Inclusion Plan at ELC level. In Ireland, unlike many other countries, the IEP process is not underpinned by legislation; and in 2006 the NCSE compiled comprehensive guidelines in relation to the IEP process in order to support a uniform approach which reflects international practice (Ring, Daly and Wall 2018). The IEP is a written document prepared for a named child and it specifies the learning goals that are to be achieved over a set period of time and the teaching strategies, resources and supports necessary to achieve these goals (NCSE 2006). The NCSE (2006) further advises that IEPs should be individualised and child-centred; inclusive; collaborative and accessible. International and national guidelines on the IEP process suggest that the process is best supported by collaboration between parents, the child, teachers and external professionals such as a psychologist, speech and language therapist, occupational therapist and others who are working with the child (Ring et al. 2018a). Although not mandated by legislation, according to McCarthy (2006) the IEP process has been embraced by many teachers and education settings in Ireland concerned with promoting good practice in supporting inclusion.

However it is important that whole-setting and individual planning is not considered in isolation from the myriad influences of in the child's environment and to this end, the model developed by the EASNIE presents a useful framework within which to locate and consider planning. In 2017, EASNIE presented a new contribution towards improving inclusive early childhood education (IECE), an ecosystem model of IECE for policy-makers and other stakeholders wishing to collaborate towards effective action in this field (EASNIE 2017a; 2017b; 2017c; 2017d). This model can support policy-makers and practitioners to collaborate in planning, reviewing and improving quality. It serves as a framework for planning, improving, monitoring and evaluating IECE quality at local, regional and national levels (EASNIE 2017b). The model is inspired by three major frameworks; the structure-process-outcome framework used by European and international policy-makers (European Commission (EC) 2014; Organisation for Economic Co-operation and Development (OECD) 2015); the ecological systems framework (Bronfenbrenner and Morris 2006) and the inclusive education perspective (EASNIE 2015). It incorporates all the principles of the EC and OECD frameworks for quality early childhood education and also enhances their applicability by locating them at different ecological levels (inclusive early childhood education setting, home/community and regional/national levels). The model places the IECE outcomes for children at its centre, surrounded by the pre-school processes and surrounding structures in the microsystem, the structural factors in the home and community at the mesosystem level, and the regional/national structures at the macrosystem level (EASNIE 2017b). This combined model provides a clear, comprehensive and situated portrayal of the issues related to improving quality in IECE and the associated implications for whole-setting and individual planning processes. Using this framework, policy-makers and practitioners can consider their own priority needs and goals within the model's comprehensive picture of the issues relevant in providing for quality IECE (EASNIE 2017a; 2017b; 2017c; 2017d).

> **Key Signposts: Planning Frameworks**
>
> - Effective planning for inclusion is a proactive rather than a reactive process.
> - Development planning at whole-school and early learning and care (ELC) setting level is an ongoing process that enables schools and ELC settings to enhance quality and manage change.
> - The Individual Access and Inclusion Plan at ELC level and the individualised planning process at primary and special school learning are useful planning framework for the individual planning process (National Council for Curriculum and Assessment (NCCA) 2006; Access and Inclusion Model (AIM) 2017).
> - Strategic planning facilitates the inclusion of all children through the equitable and effective deployment of resources, funding and staffing.
> - Using the framework developed by the European Agency for Special Needs and Inclusive Education (EASNIE) can support policymakers and practitioners in considering their own priority needs and goals within the model's comprehensive picture of the issues relevant in providing for quality inclusive early childhood education (IEC) (EASNIE 2017a; 2017b; 2017c; 2017d).

Collaborative Practice

Lohmann, Hathcote and Boothe (2018: 25) noted the 'critical' importance of partnership between families and schools for children with additional needs. Furthermore, their view is that a child's education, both academic and social, is significantly improved through effective collaborations between families and schools. Inclusive learning environments pivot on a shared responsibility by all parties working together for the benefit of the child. 'Collaborative planning supports continuity and positive transitions within, and between early childhood settings, as well as enhancing holistic and integrated approaches to achieving learning and development outcomes' (Flottman, McKernan and Tayler 2011: 12). Further support for collaborative planning is evident in the IDG's (2015) publication, which advises inclusive education is enhanced through a collaborative approach. This is further confirmed by research conducted by Lynch and colleagues (2020) in evaluating an ELC and in-school therapy support demonstration project in Ireland, where the focus of the project in building relationships and establishing collaborative practices was identified as a particularly positive element that contributed to the project's effectiveness. As stated by Graham (2017: 59) 'when teams have a shared way of working with common values, it becomes second nature among the team to consider any special requirements when planning and making decisions and carrying out daily activities.'

Síolta: The National Quality Framework for Early Childhood Education (CECDE 2006a) advocates a collaborative approach in meeting the needs of all children in the early years, with one of its sixteen quality standards dedicated to the significance of planning in providing for quality practice. This quality standard states that good practice is a key factor in supporting a child's learning and development and, is rooted in quality issues and how these are translated into practice (CECDE 2006a; 2006c).

McPartland (2012) advises that planning for collaboration and deliberation on key issues in ELC settings should not cease once the plan has been put into action but rather should be embedded in a setting's daily practice. In this context, adopting a reflective planning cycle provides the opportunity for consistent self-reflection, team-reflection and evaluation. Evaluating plans allows early childhood teachers to determine a child's progression in their learning and development, and to share this information in facilitating and leading future plans. Allocating time for regular review of plans allows for stakeholders to be effective in their work (McPartland 2012).

In essence collaboration is an inclusive process, whereby the child and all those involved in supporting the child's learning and development have a voice and are listened to. Planning to include the communities that are represented in the setting will ensure each child's cultural identity is represented (Graham 2017). This is a vital part of supporting the inclusion of all children within the setting, with Graham (2017) further noting that harnessing community will also strengthen children's understanding and awareness of diversity and inclusion. This allows children to start to appreciate and respect difference and it is important that early childhood teachers build on this understanding to support the development of more formalised attitudes to diversity as part of curriculum planning opportunities to reinforce this culture of acceptance.

There is no one definite approach associated with effective planning. Significantly the approach adopted is not the core concern but rather the key underpinning principle of placing the child at the centre of the planning. Child-centred planning, which embraces each child's individual strengths, needs and interests can contribute greatly to the provision of inclusive learning experiences.

> ### Key Signposts: Collaborative Practice
>
> - Adopting a collaborative approach supports quality practice and promotes an inclusive space for learning and development for all children.
> - Collaborative planning supports continuity and positive transitions within and between early childhood settings, as well as enhancing holistic and integrated approaches to achieving learning and development outcomes (Flottman, McKernan and Tayler 2011).
> - Utilising a reflective planning cycle provides the opportunity for consistent self-reflection, team-reflection and evaluation.
> - Allocating time for regular review of plans allows for stakeholders to be effective in their work (McPartland 2012).
> - In essence collaboration is an inclusive process, whereby the child and all those involved in supporting the child's learning and development have a voice and are listened to.
> - Planning to include the communities that are represented in the setting, will ensure each child's cultural identity is represented (Graham 2017).
> - Child-centred planning, which embraces each child's individual strengths, needs and interests can contribute greatly to the provision of inclusive learning experiences.

Overcoming the Challenges to Effective Collaboration

Among the challenges to effective collaboration in early childhood education that have been identified are the lack of a shared language and time and space for collaboration. The diversity of professionals working in the ELC sector in particular may lead to challenges, as professionals with different backgrounds may not share a common language or way to describe young children's learning and development (Wesley and Buysse 2001; Lumsden 2005; Weiner and Murawski 2005; Lynch et al. 2020). However, while it is important to acknowledge the existence of these challenges, challenges to implementing a collaborative approach should not impede early childhood teachers adopting a shared and collaborative approach to planning. Understandably, there may be frustration stemming from the amount of time early childhood teachers and parents have available for collaboration and of course, space to speak and collaborate in confidence can also present as a challenge for families. However, through prioritising the building of respectful, trusting, meaningful and mutually supportive relationships, these challenges can be overcome (Mac Naughton and Hughes 2011). Table 10.1 provides some pointers for developing collaborative communication culture.

Table 10.1. Pointers for Developing a Collaborative Communication Culture

- Recognise the parents' expertise and knowledge about their child as an instrumental source in supporting each individual child on his/her learning and development journey.
- Use written records to support conversations with parents and other professionals.
- Maintain discretion and confidentiality in all communications.
- Remain mindful of the language you are using to communicate with families and other professionals, keeping it appropriate, respectful and inclusive.
- Spend time actively listening to other relevant stakeholders – remembering that listening is effortful.
- Proactively identify and plan next steps.

Whole-Setting and Individual Planning

> ### Key Signposts: Overcoming the Challenges to Effective Collaboration
>
> - Among the challenges to effective collaboration in early childhood education that have been identified are the lack of a shared language and, time and space for collaboration.
> - While it is important to acknowledge the existence of these challenges, challenges to implementing a collaborative approach should not impede early childhood teachers adopting a shared and collaborative approach to planning.
> - Through prioritising the building of respectful, trusting, meaningful and mutually supportive relationships, challenges to effective collaboration can be met (Mac Naughton and Hughes 2011).
> - Effective collaboration can be achieved by, *interalia*, acknowledging parents' expertise; maintaining written records; maintaining discretion and confidentiality; using appropriate language; adopting an active listening disposition and actively planning and agreeing next steps.

Involving Children in the Planning Process

In Chapter 2 of this publication, Ring, Harte and Harmon have examined a range of research concerning the value of creating early childhood environments where children's right to participate is visible and where children's voices are embedded in the fabric and acoustic of the setting is explored. The authors have provided a range of strategies to support early childhood teachers in meaningfully harnessing all children's voices in ELC, primary and special school settings. The authors conclude that the rationale for capturing children's voices is threefold in terms of being a matter of human rights and social justice; optimising children's learning and development and central to the concept of democracy in education. It is imperative therefore that children are meaningfully included in the planning processes, which directly impact on their wellbeing, learning and development in the early years.

The voice of the child and the child's involvement in the planning process should be central in all discussions regarding whole-school or whole-setting planning. This is reflected in the key principles as presented by the EASNIE (2011), which start by putting the child at the heart of the planning process. Furthermore, there is increased acknowledgement of the importance of the overall wellbeing of the child and the factors that influence this. One of these factors, which is clearly recognised in the Wellbeing Policy Statement and Framework for Practice 2019–2023, is the importance of having systems in place to encourage the voice of the child (Government of Ireland (GoI) 2018a). This document also notes that children should be also involved in planning the school's extra-curricular programme.

In Ireland the demographic landscape is ever-changing; this is reflected in our ELC settings, our schools and in our after-school provision. The voice of each and every child should be reflected in the planning process; including children who are from a variety of ethnic and cultural backgrounds, children from the travelling community, children who do not have English as their first language, children with additional needs, refugees, asylum seekers and children from families of gay or lesbian parents. Inclusive practice is about accommodating and respecting difference as the norm in daily life (Graham 2017). Influenced by research in early childhood, the image of the child has shifted from that of being weak, vulnerable, helpless, dependent on adults and not capable of having a voice in matters that affect them to being strong, confident, competent and capable of having a voice in all matters that affect them (Malaguzzi 1993; Sorin 2005; Ring et al. 2018b; Moloney and McCarthy 2018; Ring et al. 2019b). This image is reflected in a range of policy and curriculum documentation in Ireland, including Aistear – the Early Childhood Curriculum Framework (NCCA 2009), Síolta, the National Quality Framework (CECDE 2006); the Primary School Curriculum (NCCA 1999; 2019); the Draft Primary Curriculum Framework (NCCA 2020) and First Five: A Whole-of-Government Strategy for Babies, Young Children and their Families 2019–2028 (GoI 2018b).

In ELC settings the emergent curriculum focuses on the early childhood teacher being responsive to the children's interest in creating meaningful and engaging learning experiences (NCCA 2009). The philosophy of the emergent curriculum is that it is child-led and builds on the child's strengths and interests. It is only when we allow children to assume a central role in planning that we can support children to be competent and confident learners. Learning is more meaningful, motivating and enjoyable for children when based on their skills, strengths and interests (NCCA 2009). Graham (2017) describes the powerful impact of consulting with children and involving them in all decisions and actions relative to them both big and small. There are many and varied ways to do this depending on the age and stage of the child and five examples of such approaches are now detailed below. Recent curriculum developments at primary level in Ireland also highlight the importance of child agency and allocating the children a central role in the learning and teaching process (Ring et al. 2018b; NCCA 2019; 2020).

The Mosaic Approach

The Mosaic Approach is a child-friendly approach to listening to children and recording their voice that acknowledges both child and adults as co-constructors of meaning using both visual and verbal methods (Clark and Moss 2011). It is a particularly useful method in including children from different backgrounds as it uses different methods in recognition of the different languages and voices of children by allowing the children to be active participants and to highlight their role as experts and agents in their own lived experiences (Clark and Moss 2011). It is also an adaptable approach and could be applied to different contexts and settings in the field of early childhood and after-school settings. The Mosaic Approach uses multiple methods to engage children in research; this approach makes use of children's drawings, tour mappings and children's photographs (Clark 2017). Findings from these methods can be brought back to children to have further discussions and hence inform planning (Clark and Moss 2011). Ultimately the Mosaic Approach has paved the way for children to have a central role in creating learning spaces that suit their needs. The methods discussed below can also be beneficially incorporated in the Mosaic Approach.

Consultation with Children

Conversations and group discussions with children can be carried out with small groups or indeed larger groups (Turner, Ring and O'Sullivan 2019). Children can talk about themselves, their likes, dislikes and interests, which can form the basis for curriculum planning. Flexibility is important in order to get the most input from children. Clark and Moss (2011) advocate that such discussions or 'conferences' need to be conducted on the move and conducted indoors or outdoors. Asking the children open-ended questions allows children to 'structure the nature and extent of their response' (Lindsay, Dockrell and Lewis 2000:55).

Visual Schedules and Choice Boards

All children, irrespective of age or capacity can contribute to discussions around their learning and teaching experiences and as educators, it is our responsibility to seek and elicit their views. AsIAm (2020: 8) advise that it is important to remember that 'spoken language is only one of the many ways in which students communicate their thoughts, ideas, feelings and information'. Children who experience challenges in making choices through language can be offered choices of activities in other forms. Through observing children, we can understand how they communicate with us. Children communicate in a myriad of ways from the moment they are born being tuned into to gestures, body-language, physical movements, sounds, smiling, laughing, crying and indicating preferences for particular activities, people and places allows us to understand how children are communicating with us (AsIAm 2020). For example, where children do not communicate verbally, the use of photographs of activities and choice boards provides children with the opportunity to express themselves and interact with the teacher (AsIAm 2020).

Children's Drawings

Veale (2005) says that drawings can provide the teacher with an insight into children's lived experiences. It is important to provide a variety of tools for the child so that they have the option of a range of implements and materials to engage in the drawing process. In early childhood, children enjoy letters, shapes and playing around with scribble and they quickly learn that letters and words can communicate meaning (Coates and Coates 2015). The mindful teacher can use these examples of such communication along with mathematical graphics, writing or reading with older children to hear their voice and engage them in the planning process. There has been a range of research conducted in Ireland that has successfully captured children's voices through the use of drawings (Daly et al. 2016; Ring and O'Sullivan 2016; Turner et al. 2019; Lynch et al. 2020).

Children as Photographers

The use of either disposable or digital cameras as a tool for children is also part of the Mosaic Approach and can be beneficial in capturing the children's lived experiences in their home, in consultation with parents or carers (Clark and Moss 2011). This method can particularly support children who are pre-verbal or children who do not have English as their first language and these photographs can be the children's voice in curriculum planning as noted by Clark and Moss below:

> Cameras offer young children the opportunity to produce a finished product in which they can take pride. Children who have seen members of their family take photographs, poured over family albums or looked at photographs in books and comics, know that photographs have a value in the 'adult world.' This is not always the case with children's own drawings and paintings. (Clark and Moss 2011: 28)

Ring and O'Sullivan (2018 cited in Ring et al. 2019b) recently developed a child-led approach, 'exploring and telling' in eliciting the voices of young autistic children in ELC settings in Ireland. The approach utilises autophotography, and the child is invited to wear a camera, to help the researcher understand the child's perspective of what is happening in the ELC setting. The video/photographs are subsequently downloaded to a visual display unit and the researcher engages in discussion with the child. The process is based 'on cultivating collaborative dialogue; inclusive democratic deliberation and co-participation' (Denzin and Lincoln 2018, cited in Ring et al. 2019b).

> **Key Signposts: Involving Children in the Planning Process**
>
> - Research indicates that listening to children and incorporating their expressed views in planning yields significant dividends in terms of contributing to creating meaningful and engaging learning and teaching experiences for children.
> - An emergent curriculum build's on a child's strengths and expressed interests.
> - All children, irrespective of age or capacity have a voice and our responsibility is to capture and incorporate the views of all children.
> - A range of methods are available to support teachers in early learning and care (ELC), primary and special schools in eliciting children's views. These methods include the Mosaic Approach (Clark and Moss 2011); consultation with children; visual schedules and choice boards; children's drawings and photography.

Conclusion

A collaborative approach to planning for young children is essential to ensure the best outcomes. This involves careful observation and documentation with regard to children's learning and development, representing individual strengths and needs, and keeping children at the heart of planning. Planning works best when all parties work together: teachers, parents, other professionals and most importantly the children themselves. The planning process must be inclusive of diversity, and community involvement ensuring each child's cultural identity is represented. The planning process must acknowledge that all children have a voice and this voice should be heard and reflected in all matters affecting them. Central to this is how adults view all children and how they respect the importance of actively listening to children and documenting their views and opinions. Planning should be supported by regular reflection and further actions in order to remain effective. Good practice essentially requires a cycle of observation, planning, action and evaluation to be undertaken on a regular basis. The power of planning, both at individual and whole-setting level for optimising children's outcomes at this critical phase of their development cannot be underestimated.

Bibliography

Access and Inclusion Model. (2017). *Guidelines for Completing an Individual Access and Inclusion Plan*. Dublin: Government of Ireland, <https://aim.gov.ie/wp-content/uploads/2016/12/aim-level-4-individual-access-and-inclusion-plan.pdf>, accessed 6 August 2019.

AsIAm. (2020). *Bridge Back to School: Am Autism-Friendly Learning Resource for Summer 2020*. Dublin: AsIAm, <https://asiam.ie/wp-content/uploads/2020/07/Digital-copy-of-Bridge-back-to-school-3.pdf>, accessed 15 September 2020.

Bronfenbrenner, U., and Morris, P. A. (2006). 'The Bioecological Model of Human Development', In W. Damon and R. M. Lerner (eds), *Handbook of Child Psychology, Vol. 1: Theoretical Models of Human Development* (6th ed.), pp. 793–828. New York, NY: Wiley.

Centre for Early Childhood Development and Education. (2006a). *Síolta: The National Quality Framework for Early Childhood Education*. Dublin: Centre for Early Childhood Development and Education, <http://siolta.ie/media/pdfs/final_handbook.pdf>, accessed 08 September 2020.

Centre for Early Childhood Development and Education (CECDE). (2006b). *Síolta Research Digest: Standard 8 Planning and Evaluating*. Dublin: Centre for Early Childhood Development and Education, <http://siolta.ie/media/pdfs/Research%20Digest%20-%20Planning%20and%20Evaluation.pdf>, accessed 24 January 2020.

Centre for Early Childhood Development and Education (CECDE). (2006c). *Síolta Research Digest*. Dublin: Centre for Early Childhood Development and Education, <http://siolta.ie/research_digests.php>, accessed 21 May 2019.

Clark, A. (2017). *Listening to Young Children: A Guide to Understanding and Using the Mosaic Approach*. London: Jessica Kingsley Publishers.

Clark, A., and Moss, P. (2011). *Listening to Young Children: The Mosaic Approach* (2nd ed.). London: National Children's Bureau Enterprises Ltd.

Coates, E., and Coates, A. (2015). 'Recognising the Sacred Spark of Wonder: Scribbling and Related Talk as Evidence of How Young Children's Thinking May Be Identified'. In S. Robson and S. Flannery Quinn (eds), *The Routledge International Handbook of Children's Thinking and Understanding*, pp. 306–317. Abingdon: Routledge.

Daly, P., Ring, E., Egan, M., Fitzgerald, J., Griffin, C., Long, S., McCarthy, E., Moloney, M., O'Brien, T., O'Byrne, A., O'Sullivan, S., Ryan, M., Wall, E., Madden, R., and Gibbons, S. (2016). *An Evaluation of Education Provision for Students with Autism Spectrum Disorder in Ireland*. Trim: National Council for Special Education, <https://ncse.ie/wp-content/uploads/2016/07/5_NCSE-Education-Provision-ASD-Students-No21.pdf>, accessed 15 September 2020.

Department of Education and Skills. (2016a). *A Guide to Inspection in Primary Schools*. Dublin: Department of Education and Skills, <https://www.education.ie/en/Publications/Inspection-Reports-Publications/Evaluation-Reports-Guidelines/A-Guide-to-Inspection-in-Primary-Schools.pdf>, accessed 14 September 2020.

Department of Education and Skills. (2016b). *Looking at our School 2016: A Quality Framework for Primary Schools*. Dublin: Department of Education and Skills, <https://www.education.ie/en/Publications/Inspection-Reports-Publications/Evaluation-Reports-Guidelines/Looking-at-Our-School-2016-A-Quality-Framework-for-Primary-Schools.pdf>, accessed 30 August 2020.

Department of Education and Skills. (2018). *A Guide to Early Years Education Inspection (EYEI)*. Dublin: Department of Education and Skills, <https://www.education.ie/en/Publications/Inspection-Reports-Publications/Evaluation-Reports-Guidelines/guide-to-early-years-education-inspections.pdf>, accessed 06 September 2020.

European Agency for Special Needs and Inclusive Education. (2011). *Key Principles for Promoting Quality in Inclusive Education. Recommendations for Practice*.

Odense, Denmark: European Agency for Special Needs and Inclusive Education, <https://www.european-agency.org/sites/default/files/key-principles-for-promoting-quality-in-inclusive-education-recommendations-for-practice_Key-Principles-2011-EN.pdf>, accessed 20 May 2019.

European Agency for Special Needs and Inclusive Education. (2015). *Agency Position on Inclusive Education Systems*. Odense, Denmark: European Agency for Special Needs and Inclusive Education, <https://www.europeanagency.org/publications/brochures-and-flyers/agency-position-on-inclusion-educationsystems-flyer>, accessed 23 May 2019.

European Agency for Special Needs and Inclusive Education. (2017a). *Inclusive Early Childhood Education: Literature Review* (F. Bellour, P. Bartolo, and M. Kyriazopoulou, eds). Odense, Denmark: <https://www.european-agency.org/sites/default/files/IECE%20Literature%20Review.pdf>, accessed 03 July 2020.

European Agency for Special Needs and Inclusive Education. (2017b). *Inclusive Early Childhood Education: New Insights and Tools – Contributions from a European Study* (M. Kyriazopoulou, P. Bartolo, E. Björck-Åkesson, C. Giné, and F. Bellour, eds). Odense. Denmark: European Agency for Special Needs and Inclusive Education, <https://www.european-agency.org/sites/default/files/IECE_Synthesis_Report_2017.pdf>, accessed 14 September 2020.

European Agency for Special Needs and Inclusive Education. (2017c). *Inclusive Early Childhood Education: New Insights and Tools – Final Summary Report* (M. Kyriazopoulou, P. Bartolo, E. Björck-Åkesson, C. Giné, and F. Bellour, eds). Odense, Denmark: European Agency for Special Needs and Inclusive Education, <https://www.european-agency.org/sites/default/files/IECE-Summary-ENelectronic.pdf>, accessed 21 January 2020.

European Agency for Special Needs and Inclusive Education. (2017d). *Inclusive Early Childhood Education Environment Self-Reflection Tool* (M. Kyriazopoulou, P. Bartolo, E. Björck-Åkesson, C. Giné, and F. Bellour, eds). Odense, Denmark: European Agency for Special Needs and Inclusive Education, <https://www.european-agency.org/resources/publications/inclusive-early-childhood-education-environment-self-reflection-tool>, accessed 06 September 2020.

European Commission. (2014). *Proposal for Key Principles of a Quality Framework for Early Childhood Education and Care. Report of the Working Group on Early Childhood Education and Care under the Auspices of the European Commission*. Brussels: European Commission, Directorate-General for Education and Culture, <https://ec.europa.eu/assets/eac/education/policy/strategic-framework/archive/documents/ecec-quality-framework_en.pdf>, accessed 14 September 2020.

Flottman, R., McKernan, A., and Tayler, C. (2011). *Victorian Early Years Learning and Development Framework: Evidence Paper Practice Principle 2: Partnership with Professionals*. Melbourne: University of Melbourne, <https://education.vic.gov.au/Documents/childhood/providers/edcare/pracpartner.pdf>, accessed 04 October 2020.

Government of Ireland. (2018a). *Wellbeing Policy Statement and Framework for Practice 2018–2023*. Dublin: Government Publications Office, <https://www.education.ie/en/Publications/Policy-Reports/wellbeing-policy-statement-and-framework-for-practice-2018%E2%80%932023.pdf>, accessed 14 September 2020.

Government of Ireland. (2018b). *First Five: A Whole-of-Government Strategy for Babies, Young Children and Their Families 2019–2028*. Dublin: The Government Publications Office, <https://assets.gov.ie/31184/62acc54f4bdf4405b74e53a4afb8e71b.pdf>, accessed 04 July 2020.

Graham, I. (2017). *Realising Potential: Equality, Diversity and Inclusion Practice in Early Years*. Dublin: Barnardos.

Inter-Departmental Group. (2015). *Supporting Access to the Early Childhood Care and Education Programme for Children with a Disability*. Dublin: Inter-Departmental Group, <http://nda.ie/nda-files/Supporting-Access-to-the-Early-Childhood-Care-and-Education-for-Children-with-a-Disability.pdf>, accessed 21 January 2020.

Kelly, M. (2000). *Good Practice Self-Assessment Manual – A Personal Resource Manual for Child Care Providers*. Dublin: National Children's Nurseries Association.

Lindsay, G., Dockrell, J. E., and Lewis, A. (2000). 'Researching Children's Perspectives: A Psychological Dimension'. In A. Lewis and G. Lindsay (eds), *Researching Children's Perspectives*, pp. 45–58. Buckingham: Open University Press.

Lohmann, M., Hathcote, A., and Boothe, K. (2018). 'Addressing the Barriers to Family-School Collaboration: A Brief Review of the Literature and Recommendations for Practice', *International Journal of Early Childhood Special Education*, 10(1), 26–32, <https://www.int-jecse.net/data-cms/articles/20200531114616pm454424.pdf>, accessed 14 September 2020.

Lumsden, E. (2005). 'Joined Up Thinking in Practice: An Exploration of Professional Collaboration'. In T. Waller (ed), *An Introduction to Early Childhood: A Multidisciplinary Approach*, pp. 39–54. London: Paul Chapman Publishing.

Lynch, H., Ring, E., Boyle, B., Moore, A., O'Toole, C., O'Sullivan, L., Brophy, T., Frizelle, P., Horgan, D. and O'Sullivan, D. (2020). *Evaluation of In-School and Early Years Therapy Support Demonstration Project*. Trim: National Council for Special Education, https://ncse.ie/wp-content/uploads/2020/11/Demo-project-evaluation-fInal-for-web-upload.pdf, accessed 04 January 2021.

Mac Naughton, G., and Hughes, P. (2011). *Parents and Professionals in Early Years Settings*. Maidenhead: Open University Press.

Malaguzzi, L. (1993). 'For an Education Based on Relationships', *Young Children*, November, 9–13.

McCarthy, J. (2006). 'The IEP Process: Current Practice and Perspectives', *REACH Journal of Special Needs Education in Ireland*, 19(2), 112–121.

McPartland, E. (2012). *Supervision and Leadership in Childcare*. Dublin: Gill & Macmillan.

Moloney, M., and McCarthy, E. (2018). *Intentional Leadership for Effective Inclusion in Early Childhood Education and Care*. London: Routledge.

National Council for Curriculum and Assessment. (1999). *Primary School Curriculum*. Dublin: National Council for Curriculum and Assessment.

National Council for Curriculum and Assessment. (2009). *Aistear: The Early Childhood Curriculum Framework*. Dublin: National Council for Curriculum and Assessment, <https://www.ncca.ie/en/early-childhood/aistear>, accessed 29 October 2019.

National Council for Curriculum and Assessment. (2015). *Aistear/Síolta Practice Guide*. Dublin, National Council for Curriculum and Assessment, <www.ncca.ie/en/Practice-Guide>, accessed 04 July 2020.

National Council for Curriculum and Assessment. (2019). *Primary Language Curriculum*. Dublin: National Council for Curriculum and Assessment, <https://www.curriculumonline.ie/getmedia/2a6e5f79-6f29-4d68-b850-379510805656/PLC-Document_English.pdf>, accessed 12 January 2020.

National Council for Curriculum and Assessment. (2020). *Draft Primary Curriculum Framework. For Consultation*. Dublin: National Council for Curriculum and Assessment, https://ncca.ie/media/4456/ncca-primary-curriculum-framework-2020.pdf, accessed 06 September 2020.

National Council for Special Education. (2006). *Guidelines on the Individual Education Plan Process*. Trim: National Council for Special Education, <https://ncse.ie/individual-education-plans>, accessed 9 May 2019.

National Council for Special Education. (2010). *Literature Review of the Principles and Practices Relating to Inclusive Education for Children with Special Educational Needs*. Trim: National Council for Special Education, <https://ncse.ie/wp-content/uploads/2014/10/NCSE_Inclusion.pdf>, accessed 22 May 2019.

National Council for Special Education. (2011). *Inclusive Education Framework, a Guide for Schools on the Inclusion of Pupils with Special Educational Needs*. Trim: National Council for Special Education, <https://ncse.ie/wp-content/uploads/2014/10/InclusiveEducationFramework_InteractiveVersion.pdf>, accessed 14 September 2020.

National Council for Special Education. (2017). *Delivering for Students with Additional Care Needs. The Right Support at the Right Time in Schools. A Proposed Model of Support.* Trim: National Council for Special Education, <https://ncse.ie/wp-content/uploads/2018/05/NCSE-Delivering-Students-Care-WGR02.pdf>, accessed 14 September 2020.

National Council for Special Education. (2018). *Comprehensive Review of the Special Needs Assistant Scheme. A New School Inclusion Model to Deliver the Right Supports at the Right Time to Students with Additional Care Needs*, <http://ncse.ie/wp-content/uploads/2018/05/NCSE-PAP6-Comprehensive-Review-SNA-Scheme.pdf>, accessed 6 January 2020.

New Zealand Ministry of Education. (1996). *Te Wharike: Early Childhood Curriculum.* Wellington: New Zealand, <http://www.minedu.gov.nz/index>, accessed 21 May 2019.

Organisation for Economic Co-operation and Development. (2015). *Starting Strong IV: Monitoring Quality in Early Childhood Education and Care.* Paris: Organisation for Economic Co-operation and Development Publishing.

Ring, E. (2016). 'National Higher Education Programme for Inclusion Coordinators in Early Years' Settings', *Education Matters*, 131.

Ring, E., Daly, P., and Wall, E. (eds). (2018a). *Autism from the Inside Out: A Handbook for Parents, Early Childhood, Primary, Post-Primary and Special School Settings.* Oxford: Peter Lang.

Ring, E., Kelleher, S., Breen, F., Heeney, T., McLoughlin, M., Kearns, A., Stafford, P., Skehill, S., Campion, K., Comerford, D., and O'Sullivan, L. (2019a). *Interim Evaluation of the Leadership for Inclusion in the Early Years (LINC) Programme.* Limerick: Mary Immaculate College, <https://documentcloud.adobe.com/link/track?uri=urn:aaid:scds:US:d8c95d7d-2d75-40a8-9f65-b6582908c08d>, accessed 6 January 2019.

Ring, E., and O'Sullivan, L. (2016). 'The Importance of Including the Child's Voice in the Transition Process: Signposts from a National Evaluation of Concepts of School Readiness in Ireland', *Children's Research Digest*, 3(2), 37–44.

Ring, E., O'Sullivan, L., O'Keeffe, S., Ferris, F., and Wall, E. (2019b). *An Evaluation of Teach Me As I Am Early Years Programme.* Dublin: AsIAm, <https://asiam.ie/wp-content/uploads/2019/04/TeachMeAsIAm-booklet.pdf>, accessed 15 September 2020.

Ring, E., O'Sullivan, L., Ryan, M., and Burke, P. (2018b). *A Melange or a Mosaic of Theories? How Theoretical Perspectives on Children's Learning and Development Can Inform a Responsive Pedagogy in a Redeveloped Primary School Curriculum.* Dublin: National Council for Curriculum and Assessment, <https://www.ncca.ie/media/3863/seminar_four_er_los_mr_pb_paper.pdf>, accessed 16 January 2020.

Sorin, R. (2005). 'Changing Images of Childhood: Reconceptualising Early Childhood Practice', *International Journal of Transitions in Childhood*, 1, 12–21.

Turner, S., Ring, E., and O'Sullivan. (2019). 'The Transformative Power of Child Voice for Learning and Teaching in Our Classrooms: Signposts for Practice from Research Findings in a Primary School in Ireland', *Learn*, 7–17.

Veale, A. (2005). 'Creative Methodologies in Participatory Research with Children'. In S. Greene and D. Hogan (eds), *Researching Children's Experience: Approaches and Methods*, pp. 253–272. London: Sage Publications.

Weiner, I., and Murawski, W. W. (2005). 'Schools Attuned: A Model for Collaborative Intervention', *Intervention in School & Clinic*, 40(5), 284–290.

Wesley, P. W., and Buysse, V. (2001). 'Communities of Practice: Expanding Professional Roles to Promote Reflection and Shared Inquiry', *Topics in Early Childhood Special Education*, 21(2), 114–123.

PATRICIA M. DALY

Chapter 11 Assessed Needs as Signposts for Learning and Development

ABSTRACT
The presence of children with assessed needs is not only to be expected in early childhood classes but to be welcomed. This chapter focuses on creating inclusive early childhood experiences for all children in early learning and care (ELC), primary and post-primary settings. It is important to note that all children are children first – they share the same learning needs and repertoires including curiosity, playfulness, exploration and a keen desire to learn. Their assessed needs signal our role to provide supports in ways that are discrete, sensitive and of benefit to all children. This chapter will focus on a conceptual understanding of behaviour as communication, both verbal and non-verbal. Teachers are situated as critical interpreters within a framework for 'seeing' behaviour as communicative, the various ways children with additional needs in early childhood classes show these needs, for understanding the message and responding to it. Particular assessed needs are presented as signposts for a range of sample supports to provide meaningful access for children with these needs. Patterns in recommended supports are then connected to the concepts of Universal Design for Learning (UDL).

Introduction

As noted in the opening chapter of the book, the Leadership for Inclusion in the Early years (LINC) Programme prepares early childhood teachers to serve in a leadership role in their classrooms and settings to ensure the inclusion of children with assessed needs (Ring et al. 2019). This in turn supports the implementation of Level 3 of the Access and Inclusion Model (AIM) in operation in Ireland since 2016 (Inter-Departmental Group (IDG) 2016) by contributing to the creation of a qualified and competent early childhood workforce. Since one early childhood teacher per early learning and care (ELC) setting Early Childhood setting is entitled to access the LINC programme, the leadership skills they develop are critical to facilitate cascading their knowledge and understanding across the other professionals in their setting. This chapter provides a glimpse of the knowledge, skills and attitudes promoted by the LINC programme and essential for working well with children with assessed needs. The chapter's focus is on children from ages 2 ½ to 5 ½ years of age approximately, in early childhood classes at ELC, primary and special schools who have an 'assessed need', which has implications for teaching and learning. These assessed needs indicate that additional supports may be needed to ensure development and learning are supported adequately in an inclusive environment. Inclusive environments differ from specialised environments that are constructed to serve the needs of cohorts of children with particular assessed needs. All children participate, learn and develop together in inclusive environments with the addition of supports based on the specialised knowledge and skills of a qualified and competent workforce as envisaged by the AIM model.

The White Paper on Early Childhood Education (Department of Education and Skills (DES) 1999) identified three reasons to educate young children with special educational needs in inclusive environments. These are: (1) the importance of early learning as a foundation for all later growth and development, (2) the potential for amelioration of the effects of a learning difficulty with early expert support and teaching, and (3) the support good quality early education provides to the families of children with additional needs. In a research report on inclusion and inclusive practices in early childcare centres in the south and west regions of Ireland, Moloney and McCarthy (2010) noted the importance of informed planning and practice by staff in order to achieve the goals of inclusion for children with additional needs. Merely placing children in early childhood classes did not, by itself, ensure that relevant practices would follow without a national framework and commitment to this.

Acceptance and belonging are critical aspects of positive learning environments and there is evidence of lower social acceptance and a weaker sense of belonging among children with additional needs in mainstream settings, peaking in the beginning of post-primary school settings (Frederickson et al. 2007). The adults in early childhood classes lead opportunities for all children to feel they are accepted and belong. In a study of three early childhood classes, classroom climate elements: emotional support, classroom organisation and instructional support (Moen et al. 2019) found that while all three were important, emotional support was the only aspect that was statistically significant. Children in classrooms where there were high levels of positive emotional support from adults demonstrated closer relationships with the adults and fewer negative interactions with peers. This type of support was led by the teacher and meant high levels of enjoyment of activities, positive interaction by teachers to children and between children and significant positive signalling by adults. These findings resonate with the discussion previously by Ryan in Chapter 4.

Acceptance by peers is also important for children with assessed needs in early childhood classes. Syrjämäki, Pihlaja and Sajaniemi (2019) noted the value for learning and developing socially of 'horizontal' relationships with peers versus vertical ones with adults. Initiatives to play in peer-to-peer contexts included verbal calls, proximity to, and non-verbal indications – looking at, nodding to and pointing to. When children with additional needs have weaker repertoires of these initiatives, the adults need to notice and provide opportunities to learn them and for peers to notice weaker versions of these invitations to play. In an interesting study of the social networks of children with and without additional needs in inclusive settings, Chen, Justice and Sawyer (2019) used teachers as informants, and predicted that children with additional needs would have fewer friendship networks and more conflict networks than those without. The study found fewer play networks for those with additional needs overall but no differences in the numbers of conflict networks formed. This study also highlighted two patterns of play networks. First, children tended to play with same gender peers, and second, peers also tended to play with peers with similar assessed needs. Finally, the number of children in early childhood classes was negatively associated with the development of social networks of both kinds. In other words, settings with more children inhibited the development of social networks.

> **Key Signposts: Introduction**
>
> - Staff in early childhood classes who have expertise in meeting the needs of children with identified needs should be enabled to cascade this expertise to all staff.
> - Inclusive early childhood classes provide important opportunities for children with additional needs to flourish, with the potential for long-term positive outcomes.
> - Emotional support from adults in early childhood classes is more important than instructional support and classroom organisation.
> - Children with additional needs may have weaker repertoires of play initiatives and peers may need prompting to notice these initiatives.
> - Children with additional needs tend to have fewer friendship networks but similar numbers of conflict networks then their peers.

Behaviour as Communication

There are many ways of viewing children's behaviour and the behavioural approach (Skinner 1963, Sundberg and Partington 2013, McClannahan and Krantz 2005) can be very helpful for teachers' understanding of the social functions of behaviour for young children. The field of applied behaviour analysis (ABA) has contributed mostly to our understanding and education of young autistic children since the development of the early intensive behavioural intervention (EIBI) approach (Raches et al. 2018). Early intensive behavioural intervention focuses on both a particular understanding of behaviour that allows for effective positive interventions as well as the development of prosocial language and learning skills. This approach to interpreting children's behaviours offers significant insight for working with all children with assessed needs in early childhood classes. Essentially, behaviour is understood within the broad context of its occurrence including both distal and proximal events. Without seeing the context in which behaviour occurs as critical, teachers may respond to the presentation of some behaviours of the child simply as 'bold'. Thinking about all behaviour as communicative has fundamentally changed how we respond when faced with behaviour that challenges us in learning environments. For example, Iwata and colleagues (1994) noted that in a leading international refereed journal on behaviour analysis, the acceptance of communicative intent as key for developing therapeutic interventions for people with additional needs has led to a significant increase in published positive constructive interventions compared to the use of punishment. This is important for adults working in the early years as misinterpreting behaviour at this level sets the tone for negative learning experiences for very young children. It is even more important to understand behaviour as communicative when working in inclusive environments with young children whose communication skills may be extremely limited by an assessed need. Therefore the child may communicate through other means such as pushing, grabbing, shouting, crying and hiding. In the previous chapter, Donnellan, Joyce and Ryan have discussed the myriad of ways that young children communicate and our role as early childhood educators in responding to the diverse ways children make their thinking visible to us.

Communication and Context

A child's behaviour is seen first in the immediate context in two ways. It may be a response to some other event in the environment, which acts as a trigger or antecedent event. For example, another child takes a toy without asking and the child reacts by crying and pointing to the 'taker'. Or, the child is engaged in an activity using a tablet and the adult tells him to shut off the programme and come to the table for a snack. The child is not ready to stop his fun activity and resists by trying to hide the tablet by going under the table. The second aspect of the environmental understanding of behaviour is what happens after the child's behaviour – the consequence. This includes any consequence the child experienced in the past and has learned from. Learning takes place mostly between the behaviour and whatever consequence the child experiences. Negative consequences are felt as punishment and are intended to reduce or eliminate the behaviour. Positive consequences are felt positively by the child and teach the child to engage in that behaviour more frequently. All children learn very quickly from the consequences of their behaviour. However, the careful and systematic use of observational skills by adults in the environment are needed to ascertain whether a particular consequence works as it is intended. For example, an adult who follows a child around the room trying to get the tablet from him by cajoling and giving him a lot of attention, even negative attention, can lead to the fun of the chase. The consequence intended to stop a behaviour in fact encourages it. Another example is when a child values the attention of the adult and approaches to show something she made. The adult is busy with another child and ignores her. She learns quite quickly not to make the effort to engage the adult as her efforts do not result in the attention she is seeking. Often, the adult is unaware of the initiation, which occurred in a very busy environment and can be surprised that the child rarely engages with her.

Distal influences on children's behaviour, called setting events, can be experienced by the child as internal, or can be ambient in the environment, or can be more distant events that happened the previous evening, or early that morning. Examples include not feeling well or having a sore tooth (internal), a lot of loud excited shouting by one or more peers during play (ambient noise) and being brought to the early childhood setting by a different adult from the usual one (early event). These events more distant from the behaviour of concern affect a child's motivation to engage in any tasks that may be perceived negatively by him or more difficult to do. In practice, if a child is feeling unwell (internal setting event), being asked to take another bite of an unappetising sandwich can be the trigger or antecedent that sets off a behaviour that can be challenging to manage. The child already feels unwell and probably not hungry so her motivation for eating is low. Not all behaviours that challenge adults have a setting event but if a behaviour seems unpredictable to the adults in an environment, some setting event may be acting in the background (Alberto and

Troutman 2013). An excellent way to find out about potential setting events is to maintain close contact with families who can share this information.

Table 11.1 shows examples of these antecedent, behaviour and consequence (ABC) of behaviour, some with setting events. Seeing them live in complex environments can be difficult at first but careful observation can quickly build adult skills of recording these in an effort to understand the communicative intent of some behaviours. Essentially there are four key intentions evident in children's behaviours when typical communication channels are weak or not evident. They are to gain adult or peer attention, to get an object, toy, crayon, tablet, or role (to be first in line), to avoid or stop some activity or event experienced as negative, frightening, or difficult, and finally, to gain or escape something sensory for the child. These are shown with other examples in Table 11.2.

As children learn quickly what particular behaviours achieve for them, these 'functions' then become communicative 'intents' for future behaviour. In essence, the children have learned potentially inappropriate ways of getting their needs met. Dunfield, Kuhlmeier and Murphy (2013) found that very young children associated clear communicative intent with engaging in co-operative activities with peers. Here are the four functions of behaviours that may challenge adults in early childhood classes.

Given the approach to understanding behaviour as communication described above, adults in early childhood classes can promote good communication by understanding what a child is saying when using behaviour other than language to communicate. It is important not to put values on these functions of the child's behaviour. Wanting attention or an item, not wanting to stay in an overly warm part of the room, or scratching to relieve an itch are simply the needs of the child. The goal then is to teach the child more socially acceptable ways to get their needs met (Cooper, Heron and Heward 2019).

Table 11.1. Elements of Behaviour Interactions in an Early Childhood Class

Setting Event	Antecedent / Trigger	Behaviour	Consequence
Child is hungry but has very little language	Child sees snacks being prepared	Child runs to the snack table and grabs a snack	Adult demands the snack from the child, who gives it to her and runs crying to her chair
Child is hungry but has very little language	Child sees snacks being prepared. Adult notices her interest and knows that she is probably hungry	Child runs to the snack table but the adult steps between the table and child with a small piece of a snack and gives it to the child saying: 'you are very hungry – here you are!'	The child takes the snack back to her chair and happily eats it.
	Child A is drawing a picture using crayons. He likes red, orange and yellow crayons only. Child B gives him blue, black and brown crayons and takes a red one.	Child A runs after Child B, pushes him and takes back his red crayon. Child B cries.	Adult reprimands Child A for pushing and grabbing. She removes all crayons from him for the day. Child A is still upset when his mother picks him up at the end of the day.
	Child A is drawing a picture using crayons. He likes red, orange and yellow crayons only. Child B gives him blue, black and brown crayons and takes a red one.	Child A runs after Child B but the adult immediately intervenes, steps between the boys and asks Child B to ask if he might borrow it only for a minute. Child A agrees to the short loan and is warmly praised by the adult as he goes back to his table. The adult casually moves the darker crayons to the side but leaves them on the table.	Child B uses the crayon and then, once prompted by the adult, brings it back and thanks Child A.

Table 11.2. Functions of Behaviours that Challenge Adults

Functions	To gain attention from an adult or peer	To get an object, toy, crayon, role, privilege	To avoid or escape some aversive or difficult situation	To gain or avoid a sensory experience
Examples	Pulls hair of peer, runs roughly at a peer to initiate playing a game	Screams to get a yellow truck out of reach Pushes peer to be at front of the line to go outside Charges at peer on swing to get access to the swing	Leaves the art table when wet art materials are presented Cries when asked to persist putting on own coat	Scratches arm to the extent the skin is broken to get relief from an itch Walks around the play area with hands over ears to block out loud noise of peers playing
	Repeatedly approaches one adult only with questions or work to get their attention			

 Key Signposts

- Behaviours that adults may find challenging should be seen as communicating a need or want by the child rather than 'bold'.
- Behaviours are best understood within their temporal context including any immediate antecedent triggers as well as current and previous consequences that enable learning.
- Behaviours are also influenced by more remote or distant events including internal feelings and ambient environmental aspects.
- Key needs expressed through behavioural communication are to get attention, to get an object or role, to avoid or escape some aversive event and to get or avoid a sensory feeling.

Rules and Children with Additional Needs

When children use non-typical ways to communicate their needs and wants, staff play a significant role in promoting both language development and self-regulation. Most rules in early childhood classes are verbally enforced and even very young children benefit from understanding the reasoning behind rules. Brennan's (2013) research on rule transgressions by young children explains that rules are considered to have 'force' which is predominantly felt when a rule is broken. For young children, rules are learned through their participation in social situations where the rules are context-specific to those situations. Both developmental and sociocultural theories provide explanations for rule infringement by young children. In the first case, development theory would explain rule breaking as the inability of the child to self-regulate when a rule infringes on their autonomy or wants. Sociocultural theory views rule breaking as the child's testing the control over their behaviour by others. Brennan further discusses the importance of developing a sense of remorse in young children for breaking rules as the feeling of remorse can activate several appropriate behaviours including the development of self-regulation that would support fewer instances of rule breaking, and making amends may be motivated. Teaching rules can be complex as the degree to which children comply is influenced by the amount of effort and self-regulation required. Rule following and rule breaking both seem developmental and young children are aware of the power of rules, for membership in prestigious groups. Difficulties, however, arise when some children with assessed needs do not notice rules that are invisible, implicit or covert and known only when transgressed. This leads to 'invisible pedagogies', which advantage those children who know the rules. For example, for autistic children, most social rules are exactly this – invisible, implicit and covert.

It would seem advisable for adults in early childhood classes to ask what a child is communicating when she breaks a rule. Trying to see rules from the child's perspective is also warranted. If a child breaks a rule because a trigger event upsets her capacity to regulate her emotions, if she is tired, frustrated, angry or distressed, a full understanding of this is very helpful in guiding the adult to provide support and acceptance of an emotional state rather than providing a consequence for breaking the rule. Rule transgressions may be adaptive for children when their emotions block their capacity to adhere to a rule. Brennan (2013) reminds us that our response as adults to children's flagrant breaking of rules can test our self-regulation also. Ultimately, given the potential for language delays and self-regulation challenges in young children with assessed needs, it is for adults to determine whether the child knows what to do, how to do it, and can do it in the heat of the moment, or is reacting by using the only communication capacity he has in a stressful situation. Both developmental stage and the presence of an assessed need must influence this determination appropriately.

Assessed Needs as Signposts for Supports

Specific assessed needs will now be addressed for early childhood classes as signposts for particular supports. For each assessed need presented, key signposts for support are listed and specific implications for addressing these are provided. These come from both the Signposts published by the Special Education Support Service (SESS) (SESS 2008) and the *Diagnostic and Statistical Manual of Mental Disorder*, 5th Edition (American Psychiatric Association (APA) 2013). Physical needs are presented first. These include Spina Bifida, Muscular Dystrophy and Cerebral Palsy, followed by assessed needs that more directly affect learning and development: Prader-Willi syndrome, autism spectrum difference (ASD) and Down syndrome. It is important to note here that any descriptions or definitions of assessed needs simply provide information about those needs, not about the specific children who experience those needs (Tynan 2019).

Regardless of assessed need, the following aims should guide interventions and supports, all of which should:

- Promote and facilitate access to all the parts of the instructional setting;
- Promote and facilitate independence in all activities if possible;
- Consider partial participation rather than merely observing peers doing an activity;
- Watch for small changes in physical, emotional and intellectual learning in all children
- Communicate with families;
- Respond to the most likely communicative intent of behaviour that challenges adults and peers.

Key Signposts

- Rules for behaving tend to show their force mostly when broken.
- Overt clear rules support all children to belong to groups that observe those rules.
- Hidden, covert or assumed rules advantage children who know them and children with additional needs tend to not know these hidden ways of behaving. Social behaviour is a key area with such hidden rules.
- It is important for adults in early childhood classes to view rule infractions from the point of view of the child, as communicating a message, and as potentially adaptive for the child.

Assessed Needs with a Physical Focus

The following presents in tabular form some key signposts for supporting children with any of three assessed needs. Each signpost leads to specific suggestions for supporting children in early childhood classes. These suggested supports would need to be tailored to individual children in specific settings. Children with the same assessed need will vary considerably in their strengths and needs from each other. Staff in leadership positions in ELC, primary and special school settings can facilitate an understanding of these signposts among the rest of the staff through targeted continuing professional development (CPD) and modelling.

In Table 11.3, it should be clear that there are common supports that can be provided for children with different assessed physical needs. These include planning for management of the physical environment, for interactions with particular children, for adapting materials and objects and for maintaining close family links. Hebbeler and Spiker (2016) remind us that children with physical disabilities are more limited in their access to the world around them. They may need to access parts of their environment through the intervention of adults or others. Using particular supports tailored to individual children can make the difference to their access to the world around them, either facilitating or denying it. They also recommend that naturalistic and embedded instruction be used to include children with assessed needs. In other words, they should learn skills in natural environments using regular activities as teaching tools and opportunities (Hebbeler and Spiker 2016).

Table 11.3. Physical Assessed Needs – Signposts and Supports

Assessed Need	Signposts for Support	Sample Supports
Spina Bifida Widely varying condition resulting from a spinal column defect (Special Education Support Service (SESS) 2008)	Likely to use a wheelchair Difficulties with bowel and bladder control May have co-ordination difficulties May have short-term memory, speech and vision difficulties	Position yourself at eye-level for all interactions if possible Adjust the physical environment to allow for movement and table space for activities Consult with family re occupational therapy suggestions for activities that support co-ordination and tracking Give sufficient time to do activities and play games Ask the child what would help

Assessed Need	Signposts for Support	Sample Supports
Muscular Dystrophy A progressive, neuro-muscular condition resulting in deterioration of muscles.	May not feel steady while standing or sitting May have difficulty using some objects and toys May have difficulty with objects that are heavy	Adjust the physical environment if the child uses a wheelchair to allow movement and table use Get physical therapist advice re chair and standing supports
(SESS 2008)		Use peers positively to engage in play and other activities to keep muscles strong as possible Adjust objects using lighter ones when possible Consult with family Ask the child what would help
Cerebral Palsy A widely varying, non-progressive condition resulting in movement and posture difficulties resulting from brain injury.	May use a wheelchair. May lack control over gross and fine-motor skills May have speech difficulties or may lack speech capacity Likely to have no intellectual differences	Adjust the physical environment if the child uses a wheelchair to allow movement and table use Learn what technological supports work for the child to enable play and interaction with objects Consult with family and occupational
		therapist for ways to support communication for the child Teach peers to recognise communicative initiatives from the child. Position yourself at eye-level for all interactions if possible Ask the child what would help

> **Key Signposts**
>
> - Regardless of assessed need, all interventions for children should promote independence, attend to children's communicative intent and promote access to activities and items.
> - Assessed needs that are mostly physical in nature dictate the types of supports most useful for children in early childhood settings at early learning and care (ELC), primary and special school levels.
> - Environmental management, communication with families, input from therapists when needed, and adaptation of games and objects are primary supports for physical assessed needs.

Assessed Needs with Intellectual and Learning Focus

The following presents in tabular form key signposts for support for children with any of four assessed needs that may directly affect children's learning and development. The supports suggested will need to be tailored for individual children to meet their specific needs and use their strengths.

Looking at the sample supports suggested for the assessed needs in Table 11.4, some commonalities should also be evident. These include but are not limited to environmental management, use of visual supports, engagement with the family, use of peers, motivation and making explicit daily activity structures available to the children. Environmental management includes thinking about the physical layout and use of all environmental objects in space (Mercer and Mercer 2005). Visual supports (Earles-Vollrath et al. 2006; Cohen and Gerhardt 2016) include clear visual guides inclusive or exclusive of words that support children to learn and use social and behavioural routines and systems, manage their behaviour and stay aware of the structure or roadmap of activities for each day. Family engagement (Dardig 2016) includes using naturally occurring opportunities such as chatting with a parent when the child is dropped off or picked up from the setting and more structured methods such as setting up and keeping a simple home-school journal to relay information, concerns and achievements. Using peers to support others in play and other daily routines can be explicitly encouraged and also allowed to occur naturally and builds skills of both the helper and helped (Katz et al. 2013; Keane 2014). Motivation refers to any deliberate system of positive consequences put in place for an individual or group of students such as a token system, activity rewards, or access to a preferred activity (Alberto and Troutman 2013). In terms of setting up specific consequences to motivate children, Sigler and Aamidor (2005) identify three key elements which serve to indicate to a child that specific behaviours are liked and they should do them more often. These are: tell the child what to do, use natural consequences (join in in a game or activity, use verbal approvals rather than adding tangibles), and whereas you can ignore unwanted behaviour you must stop dangerous behaviour, redirect to an alternative activity, engage and then give a positive consequence. Explicit daily structures are individually constructed personal schedules of activities, frequently requiring the child to move an object or word for each activity completed. These daily schedules serve to structure the day for children, reduce anxiety and increase the predictability of events in the environment. They are a particular form of visual support.

Table 11.4. Assessed Needs with Intellectual Focus: Signposts and Supports

Assessed Need	Signposts for Support	Sample Supports
Prader-Willi syndrome A congenital condition caused by an abnormality on chromosome 15 (Special Education Support Service (SESS) 2008)	Likely to have mild general learning disability (but may not) Delayed motor development Short-term memory deficits but long-term memory strengths	Provide multiple opportunities for playing games and doing learning activities in interesting ways As the child tires easily, introduce physical and demanding skills early in the day
	Strengths at sedentary activities like drawing, computer work and colouring May have poor co-ordination and balance May have poor auditory processing skills May have poor ability to acquire social skills without explicit instruction and supports	Alternate easy skills with more challenging ones giving opportunities for rest Showcase activity products (drawings, e.g.) Provide sufficient physical space for the child to move and be supported
	May get frustrated easily by difficult tasks and engage in behaviours that challenge adults and peers Intense craving for food and will seek food consistently	Use visual supports for all activities such as simple pictures of routines, calming strategies and sequences Teach social routines and rules explicitly, with visual supports and peer engagement
		Use timers and positive consequences for engaging in difficult activities – keep interactions positive Have a visual schedule of activities and support the child in understanding and using this. Discuss dietary control with family

Assessed Need	Signposts for Support	Sample Supports
Autism spectrum difference A neurological condition with widely varying characteristics. No known cause yet. (DSM-V 2013; Daly 2020)	Social Communication and Social Interaction difficulties including: • Initiating conversations with peers • Responding to social initiatives of peers • Back-and-forth conversation • May not notice non-verbal aspects of communication • Difficulty making friends	Pair with peer models who are kind and caring Show key communication skills using videos Teach social routines and rules explicitly, with visual supports and peer engagement
	Restricted Patterns of Behaviour and Interests including: • Using toys and objects in repetitive and different ways • May echo other's speech • Repetitive speech patterns	Teach clear obvious non-verbal communication signals first Structure game-playing with key peers for short periods of time Echolalia teaches a lot about the child's speech and articulation capabilities
	• Upset by unplanned changes to routines • Strong interests in particular objects, events or people. Can engage in these interests excessively	Have a visual schedule of activities and support the child in understanding and using this Use keen interests for teaching as much as possible
	• Strong sensory differences particularly related to sounds – sensory seeking or sensory avoidant	Allow access to keen interests after short amounts of engagement in more difficult activities ensuring the child is successful Respect the child's need for sensory supports and never make these contingent on any other behaviours
	• May engage in behaviours that challenge adults when anxious, stressed, tired or ill	Have personal quiet space for the child to self-regulate emotions, and allow to use as needed Consult with family to learn about external events that may affect child's behaviour

Needs as Signposts for Learning and Development

Assessed Need	Signposts for Support	Sample Supports
Down syndrome The most common developmental condition caused by an abnormality in chromosome pair 21 (Daly 2020)	Some level of general learning disability will be present Language learning may be delayed May have hearing difficulties and is vulnerable to upper respiratory diseases resulting in absences	Provide multiple opportunities for playing games and doing learning activities in interesting ways Listen carefully to the child's language efforts and repeat back what you hear for verification Use visual supports for instruction and
	Receptive language is stronger than spoken language May be very socially aware and 'savvy' with peers Keenly aware of your approval and disapproval	routines Support the child explicitly when back in Early Childhood classes after an absence Provide partial responses giving the child the opportunity to fill in with key words Use songs and music and drama to support
	Awareness of own skill levels may lead to avoidance of difficult tasks May be difficult to motivate to try or persist with difficult tasks	articulation development Use buddy systems and peers to support engagement in specific tasks. Focus on the child's strengths at first.
		Differentiate tasks so the child can be successful and earn your approval – use verbal and non-verbal means for this Consider overt motivational systems such as tokens for engaging in difficult tasks Use timers for very short periods Connect new tasks to known ones

> **Key Signposts**
>
> - Assessed needs involving intellectual functioning also indicate the need for both general and particular supports in early childhood classes.
> - Common supports include environmental management, clear and unambiguous use of visual supports for routines, for behaviour sequences and for reducing the unpredictability of the sequence of daily events. They also include close communication with families and the use of peers in prompted and unprompted ways.
> - Providing additional overt structure to the day and to individual activities reduces anxiety and promotes opportunities for better and more successful learning by children with additional needs in early childhood classes.

Universal Design for Learning (UDL)

The valuable support discussed will now be considered within the framework of Universal Design for Learning (Rose, Gravel and Gordon 2014). Universal Design for Learning (UDL) is a concept derived from architecture where homes are constructed for the lifetime of their occupants (Grey et al. 2019). They are built to be both child-friendly and accessible to older people from the start. Ideally, no retro-fitting is needed in such homes. This concept was adopted as an instructional and learning framework to support the access and education of all children in inclusive engaging environments. Universal Design for Learning according to Rose et al. (2014), provides for multiple means of representation, multiple means of action and expression and multiple means of engagement. In practice, representation means that educators in all settings arrange for multiple ways for children to access information including multisensory options, use of multimedia, careful teaching of language, both symbolic and linguistic, and considers the learning and knowledge the child brings to the teaching and learning environment. Further, representation also includes consideration of maintenance and generalisation of learning. Action and expression for educators means that both physical actions using multiple tools, verbal and other communication tools are used and valued. Finally, engagement means that educators find multiple ways of attracting interest to learning activities and play, offering and supporting choices by children, promoting sustained engagement and effort and providing opportunities for self-regulation including building coping skills. Essentially, UDL considers the needs of all learners from the design stage of all instructional and learning opportunities. Access and engagement are key. Given the focus of this chapter on children with additional needs in early childhood settings, adults can meaningfully plan for the full inclusion of all children by applying UDL principles from the outset. When we assume that children with different strengths and needs will be in our educational environments, when we know their families have the same hopes and expectations of all other families for their children, then putting in place as many environmental and interactional supports as possible is much more likely to ensure a genuine welcome and successful access by all children to their meaningful education. Table 11.5 places some of the common supports recommended in this chapter on the UDL framework.

Table 11.5. Common Supports Linked to Universal Design for Learning Elements

Universal Design for Learning Elements		
Representation	Expression	Engagement
Multimedia Multisensory Language / symbols Prior knowledge of child	Physical actions Multiple tools Verbal /other communication tools	Attracting interest Choices Sustained engagement Self-regulation Coping skills
Commonly Recommended Supports		
Physical environment management Maintaining strong two-way family links	Physical environment management Maintaining strong two-way family links	Physical environment management Maintaining strong two-way family links
Use of visual supports Individual daily schedule Motivation	Use of visual supports Individual daily schedule Adapting objects, toys and materials Motivation	Use of visual supports Individual daily schedule Using peers to support engagement, play and build social repertoires Motivation

In line with the ecological lens suggested by Ring in Chapter 1, it can be seen from Table 11.5 that some specific supports for children with additional needs enable the three elements of UDL to be effective. For example, close two-way family communication facilitates the adults in the early childhood class to know and select particular multisensory or multimedia means of accessing content. It also influences what tools children might use to express their learning, and promotes engagement at deeper and more sustained levels by children. Similarly, the arrangement of the environment enables access to items and peers, supports the use of communication, and encourages sustained engagement in play and other key activities. Motivation attracts children to access items and activities, helps them to express themselves in effective ways and supports them to engage in more difficult activities thereby building endurance. Although the specific supports selected for individual children will vary, the expectation that communication with families will inform these choices, that careful arrangement of the environment will enable access, and that motivation supports all three areas applies to all children with additional needs. Each support suggested in this chapter will benefit not only the child it is intended for, but others in early childhood classes also. When UDL becomes the norm for designing better instructional and learning environments, and when teachers and other adults in these settings view additional needs as signposts for devising supports for children, then children who would otherwise remain on the margins of good practice will be placed at the centre and all children will benefit.

Once the UDL model for designing instruction and learning activities is in place, there are several level systems of support available to early childhood teachers to work well with children who have additional needs in their classes. These include Response to Intervention (RtI) (Sugai and Horner 2009), Positive Behaviour Support (PBS) (Bradshaw et al. 2015) and the Continuum of Support model (National Educational Psychological Service (NEPS) 2007; National Council for Special Education (NCSE) 2018). All contain a broad level of additional supports for all children in a setting, followed by a more intensive range of supports for that smaller group of children for whom the broad level is not sufficient. This is then followed by a third level of support, which targets individual children and designs interventions specifically for the focus child. There is considerable research support for the effectiveness of these systems (Bradshaw et al. 2015; Sørlie et al. 2018; Lynch et al. 2020).

> ### Key Signposts
>
> - Universal Design for Learning (UDL) has three key elements: multiple means of representation (providing access to learning activities and events), multiple means of expression (showing what one has learned) and multiple means of engagement allowing for individual interests, choices and self-regulation.
> - UDL is a way of considering the environment and all instructional opportunities to ensure as much as possible that they are accessible to all children in early childhood education. UDL is intended to support all children's engagement and success in learning activities.
> - Noting several common supports for children with various assessed needs, these common supports fit into the model of UDL.
> - While observing the guidelines and principles of UDL in early childhood classes, particular and individually targeted supports may also be warranted to ensure access and successful learning for all children.

A Note on Independent Toileting

Wheeler (2007) identifies several compelling reasons for teaching all young children to toilet independently if possible. These are the impact on families of having a child who is incontinent, socially and financially, the expectations of teachers at higher grade levels that these skills should have been taught and learned at an earlier age, and the impact of incontinence on social relationships for the child and family. Children with additional needs in early childhood classes may need support for independent toileting. As can be seen from the signposts in Table 11.3, some areas of assessed need include difficulties with bowel and bladder control. It is beyond the scope of this chapter to provide a detailed description of how best to plan for supporting independent toileting, but some guidelines are provided here.

Learning to use the toilet is a developmental set of skills for all children and includes knowing when they need to use the toilet and the chain of behaviours involved in using it. These behaviours are entering the bathroom, undressing, sitting on the toilet, voiding appropriately, wiping, flushing, dressing and washing and drying hands. Some of these skills can happen in different orders such as wiping and then flushing or wiping, dressing and then flushing. Children with additional needs can have particular difficulties with all or some elements of this process. General guidelines would advise the following: that the child should be at least 2 years of age and should have the physical ability to sit and hold her body in an upright position prior to commencing a programme. She should be co-operative with undressing and dressing to the extent that toileting requires. She should not have any medical reason that contraindicates starting this training. The process used should be exclusively positive, developmentally appropriate and have family support.

Difficulties that children with additional needs may have around learning to use the toilet include lack of awareness of their need to eliminate, anxiety about sitting on the toilet such that they cannot relax sufficiently to eliminate and sensory avoidant behaviours related to voiding or flushing. Supports for teaching toileting include the use of visuals, social stories (Gray 2015), teaching the various elements of the chain separately if necessary, and careful observation of fluid and food intake to inform the best times to prompt toilet use. There is a very small but growing body of research evidence to support the use of video modelling to teach toileting. However, use of video for such a sensitive set of behaviours needs careful consideration as noted by Drysdale et al. (2015) who combined animation with videos of the children using big loose clothing to ensure their privacy. Finally, advice from an occupational therapist (OT) might be in order when working with some children.

> **Key Signposts**
>
> - Learning to use the toilet independently is important for children with additional needs in early childhood classes to promote peer social relationships and reduce expense and social impact on families.
> - Toileting includes a sequence of steps that occur in a chain. Children with additional needs should be older than 2 years of age, have full family support, and allow adults to assist in relevant dressing and undressing before a toileting programme can be commenced.
> - Some children with additional needs may not be aware of their need to use the toilet, may have anxiety about various steps in the process and may have sensory difficulties with some steps.
> - Both social stories (Gray 2015) and very sensitive use of video modelling (Drysdale et al. 2015) have been useful in toileting programmes.

Conclusion

Children with additional needs benefit hugely from attending inclusive early childhood classes in ELC, primary and special school settings. Their particular individual needs and strengths dictate for adults the type and extent of supports needed for their engagement and success in these settings. As discussed by Barr and Hilliard in Chapter 5, close communication with families is key for informing the selection and use of various targeted supports for children.

Bibliography

Alberto, P. A., and Troutman, A. C. (2013) *Applied Behaviour Analysis for Teachers* (9th ed.). New York, NY: Pearson.

American Psychiatric Association. (2013). *Diagnostic and Statistical Manual of Mental Disorder* (5th ed.). Washington, DC: America Psychiatric Association.

Bradshaw, C. P., Wassdorp, T. E., and Leaf, P. J. (2015). 'Examining Variation in the Impact of School-Wide Positive Behavioral Interventions and Supports: Findings from a Randomized Controlled Effectiveness Trial', *Journal of Educational Psychology*, 107, 546–557.

Brennan, M. (2013). 'Rule Breaking in the Child Care Centre: Tensions for Children and Teachers', *International Journal of Early Childhood*, 48, 1–15.

Chen, J., Lin, T. J., Justice, L., and Sawyer, B. (2019). 'The Social Networks of Children with and without Disabilities', *The Journal of Autism and Developmental Disorders*, 49, 2779–2794.

Cohen, M. J., and Gerhardt, P. F. (2016). *Visual Supports for People with Autism: A Guide for Parents and Professionals* (2nd ed.). Bethesda, MD: Woodbine Press.

Cooper, J. O., Heron, T. E., and Heward, W. L. (2019). *Applied Behavior Analysis* (3rd ed.). Columbus, OH: Pearson Merrill Prentice Hall.

Daly, P. (2020). *Small Changes Can Make Big Differences: Behaviour Management through the Lens of Special Educational Needs*. Limerick: Curriculum Development Unit, Mary Immaculate College.

Dardig, J. (2016). *Involving Parents of Students with Special Needs: 25 Ready-to-Use Strategies*. New York, NY: Skyhorse Publications

Department of Education and Skills. (1999). *Ready to Learn: White Paper on Early Childhood Education*. Dublin: Stationery Office.

Drysdale, B., Yun Qi Lee, C., Anderson, A., and Moore, D. W. (2015). 'Using Video Modeling Incorporating Animation to Teach Toileting to Two Children with Autism Spectrum Disorder', *Journal of Developmental and Physical Disabilities*, 27(2), 149–165.

Dunfield, K. A., Kuhlmeier, V. A., and Murphy, L. (2013). 'Children's Use of Communicative Intent in the Selection of Cooperative Partners', *PLoS ONE*, 8(4), e61804.

Earles-Vollrath, T. L., Tapscott Cook, K., and Ganz, J. B. (2006). *How to Develop and Implement Visual Supports* (E-Book 13886, ISBN: 9781416406341). Texas: Pro-Ed Series on Autistic Spectrum Disorders.

Frederickson, N., Simmonds, E., Evans, L., and Soulsby, C. (2007). 'Assessing the Social and Affective Outcomes of Inclusion', *British Journal of Special Education*, 34, 105–115.

Gray, C. (2015). *The New Social Story Book TM*. Texas: Future Horizons.

Grey, T., Corbett, M., Sheerin, J., Heeney, T., Ring, E., and O'Sullivan, L. (2019). *Universal Design Guidelines for Early Learning and Care Settings*. Dublin: Department of Children and Youth Affairs in collaboration with the Centre for Universal Design, National Disability Authority, <https://aim.gov.ie/wp-content/uploads/2019/06/universal-design-guidelines-for-elc-settings-introduction-1.pdf>, accessed 6 January 2019.

Hebbeler, K., and Spiker, D. (2016). 'Supporting Young Children with Disabilities in Early Childhood Special Education Classrooms', *The Future of Children*, 26(2), 185–205.

Inter-Departmental Group. (2015). *Supporting Access to the Early Childhood Care and Education Programme for Children with a Disability*. Dublin: Inter-Departmental Group, <http://nda.ie/nda-files/Supporting-Access-to-the-Early-Childhood-Care-and-Education-for-Children-with-a-Disability.pdf>, accessed 21 January 2020.

Iwata, B. A., Dorsey, M. F., Zarcone, J. R., Vollmer, T. R., Smith, R. G., Rogers, T. A., Lerman, D. C., Shore, B. A., Mazaleski, J. L., Goh, H., Edwards Cowdery, G., Kalsher, M., McCosh, K. C., and Willis, K. D. (1994). 'The Functions of Self-Injurious Behavior: An Experimental-Epidemiological Analysis', *Journal of Applied Behavior Analysis*, 27(2), 215–240.

Katz, E., and Girolametto, L. (2013). 'Peer-Mediated Intervention for Preschoolers with ASD Implemented in Early Childhood Education Settings', *Topics in Early Childhood Special Education*, 33(3), 133–143.

Keane, S. (2014). 'Aistear in a Junior Infant Classroom – Putting Theory into Practice', *An Leanbh Óg, The OMEP Ireland Journal of Early Childhood Studies*, 8, 215–226.

Lynch, H., Ring, E., Boyle, B., Moore, A., O'Toole, C., O'Sullivan, L., Brophy, T., Frizelle, P., Horgan, D. and O'Sullivan, D. (2020). *Evaluation of In-School and Early Years Therapy Support Demonstration Project*. Trim: National Council for Special Education, https://ncse.ie/wp-content/uploads/2020/11/Demo-project-evaluation-fInal-for-web-upload.pdf, accessed 04 January 2021.

McClannahan, L. E., and Krantz, P. J. (2005). *Teaching Conversation to Children with Autism: Scripts and Script Fading*. Bethesda: Woodbine Press.

Mercer, C. D., and Mercer, A. R. (2005). *Teaching Children with Learning Problems* (7th ed.). Boston, MA: Pearson.

Moen, A. L., Sheridan, S. M., Schumacher, R. E., and Cheng, K. C. (2019). 'Early Childhood Student–Teacher Relationships: What Is the Role of Classroom Climate for Children Who are Disadvantaged?', *Early Childhood Education Journal*, 47, 331–341.

Moloney, M., and McCarthy, E. (2010). *Development of a Framework for Action for the Inclusion of Children with Special Needs in Early Childhood Education Settings*. Curriculum Development Unit Mary Immaculate College Limerick in partnership with Limerick City Childcare Committee.

National Council for Special Education. (2018). *Comprehensive Review of the Special Needs Assistant Scheme. A New School Inclusion Model to Deliver the Right Supports at the Right Time to Students with Additional Care Needs.* Trim: National Council for Special Education, <http://ncse.ie/wp-content/uploads/2018/05/NCSE-PAP6-Comprehensive-Review-SNA-Scheme.pdf>, accessed 06 January 2020.

National Educational Psychological Service. (2007). *Special Educational Needs, A Continuum of Support. Guidelines for Teachers*, <https://www.education.ie/en/Schools-Colleges/Services/National-Educational-Psychological-Service-NEPS-/neps_besd_continuum_teacher_guide.pdf>, accessed 15 September 2020.

Raches, C., Tomlin, A. M., and Pratt, C. (2018). 'Integrating Applied Behavior Analysis and Infant/Early Childhood Mental Health: Implications for Early Intensive Intervention in Autism', *Review Journal of Autism and Developmental Disorders*, 6, 246–254.

Ring, E., Kelleher, S., Breen, F., Heeney, T., McLoughlin, M., Kearns, A., Stafford, P., Skehill, S., Campion, K., Comerford, D., and O'Sullivan, L. (2019). *Interim Evaluation of the Leadership for Inclusion in the Early Years (LINC) Programme.* Limerick: Mary Immaculate College, <https://documentcloud.adobe.com/link/track?uri=urn:aaid:scds:US:d8c95d7d-2d75-40a8-9f65-b6582908c08d>, accessed 6 January 2019.

Rose, D. H., Gravel, J. W., and Gordon, D. T. (2014). 'Universal Design for Learning'. In L. Florian (ed), *The Sage Handbook of Special Education* (2nd ed.), pp. 475–489. London: Sage.

Sigler, E. A., and Aamidor, S. (2005). 'From Positive Reinforcement to Positive Behaviors: An Everyday Guide for the Practitioner', *Early Childhood Education Journal*, 32(4), 249–253.

Skinner, B. F. (1963). 'Operant Behavior', *American Psychologist*, 18, 503–515.

Sørlie, M., Idsoe, T., Ogden, T., Olseth, A. R., and Torsheim, T. (2018). 'Behavioral Trajectories During Middle Childhood: Differential Effects of the School-Wide Positive Behavior Support Model', *Prevention Science*, 19, 1055–1065.

Special Education Support Service. (2008). *Signposts: A Resource Pack for Teachers.* Cork: Cork Education Support Centre, <https://www.sess.ie/sites/default/files/Documents_Publications/SESS_Signposts_Complete_Document.pdf>, accessed 15 September 2020.

Sugai, G., and Horner, R. H. (2009). 'Responsiveness-to-Intervention and School-Wide Positive Behavior Supports: Integration of Multi-Tiered System Approaches', *Exceptionality: A Special Education Journal*, 17(4), 223–237.

Sundberg, M. L., and Partington, J. W. (2013). *Teaching Language to Children with Autism or Other Developmental Disabilities* (2nd ed.). Pleasant Hill, CA: Partington Behavior Analysts.

Syrjämäki, M., Pihlaja, P., and Sajaniemi, N. K. (2019). 'Enhancing Peer Interaction in Early Childhood Special Education: Chains of Children's Initiatives, Adults' Responses and Their Consequences in Play', *Early Childhood Education Journal*, 47, 559–570.

Tynan, F. (2019). *Wishes: Williams Syndrome: Holistic Educational Strategies*. Limerick: Curriculum Development Unit, Mary Immaculate College.

Wheeler, M. (2007). *Toilet Training for Individuals with Autism or Other Developmental Issues*. Arlington, TX: Future Horizons.

Notes on Contributors

ANNA BARR is a tutor and content developer on the Leadership for Inclusion in Early years (LINC) Programme at Mary Immaculate College (MIC), Limerick. Anna has been involved in adult education, working as a placement tutor and lecturer on early childhood programmes, and previously worked as an early childhood teacher. Anna's research interests include early childhood teacher professional development, inclusion, and digital learning; and she is currently a doctoral candidate.

PATRICIA M. DALY is a graduate of University College Cork (UCC) and completed a MA in Emotional and Behavioural Disorders (1982), and a PhD in Applied Behaviour Analysis at Ohio State University in 1986. She worked in undergraduate and graduate special education in the US until she returned to MIC, Limerick in 2007 to direct the graduate diploma in special education needs programme at the College. She has recently retired from her role as Head of the Department of Educational Psychology, Inclusive and Special Education. She has provided continuing professional development (CPD) for teachers in the area of autism and behaviour management countrywide, including with Middletown Centre for Autism in Northern Ireland.

MARIE DOHERTY is National Programme Director of the LINC Programme, at MIC, Limerick. Marie previously worked as an early years manager and teacher, a research assistant at MIC, an early years specialist and trainer at Early Childhood Ireland (ECI) and early years inspector at the Department of Education and Skills (DES). Marie has been involved in a number of national research initiatives and training programmes. Her main interests include spirituality, Inclusion, transitions, evaluation and quality, and early childhood education and care.

ANN DONNELLAN is a tutor on the LINC Programme since 2018. Ann has a BA (Hons) in Montessori Education (Cork Institute of Technology) and a Masters in Adult and Further Education (MIC, Limerick). Before joining the LINC team, Ann previously worked with Cork Education and Training Board (ETB) as a tutor delivering programmes approved by Qualifications and Qualifications Ireland (QQI) at Level 5 and 6 on the National Qualifications Framework (NFQ) Early Childhood Care and Education modules. Ann also works part-time as a facilitator for the National Parents Council (NPC), Primary delivering a wide range of training programmes to parents of children in primary school and in early learning and care (ELC) settings.

SARAH FEENEY is a primary teacher and works in Scoil Chormaic Special School in Cashel, Co. Tipperary. She completed a post-graduate Diploma in Special Educational Needs at MIC, Limerick, followed by a Masters in Special Education at St. Patrick's College, Drumcondra, Dublin. Sarah has worked as a part-time lecturer with the Department of Educational Psychology, Inclusive and Special Education at MIC, lecturing in the area of special and inclusive education. She is currently undertaking a research PhD studentship at MIC, funded by Middletown Centre for Autism, under the guidance of Dr Patricia Daly and Prof Emer Ring.

EDEL FENLON has worked in a wide variety of early childhood settings over the last thirteen years. She holds a BA in Early Childhood Studies, a post-graduate certificate in Special and Additional Learning Needs and graduated with a MA in Mentoring Management and Leadership in the Early Years in 2019. A former tutor and content developer for the awarding winning LINC Programme, she returned to practice in 2019 to lead the transition of a specialist day service for children with disabilities to an inclusive early childhood setting for all children in her local community.

MAURICE HARMON is Head of the Department of Learning, Society and Religious Education, and a Senior Lecturer in Education at MIC, Limerick. Maurice lectures in religious education at both undergraduate and post-graduate level at MIC and supervises students' research at undergraduate, Masters and PhD levels. Maurice has extensive experience in primary education and his research interests include child's voice, participatory based research, religious education, spirituality and pedagogy and curricula development in primary education. Maurice has published and presented widely in these areas

PAULA HARTE is a tutor on the LINC Programme at MIC, Limerick. She has been involved with the delivery of the LINC Programme across a variety of centres in the North West of Ireland since it was launched in 2016. Paula has previously worked as a mainstream class support assistant, an assistant pre-school manager, tutor of early childhood care and education (ECCE) studies with Donegal Education and Training Board (ETB), Lecturer in ECCE studies in both further and higher education establishments and an ECCE student placement officer. Paula is an advocate of enhancing professionalism within the ECCE sector, the promotion of inclusion for young children in mainstream settings, the enhancement of ECCE settings and family support infrastructures.

SHIRLEY HEANEY is a lecturer in the Department of Reflective Pedagogy and Early Childhood Studies, and an academic project officer with the LINC Programme in MIC, Limerick. Previously Shirley worked in the ELC sector for over ten years. During this time, she worked with children with additional needs and children from the Traveller Community. Shirley's research interests include inclusive education and child wellbeing. Shirley is currently completing her PhD on the wellbeing of children with additional needs in ELC settings in Ireland.

PAULA HILLIARD has been involved in early childhood education as a service provider for fifteen years. Paula has a passion for ensuring quality early learning experiences for all children their families and early childhood teachers. Paula has been a tutor and content developer on the LINC Programme. She has also worked as a Development Officer with Galway and Longford Childcare Committees. Paula has delivered Diversity, Equality and Inclusion training and tutored and lectured on early childhood programmes. Paula continues to mentor early childhood teachers to support children and their families experience inclusive early childhood experiences.

MARGARET JOYCE is a tutor on the LINC programme since it was launched in 2016, and has recently been appointed lead tutor with LINC. Margaret has a BA in Early Childhood Studies and Practice (NUI Galway), a Masters in Child, Family and Community Studies (DIT) and a post-graduate qualification in Special and Inclusive Education (St. Angela's college, Sligo). Margaret has previously worked as a special needs assistant (SNA), a disability co-ordinator and a facilitator for the National Parents Council (NPC). Margaret is an advocate for inclusive care and education for all children across a range of settings.

SARAH KELLEHER is an adult educator teaching in the area of early childhood education. Sarah previously worked as LINC Programme Researcher, tutor and content developer on the LINC programme at MIC, Limerick. She has extensive hands-on experience with young children and those with additional needs. Sarah's research interests include early childhood education, inclusion, child voice, blended learning and adult education.

LISHA O'SULLIVAN is Head of the Department of Reflective Pedagogy and Early Childhood Studies at MIC, Limerick. Lisha lectures in early childhood education and play at MIC and also supervises students' research at undergraduate, Masters and PhD levels. Lisha is a qualified play therapist and her research interests include inclusive pedagogy and curricula in the early years; self-regulation and play.

Prof EMER RING is Dean of Education (Early Childhood and Teacher Education) Studies at MIC, Limerick. Emer previously worked as a mainstream class teacher, a learning support teacher, a resource teacher at primary school level, a senior inspector with the Department of Education and Skills (DES) and Head of Department of Reflective Pedagogy and Early Childhood Studies at MIC. Emer has been principal investigator on a range of national research projects and her research interests include, early childhood education, the teacher education continuum, inclusion, child voice, pedagogy and autism. Emer has published and presented widely in these areas.

MARIE RYAN is an educational psychologist and lecturer in early childhood education and care in MIC. Marie previously worked as a mainstream primary school teacher and as a learning support/resource teacher. She lectures in developmental psychology, educational psychology and early childhood education across the Bachelor of Education (BEd), BEd in Education and Psychology, BA in Early Childhood Care and Education (ECCE), Bachelor of Arts in Early Childhood Practice (BAECP) and LINC Programme. Marie has published work on inclusive education, autism, teacher research and data-informed practice in education. She has a particular expertise the area of classroom assessment and is completing her PhD in the University of Cambridge in this field. Marie is co-founder of the T-REX project, along with Dr Marek McGann, and is hugely passionate about the value and potential of teacher research.

RACHAEL RYAN has been involved in the early years sector for over a decade. She qualified from MIC with a BA in Early Childhood Care and Education (ECCE), continued her studies completing a Diploma in Child Psychology and more recently a post-graduate Diploma in Teaching in Further Education. Rachael started her career in practice before becoming an early years tutor, working with Tipperary Education and Training Board (ETB), the LINC Programme. Rachael now works with City and County Childcare Committees, as a Childminding Development Officer. Rachael's interest areas are child development, emotional development and early years relationships, reflective practice and professional development.

SHARON SKEHILL is completing her PhD in Education with MIC (MIC) and lectures in the Department of Reflective Pedagogy and Early Childhood Education. She has also been involved in content development and delivery of the LINC programme. Sharon continues to work in practice in the ELC sector in an outdoor setting, and brings this experience working with staff, families and children into her research and academic work.

Reviews for the Back Cover

Reviewed by Prof Olivia Saracho, University of Maryland

The book has an important foundation for research and practice in relation to inclusion. When designing teaching plans for the classroom, it proposes a personalised educational approach that considers each student's strengths and potential. Therefore, it describes and justifies a variety of approaches that many disability specialists have tested and accepted for children who have a variety of needs. The concepts in these approaches have been implemented in many inclusion programs across the US and abroad. Such concepts have had a lasting impact on the way in which children learn and develop. They are a broad array of creative and practical practices for conceptualising and implementing inclusion. The book has a diverse content that has an up-to-date literature and is clearly written to be understood by all audiences. The book will be of great use to a wide range of professionals, researchers, practitioners and students who work with children who have additional needs and defined disabilities. The book will be among the most recommended books by experts who work and study children with disabilities.

Review by Prof Deborah Robinson, University of Derby

This book is a must for parents and early childhood teachers who want all children to be valued equally. The authors of this book have keep the principle of child centredness at the heart of this book but they also recognise that parents, families and communities are essential to the ecology of inclusion. If the principle of inclusion is important to, this book will really matter as a guide for thinking and practising in ways that deliver equity for all children.

What a fantastic book Emer,

Index

Aamidor, S. 300
Access and Inclusion Model (AIM) 6–8, 137, 154, 236, 261, 264–267, 285, 285–286
Ainsworth, M.S. 78, 158
Aistear (The Early Childhood Curriculum Framework) 32, 37, 44, 62–63, 125–126, 127, 157, 163, 165, 169, 170, 199–200
Alexander, R.J. 102, 106, 109, 113–114
'all about me' forms 136, 137, 143, 144
Allred, K.W. 242
anti-bias approach 168–170
  Derman-Sparks 168–170
applied behaviour analysis (ABA) 288
Arnold, C. 67–68
Asmussen, K. 64, 70
assessed needs 21, 285–309
  behaviour as communication 285–286, 288, 291
  communication and context 289–291
  intellectual and learning focus 299–304
  peer interaction 287, 288
  physical focus 296–299
  rules 294–295
  signposts for supports 295–296
Athey, Chris 67
attachment and relational theory 39, 77–82

Baird, L. 18
Bandura, A. 76

Barr, Anna 19, 250, 309
Beavers, E. 239
behaviourist theory 74–75, 288–289
  examples of behavioural interactions 292–293
Bereiter, Carl 74
bioecological perspective 14–17, 39, 126–129
Blatchford, P. 113–114
Bodrova, E. 188
Boivin, M. 76
Boothe, K. 267
Bornstein, M.H. 70–71
Bowlby, J. 77–78, 158
Bradley, D. 34
Bremner, A.J. 70
Brennan, M. 294, 295
Brodie, K. 65–66
Bronfenbrenner, U. 14–15, 76, 126, 128–129
Bruce, T. 67
Bruner, J. 66, 72, 73
Buchanan, M. 188, 194
buddy systems 163, 164
Buldu, M. 116

Carlson, E. 167
Carpenter, M. 73
Carroll, D.E. 194
Chen, J. 287
children's rights
  concept of agency and competence 34, 37, 75, 273
  to participate and have voice heard and valued 31–59
  policy and legislative context 34–38

choice boards 274, 276
Clare, A. 79
Clark, A. 274, 275
cognitive and constructionist educational theories 66–73
cognitive conflict 101–102, 114
cognitive psychology theory 39–40
collaborative play 188
communication diaries 136, 138, 144
Cooper, J. 48
Coughlin, A.M. 18
Csikszentmihalyi, M. 74, 87

Dahlberg, G. 217
Daly, Patricia M. 13, 21
Deegan, J. 42
Delafield-Butt, J. 72
DeLoache, J.S. 70
Derman-Sparks, L., anti-bias education 168–170
Dewey, J. 5, 21, 42, 73, 195, 216
dialogic teaching 97, 107–110, 118
direct-instruction 112, 113
Disability Act (2005) 9, 10
Doherty, Marie 19, 143, 156
Doise, W. 101
Donnellan, Ann 20–21, 289
drawings, as means of communication 275, 276
Drysdale, B. 308
Dunfield, K.A. 291
Dweck, C. 74

early childhood education
    adapting to children with different needs 185–186
    associated competencies 15–17, 70
    bioecological systems theory 14–17, 126–129, 217
    child-centred model 128–129, 173, 217
    children's drawings 275
    consultation with child 21, 32–33, 252–253, 261
    early years education-focused Inspection (EYEI) 131
    effective leadership in ELC setting 235–255
    environment as third teacher 202, 215–227
    facilitating articulation of views 48–49
    impact of high-quality experiences 130–134
    impact of inclusivity 3–4
    importance of active engagement 40–41, 71, 72, 88, 187–188
    inclusive partnership strategies 140–142, 267–268
    independent toileting 307–309
    'key person' approach 79–80, 82–85, 88, 143–144
    key quality characteristics 160–161, 200
    learning space and environment 46–47, 71
    link between home and education setting 19–20, 125, 250, 267–268
    needs assessment 21
    partnership with parents 125–147
    potential of participation 38–41
    role of adult in fostering inclusion 167–170, 173
    teacher education and qualifications 238–241
    teaching problem-solving approach to conflict resolution 170–173
    theoretical perspectives 39–41

unique learning capacity from birth to three years 61–66, 71, 87–88, 156, 173
varied settings 219, 222
wellbeing provisions 153–174
see also assessed needs; children's rights; interactions; learning theories; planning; play
Early Childhood Ireland (ECI) 7–8
Education Act (1998) 9, 125
Education for Persons with Special Educational Needs (EPSEN) Act (2004) 9–10, 125
Education (Welfare) Act (2000) 9
Edwards, C. 135–136, 217
Effective Provision of Preschool Education (EPPE) project 98–99, 100, 106, 108–109
EIBI (early intensive behavioural intervention) approach 288–289
Eisele, G. 189
Eliot, L. 83
Engelman, Siegfried 74
Epstein, Joyce 136, 138, 250
Equal Status Acts (2000–2004) 9
Erikson, E.H. 158, 216
European Agency for Special Needs and Inclusive Education (EASNIE) 15, 125, 127, 130, 141, 143, 266, 267
exploratory talk 108

Farah, M.J. 84
Featherstone, S. 79–80, 86
Feeney, Sarah 19–20
Fenlon, Edel 20
Feuerstein, R. 83
fine-motor practice 191
Finnegan, J. 84
Fisher, K.R. 112

Fitzgerald, J. 237, 245–246
Foreman, G. 135–136
friendship bench/bus 163, 164
Froebel, Friedrich 216
Furnivall, J. 78

Galton, Maurice 106
games with rules 189, 195–196, 196
Gandini, L. 135–136, 219, 220, 221
Gerber, Magda 67, 68, 69, 80–81
Gerhardt, S. 78
Gibson, E.J. 70
Giovacco Johnson, T. 188, 194
global education reform movement (GERM) 201
Goble, P. 99, 100
Goldschmied, Elinor 67, 68–69
Goodall, J. 134–140
Gopnik, A. 68, 83, 84
Gottlieb, C.D. 84
Graham, I. 244–245, 268–269, 273
Granrusten, P.T. 242
Gray, C. 67, 74, 77
Greenspan, S. 75
Grenier, J. 67

Hahn, C.S. 70–71
Hamre, Bridget 99, 100
hands-on learning 187
Harmon, Maurice 18–19, 253, 271
Harris, P. 47–48
Harte, Paula 18–19, 253, 271
Hathcote, A. 267
Hayes, N. 34
Heaney, Shirley 19–20
Hebbeler, K. 297
Heikka, J. 241–242
Hestanes, L.E. 194
heuristic play 68–69

hierarchy of needs theory 86–87
HighScope problem-solving
    approach 171–172, 173
Hilliard, Paula 19, 250, 309
Hoas Moen, K. 241
Howard, J. 189
Hub na nÓg (Young Voices in Decision
    Making) 36
Hughes, A.M. 67, 68, 82
Hujala, E. 241–242
human rights 34–35
    see also children's rights

IDZ (Intermental Development
    Zone) 103
IECE (inclusive early childhood
    education) 266
IEP (Individual Education Plan) 265
inclusion
    concept of 11–14
    current research focus 3–4
    education setting inclusion pol-
        icies 141, 142–147
    inclusive pedagogy 144–146
    Irish policy context 235–236
    leadership practice 17–18, 20–21, 235–255
    positive transition
        experiences 142–143, 144
    role of adult in fostering 167–170
INCO (INclusion CO-ordinator)
    role 8, 20–21, 235–236,
        240–244
    information sharing 250–252
    managing change 245–249
    planning 261, 265
    pressure to balance
        responsibilities 241–242, 255
    supporting diversity, equality and
        inclusion 252, 252–255

integration movement 11
intellectual and learning focus, assessed
    needs 299–304
interactional environment 225–226
interactions
    classroom 106–107
    drivers of development 97–118
    group-work 114, 115
    importance of high-quality inter-
        actions 98–100, 105, 118,
        156–158
    inter-thinking 100–105
    language and talk as teaching
        tools 104–105
    pair-work 114, 115
    pedagogical documentation 116–117,
        118, 218, 251
    peer interactions 101–103, 105,
        113–115, 173–174
    playful interactions 111–113
    role of adults 97, 99, 101–103,
        105, 225
    teaching through interactions
        (TTI) 99
    types 99
IPG (Integrated Play Groups) 204
Ireland
    early childhood education 6–11
    provision for children with add-
        itional needs 6–7, 10
IRF/E sequence (initiation, response,
    follow-up/evaluation) 107–
        108, 109–110

Jablonka, Eva 84
Jackson, S. 67
joint productive activity 108
Joyce, Margaret 20–21, 289
Justice, L. 287

Index

Kelleher, Sarah 20
Kellmer-Pringle, Mia 86–87
Kelly, M. 263
Kilkelly, U. 34, 37–38
Kirkwood, D. 239
Kuhlmeier, V.A. 291
Kutnick, P. 113–114

labelling culture 12
language development 40–41, 68–69, 84–85, 116
   infant-directed speech ('motherese') 84–85
   speaking and listening skills ('oracy') 114–115, 115, 118
Lansdown, G. 42
Lárusdóttir, S.H. 242
Laverty, V. 80
Lawton, K. 84
leadership
   development of skills 241–244, 285–286
   distributed 237–238, 241
   effective policies 237–238
Leadership for INClusion in the Early Years (LINC) Consortium 7–8, 20–21, 45, 125, 127, 140, 141, 154, 215, 218–219, 239–240, 242, 265, 285
learning theories
   theoretical perspectives 39–41
   see also attachment; behaviourist; cognitive/constructionist; hierarchy of needs; sociocultural
Lee, F.L.M. 168
Leithwood, K. 237
Leong, D.J. 188
Leong, V. 80
Lewin, K. 247–249, 255

Lindon, J. 65–66
Littleton, K. 115
Lohmann, M. 267
'loose parts' play material 69–70
Lundy, Laura 44
Lundy Model of Child Participation 33, 43–45, 46, 47, 49–51
Lynch, H. 268
Lynch, Kathleen 167

Macari, S. 70
MacBlain, S. 67, 74, 77, 80, 82
McCarthy, E. 241, 253, 265, 286
McClelland, M.M. 198
McGoldrick, D. 34–35
McPartland, E. 268
Maguire-Fong, M. 72
Malaguzzi, Loris 216, 220
Manni, L. 237, 238
Maslow, A.H. 86–87, 158
Mathers, S. 64
Melhuish, E. 8, 98, 160
Menatakis, H. 47–48
mentoring, education of ELC teachers 239–241
Mercer, N. 103, 111, 114–115
meta-cognition theory 39
MKO (more knowledgeable other) theory 66, 103
Moloney, M. 241, 245, 253, 286
Montessori, Maria 216
Montgomery, C. 134–140
Mosaic approach 273–274, 276
Moss, P. 274, 275
motivational theories 39, 74–75, 77, 87
movement breaks 163, 164
Moyles, J. 145, 237
Mugny, G. 101
multiple intelligences perspective 40

Murphy, L. 291
Murray, J. 240

National Council for Special Education (NCSE) 9–10, 263, 265
National Council for Curriculum and Assessment (NCCA) 8, 32, 33, 37, 44
Nelson, N. 106
neurocognitive
    perspectives 39–40, 82–85
    early years development 64–66
Nicholson, S. 69–70
Noddings, N. 80
Northouse, P.G. 244
Nutbrown, C. 67, 79
Nystrand, M. 109–110

Oberhuemer, P. 239
object play (constructing/making) 189, 191–192, 196
O'Brien, T. 12
Observational Research and Classroom Learning Evaluation (ORACLE) study 106, 113
O'Byrne, A. 250
O'Connor, E. 242
Odom, S.L. 200
Ombudsman for Children's Office (OCO) 36
open-door policy 141, 143
Orange, A. 239
Osgood, J. 237, 240
O'Sullivan, Jan 167
O'Sullivan, Lisha 20, 250–251, 275–276

Page, J. 79
Pairman, A. 46, 215, 226–227

parents
    continuum of parental involvement 134–140
    definition 5
    parental engagement with children's learning 135, 138–140
    parental involvement with children's learning 135–138
    parental involvement with the setting 135–136
    role in ELC setting 125–152, 259
    support strategies 19–20
Pavlov, Ivan 74
Payler, J. 240
pedagogical coaching, education of ELC teachers 239–241
peer interaction 163–164
    buddy system 204
    impact on child development 165–166
Peeters, J. 239
Perret-Clermont, A.-N. 101
Pestalozzi, Johann Henrich 97, 104–105
Peters, RDeV 76
Pettersen, J. 245
photography, as means of communication 275, 276
physical environment 222–223
physical focus, assessed needs 296–299
physical (rough and tumble) play 189, 190–191, 196
Piaget, Jean 66–67, 68, 72, 97, 100–102, 105, 114, 158, 216
Pianta, Robert 99
Picker, Emmi 80
Pihlaja, P. 287
planning
    challenges to collaboration 270–271
    child-centred 262, 269
    child's right to participate 271–277

Index

collaborative practice 267–271, 276–277
evaluation/review cycle 268, 269
frameworks 263–267
whole-setting and individual 261–277
play 68–71
  adaptations for children with additional needs 188–189, 203–204, 287–288
  associated competencies 15–17, 70
  categorising 189–190
  collaborative 188
  creating opportunities 196
  defined as a spectrum 201
  facilities 46–47
  free-play 112, 113, 197–199, 201
  'generation effect' 187
  guided-play 97, 112, 113, 201
  heuristic play 68–69
  'loose parts' play material 69–70
  peer interactions 165–166
  playful interactions 111–113, 118, 201
  social interactivity of 187–188
  suggested pedagogy 20, 185–206
  'treasure basket' play 68–69
pretend play 189, 192–194, 196
problem-solving approach 170–173

Reggio Emilia approach 116, 202, 215, 216–218
Reunamo, J. 165
revisiting 218
Rinaldi, C. 64, 116
Ring, Emer 18–19, 38–39, 86, 99, 112, 239, 241, 253, 271, 275–276, 306
Rodd, J. 237
Rose, D.H. 304
Rosselli, M. 84
Rubiano, C. 238

rules, children with additional needs 294–295
Ryan, Marie 19, 157, 225, 287
Ryan, Rachael 20–21, 289

Sajaniemi, N. 287
Salamanca World Conference Declaration Statement 3–5, 11–12
Sandilos, L.E. 99
Sawyer, B. 287
'scaffolding' concept 72, 84, 97, 110–111, 112, 118, 191
Scarpate, M. 80
schemas, repetitive actions 67
Schultz, Laura 112
Seashore-Louis, K. 237
self-regulation theory 39, 197–198, 294
sensory preferences 161, 164
setting events 290–291
settling-in policy 141, 142–143, 144
Sigler, E.A. 300
Simcock, G. 70
Síolta (The National Quality Framework for Early Childhood Education) 37, 44, 125–126, 127, 138, 144–145, 157, 171, 268
Siraj-Blatchford, I. 201, 237, 238
Skehill, Sharon 20
Skinner, B.F. 74, 75
Slee, R. 14
Smith, F. 106
social interaction 163–164
sociocultural theory 39–40, 76–77, 97–98
Sorin, R. 253
Spiker, D. 297
strengths-based approach 137
Suhonen, E. 165

sustained shared thinking (SST) 97, 108–109, 116, 118
Suwalsky, J.T.D. 70–71
Sylva, K. 106, 201
symbolic play 189, 193, 194–195, 196
Syrjämäki, M. 287

teacher education 7–8
teaching through interactions (TTI) 99
temporal environment 223–224
terminolog 4–5, 11
language of deficit 4–5, 160–161
Terreni, L. 46, 215, 226–227
Tominey, S.L. 198
Tovey, H. 69, 202
Trawick-Smith, J. 189
'treasure basket' play 68–69
Tremblay, R.E. 76
Trevarthen, C. 72
Tusla Quality and Regulatory Frameworks (QRFs) 130, 141

UDL (universal design for learning) 161–163, 164, 304–307
United Nations Convention on the Rights of the Child (UNCRC) 5, 31–32, 34–36, 37–38
Article 12 33, 35, 41–42, 44–45, 217

Universal Declaration of Human Rights (UDHR) 34
Urban, M. 238, 239

van de Pol, J. 111
van Leer, Bernard 64
visual schedules 274, 276
Volman, M. 111
Vygotsky, L.S. 66, 97, 102–103, 105, 158, 188, 216

Warnock, M. 11
Waters, J. 240
Watson, John 74
Westwood, P. 221
Wheeler, M. 307
Whitebread, D. 187, 189, 193
whole-setting approach 261
Wieder, S. 75
Willcocks, J. 106
Wiltshire, M. 171
Wolfberg, P.J. 204
Wood, E. 200

Yang, A. 84

Zosh, J. 186, 187, 201
ZPD (zone of proximal development) theory 66, 102–103, 188

www.ingramcontent.com/pod-product-compliance
Ingram Content Group UK Ltd.
Pitfield, Milton Keynes, MK11 3LW, UK
UKHW021314180426
11947UKWH00015B/1228